WHITHER

THE JERUSALEM INSTITUTE FOR ISRAEL STUDIES

WHITHER JERUSALEM?
PROPOSALS AND POSITIONS CONCERNING THE FUTURE OF JERUSALEM

by

MOSHE HIRSCH,
DEBORAH HOUSEN-COURIEL
and
RUTH LAPIDOTH

MARTINUS NIJHOFF PUBLISHERS
THE HAGUE / LONDON / BOSTON

A C.I.P. Catalogue record for this book is available from the Library of Congress.

ISBN 90-411-0077-6 (Hb)
ISBN 90-411-0078-4 (Pb)

Published by Kluwer Law International,
P.O. Box 85889, 2508 CN The Hague, The Netherlands.

Sold and distributed in the U.S.A. and Canada
by Kluwer Law International,
675 Massachusetts Avenue, Cambridge, MA 02139, U.S.A.

In all other countries, sold and distributed
by Kluwer Law International
P.O. Box 322, 3300 AH Dordrecht, The Netherlands.

Printed on acid-free paper

All Rights Reserved
© 1995 Kluwer Law International
Kluwer Law International incorporates the publishing programmes of
Graham & Trotman Ltd, Kluwer Law and Taxation Publishers,
and Martinus Nijhoff Publishers.

No part of the material protected by this copyright notice may be reproduced or
utilized in any form or by any means, electronic or mechanical,
including photocopying, recording, or by any information storage and
retrieval system, without written permission from the copyright owner.

Printed in the Netherlands

Table of Contents

PREFACE ix

ABOUT THE AUTHORS xi

Chapter One – THE LEGAL STATUS OF JERUSALEM 1
A. Legal-Historical Background 1
B. Opinions on the Legal Status of Jerusalem According to
   International Law 15
   (1) West Jerusalem 15
   (2) East Jerusalem 18
C. The Legal Status of Jerusalem According to Israeli Law 22

Chapter Two – PROPOSALS AND POSITIONS CONCERNING
THE FUTURE OF JERUSALEM 25
1. The Sykes-Picot Agreement (1916) 25
2. The British Mandate for Palestine (1922) 26
3. Proposal of Dr. Chaim Arlosoroff (1932) 27
4. The Peel Commission Report (1937) 28
5. Proposal of the Jewish Agency (1938) 29
6. Report of Sir William Fitzgerald (1945) 30
7. The Morrison-Grady Committee Report (1946) 32
8. Proposal of the Minority of UNSCOP (1947) 34
9. The Resolution on the Future Government of Palestine
   (The "Partition Resolution") of the U.N. General Assembly
   (Resolution 181 [II]) (1947) 36
10. Proposal of the Archbishop of Canterbury (1949) 39
11. U.N. Trusteeship Council: A Draft Statute for Jerusalem (1950) .. 40
12. Proposal by the Government of Israel (1950) 43
13. Proposal Submitted by Sweden (1950) 45
14. Proposal by Professor Benjamin Akzin (1967) 47
15. Proposal by Professor Avigdor Levontin (1967) 48
16. Proposal by the Government of Israel after the Six-Day War (1967-1969) 50
17. Proposal by Dr. Meron Benvenisti (1968) 52
18. Proposal by Professor Elihu Lauterpacht, CBE, Q.C. (1968). 57
19. Proposal by Professor S. Shepard Jones (1968) 59
20. The Rogers Plan (U.S. Secretary of State William Rogers) (1969) 60
21. Proposal by Evan M. Wilson (1969) 61

22. Proposal by Professor W. Michael Reisman (1970) 63
23. Proposal by Dr. Raphael Benkler (1972) 65
24. Proposals of Sen. Richard Nixon and Sen. J. William Fulbright
    (1967 and 1974) 67
25. Report of the Aspen Institute (1975)... 69
26. Report of the Brookings Institution (1975) 71
27. The Allon Plan (1976)... 72
28. Proposal by Ambassador James George (1978).. 73
29. Proposal by Dr. Shmuel Berkovitz (1978) 74
30. Proposal by Dr. Joëlle Le Morzellec (1979) 79
31. Proposal by Lord Caradon (1980)... 81
32. Proposal by Ya'akov Hazan (1980).. 82
33. Proposal by Mark Gruhin (1980) 84
34. Peace Plan by Crown Prince Fahd of Saudi Arabia (1981) 86
35. Proposal by the Honourable Terence Prittie (1981)... 87
36. Proposal by Professor Saul Cohen (1981).. 88
37. Proposal by Dr. Henry Cattan (1981)... 90
38. Proposal by Professor Gerald I.A.D. Draper, OBE (1981) 91
39. Resolution of the Arab Summit Conference at Fez (1982).............................. 92
40. Proposal by Justice Haim Cohn (1982).. 93
41. Proposal by Ambassador Gideon Rafael (1983) 95
42. Proposal by Professor Antonio Cassese (1986) 96
43. Proposal by Professor Thomas and Ms. Sally Mallison (1981, 1986) 97
44. Proposal by Dr. Walid Khalidi (1978, 1988) 98
45. Proposal by David Ish-Shalom (1987) 99
46. Proposal by Dr. Grant Littke (1988) 100
47. Proposal by John V. Whitbeck (1989-1994)... 101
48. Proposal by Raphael Cidor (1989) 103
49. Proposal by Professor Gidon Gottlieb (1989) 105
50. Proposal by Shmuel Toledano (1991).. 106
51. Proposal by Professor Daniel Elazar (1991) 107
52. Proposal by Palestinian and Israeli Peace Activists (1991) 109
53. Proposal by Dr. Sari Nusseibeh and Dr. Mark Heller (1991) 111
54. Proposal by Professor Francis A. Boyle (1992)... 113
55. Proposal by H.E. Ambassador Adnan Abu Odeh (1992)............................... 115
56. Proposal by Dr. Cecilia Albin, Moshe Amirav,
    and Hanna Siniora (1992) 117
57. Proposal by the Israel/Palestine Center for Research and
    Information (IPCRI) (1994) 121

58. Position of the Palestine Liberation Organization 126
59. Position of the Vatican 127
60. Position of Egypt 129
61. Position of the Hamas 131
62. Position of the United States 132
63. Position of Jordan 135

Chapter Three – COMPARATIVE ANALYSIS OF PROPOSALS AND POSITIONS ACCORDING TO SPECIFIC SUBJECTS 137
A. General 137
B. National Aspirations 138
C. Holy Places 140
D. Municipal Administration 143

Chapter Four – LEXICON OF TERMS 145
1. Annexation 145
2. Autonomy 146
3. Buffer Zone 149
4. Capitulations 150
5. Church of the Holy Sepulcher 150
6. Condominium 151
7. *Corpus separatum* 152
8. Demilitarization 152
9. Diplomatic Privileges and Immunities 153
10. Enclave 156
11. The Holy Places 157
12. Internationalization 160
13. Mandate 161
14. Neutrality and Neutralization 162
15. Sovereignty 163
16. *Status quo* in Religious Matters 165
17. The Supreme Muslim Council and the Supreme Islamic Authority 166
18. The Temple Mount 167
19. The U.N. Trusteeship Council 168
20. The Vatican 169
21. Waqf 170
22. The Western Wall 172

SELECTED BIBLIOGRAPHY 174

PREFACE

For historical, religious and political reasons, the status of Jerusalem has stirred widespread interest. The city's future status is a major point of contention in the Arab-Israeli conflict; but for many others as well, who are not directly involved in the conflict, the terms of the future settlement are of cardinal importance. As a result, numerous proposals for a resolution of the Jerusalem question have been put forward by individuals and institutions throughout the world. The present book describes and analyzes more than fifty of these proposals and positions. We hope that this study will benefit scholars in various disciplines, such as history, political science, international relations, and law. Naturally, we shall be more than gratified if the book also serves as a tool for those actively seeking a resolution to the Jerusalem question.

The book's structure enables the reader to follow the historical development by which certain types of proposals were espoused in a particular period and subsequently abandoned in favor of utterly different ideas as circumstances changed (for example, the solution of a British Mandate for the city proposed in the 1930s and 1940s). Some of the political models surveyed have been tried elsewhere (autonomy regimes, for example) while others have never been put into practice. Many of the proposals and viewpoints are based on the author's interpretation of the city's legal status according to international law and will therefore be of interest also to scholars and practitioners in that field.

The *first chapter* begins with a survey of the historical and legal background to the question of Jerusalem's status, from the British conquest of the city in 1917 to our own day. This background is essential for an understanding of various proposals. The second part of the chapter surveys different opinions on the city's legal status according to international law. *Chapter 1* concludes with a brief description of the city's status under Israeli law. *Chapter 2* presents a survey of the various proposals and positions regarding the city's future status. The main points of each plan are given, with special emphasis on national aspirations, the Holy Places, and municipal administration. In addition, a brief sketch is provided of the individual or institution behind each proposal, and in some cases the political background is described. The *third chapter* presents a comparative analysis of the positions and proposals surveyed in Chapter 2 according to a cross-section of the principal themes. This may be helpful both to those who are interested in a solution relating to a specific subject (Holy Places, for example) and to those who may wish to combine several proposals into a single new plan. The lexicon (*Chapter 4*) explains certain terms that appear in the book, especially in Chapter 2.

Chapters 1 and 3 were written by Moshe Hirsch, and Chapter 4 by Ruth Lapidoth. Most of the proposals dealt with in Chapter 2 were analyzed by Moshe Hirsch, and some by Deborah Housen-Couriel. As far as possible, the summaries of the various proposals have been sent to their respective authors, and we have corrected the text in accordance with their wishes.

It is our pleasant duty to thank those who contributed so much to the book. First of all we wish to thank the authors of the various proposals for having taken the time to review our summaries. Ambassador Mordechai Gazit read Chapter 1 and offered many helpful comments. Ora Ahimeir, director of the Jerusalem Institute for Israel Studies, oversaw the work and provided comfortable research conditions. Dr. Yitzhak Reiter was most helpful reviewing the lexicon entries on the "Waqf" and the "Supreme Muslim Council"; Naomi Teasdale offered illuminating comments on the entries for the "Church of the Holy Sepulcher" and "The Holy Places"; Amnon Ramon advised us on geographical questions and Dr. Ifrah Zilberman advised us on the position of Jordan; Ronit Ben Dor was of great assistance in the final research stages; Tsyiona Hizkiahu from the Jerusalem Institute for Israel Studies provided efficient and congenial administrative support; Ralph Mandel provided an excellent translation, faithful to the original and Robert Amoils's meticulous proof-reading contributed considerably to the accuracy of the text. Israel Kimhi and Vered Shatil provided the clear maps; and Esti Boehm, also from the Jerusalem Institute for Israel Studies, designed the book and gave it its special character. All of them have our deepest gratitude.

ABOUT THE AUTHORS

Moshe Hirsch

Dr. Jur. (The Hebrew University of Jerusalem); Teaching Fellow at the rank of Lecturer in International and European Law at the Faculty of Law, The Hebrew University of Jerusalem; and Researcher at the Jerusalem Institute for Israel Studies.

Deborah Housen-Couriel

Doctoral candidate at the Law Faculty of The Hebrew University of Jerusalem; and Director of the Department of Regulation and International Treaties at the Ministry of Communications of Israel.

Ruth Lapidoth

LL.M. (Jerusalem); Ph.D. (Paris); The Bessie and Michael Greenblatt Q.C. Professor of International Law at the Faculty of Law and Head of the Institute for European Studies at The Hebrew University of Jerusalem; Head of the Legal Team of the Jerusalem Institute for Israel Studies.

Chapter One

THE LEGAL STATUS OF JERUSALEM

A. Legal-Historical Background

On 9 December 1917 General Edmund Allenby entered Jerusalem following Britain's conquest of the city from the Turks. At the San Remo Conference (April 1920) the Supreme Allied Council designated Britain as the Mandatory Power to administer "Palestine" (including Jerusalem). On 24 July 1922 the Council of the League of Nations confirmed the terms of the Mandate, which came into effect on 29 September 1923. Article 2 provided that Britain was responsible for creating "such political, administrative and economic conditions as will secure the establishment of the Jewish national home, ... and the development of self-governing institutions, and also for safeguarding the civil and religious rights of all the inhabitants of Palestine, irrespective of race and religion."[1]

On 29 November 1947 the General Assembly of the United Nations adopted Resolution 181 (II) on "the Future Government of Palestine" (also known as the "Partition Resolution").[2] It recommended the establishment in the territory of the Mandate of a Jewish state and an Arab state, to be closely linked economically. The Resolution's third section, dealing with Jerusalem, recommended the creation of a separate entity (*corpus separatum*), demilitarized and neutral. A special "international regime" would be established in the city, to be administered by the Trusteeship Council on behalf of the United Nations. The Council was to draft within five months a detailed proposal for a statute for the city. As for the city's boundaries (see Map 1), these would extend to Abu Dis in the east, Bethlehem in the south, Ein Karem in the west, and Shuafat in the north (these places were to be part of the *corpus separatum*).[3]

---

[1] For the terms of the British Mandate for Palestine, 24 July 1922, see R. Lapidoth & M. Hirsch (eds.), *The Arab-Israel Conflict and Its Resolution: Selected Documents*, 1992, p. 25. The British Mandate applied to the area west of the Jordan River and to its east – today's Kingdom of Jordan. However, in accordance with Article 25 of the Mandate, and with the agreement of the Council of the League of Nations of 16 September 1922, Britain determined that the terms of the Mandate which were meant to support the establishment of the Jewish national home would not apply to the territories lying east of the Jordan. Those territories became independent in 1946. P. Malanczuk, "Israel: Status, Territory and Occupied Territories," in: R. Bernhardt (ed.), *Encyclopedia of Public International Law*, vol. 12, 1990, pp. 149, 155.

[2] For U.N. General Assembly Resolution 181(II) on the Future Government of Palestine, 29 November 1947, see Lapidoth & Hirsch, *The Arab-Israel Conflict* (*supra*, note 1), p. 33.

[3] *Ibid.*, p. 48.

2   *The Legal Status of Jerusalem*

Map 1

City of Jerusalem: Boundaries Proposed by the *Ad hoc* Committee on the Palestine Question

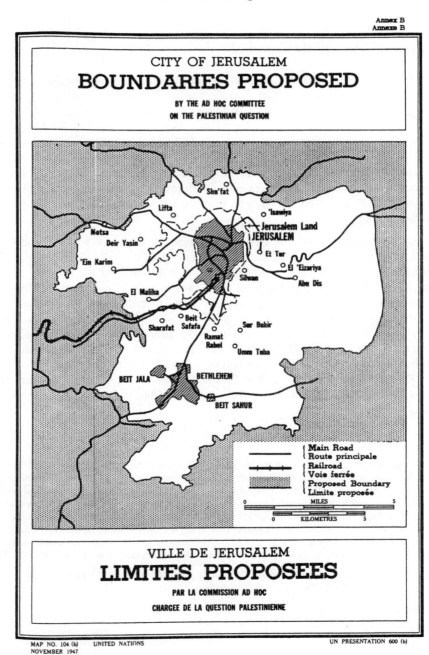

The leaders of the Jewish national institutions of the Yishuv (the Jewish community in pre-state Palestine) agreed to implement the partition plan, provided the Palestine Arabs did likewise. The latter, however, rejected strenuously the U.N. decision[4] and on the day after its adoption launched violent attacks on the Yishuv. On 14 May 1948, shortly before the termination of the British Mandate, the establishment of the State of Israel was proclaimed, triggering an invasion by Arab states (Egypt, Syria, Lebanon, Iraq, and Jordan, assisted by Saudi Arabia).[5] Jerusalem's Jewish neighborhoods came under fierce shelling by the Arab (Jordanian) Legion, supported by Egyptian units. The city was soon under siege and suffered heavy casualties. Intense fighting broke out in the city and on its access roads. On 28 May 1948 the Jewish Quarter of the Old City fell to Jordanian forces following a prolonged siege.[6] On 7 July 1948 Israel and Jordan signed, under U.N. auspices, an agreement for the demilitarization of Mount Scopus, where a Jewish enclave remained. The agreement allowed Israel to deploy a small number of policemen and civilians to maintain the buildings there. The U.N. undertook to guarantee the supply of water and essential equipment and to arrange the rotation of the Jewish personnel in a biweekly convoy.[7]

When the 1948 war ended, east Jerusalem was under the control of the Jordanian Army and west Jerusalem under the control of the Israel Defense Forces (IDF) (see Map 2). In the Israel-Jordan armistice agreement of April 1949, the two states pledged to refrain from taking "aggressive action" against each other.[8] Article 8(2) of the agreement stipulated the establishment of a joint "Special Committee" to discuss subjects raised by either party, "which, in any case, shall include the following, on which agreement in principle already exists: ... resumption of the normal functioning of the cultural and humanitarian institutions on Mount Scopus and free access thereto; free access to the Holy Places and cultural institutions and use of the cemetery on the Mount of Olives;..."[9] Despite these explicit provisions, Jordan denied Jews access to the Western Wall, prevented the reopening of the two institutions on Mount Scopus – the Hebrew University and Hadassah Hospital – and refused to make arrangements with Israel on these subjects.[10] From the end of the 1948 war until

---

[4] Hassan Bin Talal, *A Study On Jerusalem*, 1979, p. 11; J.B. Tulman, "The International Legal Status of Jerusalem," 3 *International Law Students Association Journal*, 39, 46 (1979).

[5] *Ibid.*, p. 46.

[6] T. Kollek & M. Perlman, *Jerusalem, Sacred City of Mankind: A History of Forty Centuries*, 1968, p. 250.

[7] For the agreement between Israel and Jordan on the demilitarization of Mount Scopus of 7 July 1948, see Lapidoth & Hirsch, *The Arab-Israel Conflict* (*supra*, note 1), p. 66; T. Meron, "The Demilitarization of Mount Scopus: A Regime That Was," 3 *Israel Law Review* 501 (1968).

[8] Article 1 of the Hashemite Jordan Kingdom-Israel General Armistice Agreement, 1949, 42 *United Nations Treaty Series* 304.

[9] Article 8, *ibid.*

[10] Kollek & Perlman (*supra*, note 6), p. 252.

4   *The Legal Status of Jerusalem*

Map 2
Armistice Lines in the Jerusalem Area, 1949-1967 (unofficial map)

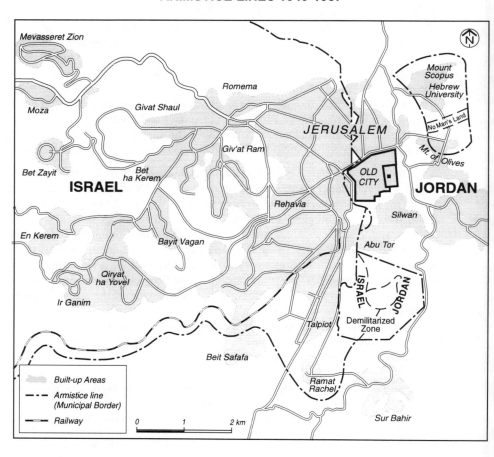

June 1967 the city remained divided between Jordan and Israel, and it suffered from occasional armed clashes between the sides.[11]

In September 1948 the Supreme Court of Israel was established in Jerusalem, and on 20 December the government decided to transfer its ministries to the city.[12] On 5 December 1949 Prime Minister David Ben-Gurion declared in the Knesset (Israel's Parliament) that Jewish Jerusalem is an organic and inseparable part of the State of Israel,[13] and the Knesset declared it the capital of Israel on 13 December 1949.[14] The Prime Minister's Office was moved to Jerusalem the next day, while the Knesset held its first session in the city on 26 December.[15]

The U.N. addressed the Jerusalem question several times between 1948 and 1953. On 26 April 1948 the General Assembly adopted Resolution 185 (S-II), requesting the Trusteeship Council to study suitable measures for the city's protection.[16] In Resolution 187 (S-II) of 6 May 1948[17] the General Assembly called for the appointment of a Special Municipal Commissioner for Jerusalem; this proposal was implemented, but in practice the appointee could not fulfill his designated duties. The General Assembly called for Jerusalem to be "placed under effective United Nations control" in Resolution 194 (III) of 11 December 1948.[18] Additional confirmation of the internationalization approach contained in the Partition Resolution was afforded by the General Assembly in Resolution 303 (IV) of 9 December 1949.[19] The General Assembly also discussed the status of Jerusalem in 1950, 1952, and 1953, but without adopting resolutions on the subject. From 1953 until 1967 Jerusalem did not appear on the agenda of the U.N.'s institutions.

Following the 1948 war, Jordan controlled the West Bank – including east Jerusalem – through a system of military governors, who applied the laws of Mandatory Palestine, subject to Jordanian legislative amendments.[20] The Palestine Arab Conference,

---

[11] N. Shur, *The History of Jerusalem*, Vol. 3, 1987, p. 855 (Hebrew).

[12] M. Brecher, "Jerusalem: Israel's Political Decisions 1947-1977," 27 *The Middle East Journal* 13, 18.

[13] *Records of Knesset Proceedings*, Second Session, 93rd meeting, 5 December 1949, p. 5; on the background to this decision, see Brecher, *op. cit.*, p. 19.

[14] *Records of Knesset Proceedings*, Second Session, 96th meeting, 13-14 December 1949, p. 6.

[15] *Records of Knesset Proceedings*, Second Session, 98th meeting, 26 December 1949, p. 313. It should be noted that the first sessions of the "Constituent Assembly" were also held in Jerusalem (at Jewish Agency headquarters); *Records of Knesset Proceedings*, 14-17 March 1949, pp. 52-55.

[16] Reprinted in R. Lapidoth & M. Hirsch (eds.), *The Jerusalem Question and Its Resolution: Selected Documents*, 1994, p. 18.

[17] *Ibid.*, p. 19.

[18] *Ibid.*, p. 30.

[19] *Ibid.*, p. 49. A detailed survey of the deliberations of U.N. institutions from 1948 to 1953 appears in E. Lauterpacht, *Jerusalem and the Holy Places*, 1968, pp. 23-32.

[20] M.M. Whiteman, *Digest of International Law*, vol. 2, 1963, p. 1163; see also Hassan Bin Talal (*supra*, note 4), p. 24.

meeting at Jericho on 1 December 1948, decided to unite the West Bank (including east Jerusalem) and the Kingdom of Jordan as a single kingdom under King Abdullah of Jordan. On 7 December 1948 the Jordanian government confirmed this decision, and on 13 December 1948 the Jordanian parliament endorsed the government's decision.[21] Four months later, general elections were held in Jordan and the West Bank for a new Jordanian parliament with equal representation for the two banks of the Jordan River. The elected National Assembly then approved the unification of the two banks, in a resolution of 24 April 1950.[22] However, the Arab League objected to the annexation of Arab Palestine by Jordan, claiming that this violated the League resolution of 12 April 1950 prohibiting the annexation of any part of "Palestine." Indeed, Egypt, Saudi Arabia, Syria, and Lebanon voted for a draft resolution to expel Jordan from the Arab League because of the annexation. Finally a compromise was worked out with the mediation of the Iraqi government, according to which Jordan declared to the Arab League, on 31 May 1950, that the annexation would not prejudice the final settlement of the Palestine question.[23] Only two states – Pakistan and Britain – recognized Jordan's annexation of the West Bank, and Britain explained that it did not recognize Jordan's sovereignty in Jerusalem but only its *de facto* authority in the eastern section of the city.[24]

On 5 June 1967 the Six-Day War broke out on the Israeli-Egyptian border. In the early hours of that morning Israel sent messages to King Hussein of Jordan, through the U.N. and the United States, stating that it did not intend to attack Jordan and that if the latter did not intervene Israel would not attack it. Nevertheless, the Jordanian Army began to shell west Jerusalem at 10:45 a.m. and its forces moved toward the city, soon capturing Government House, the seat of U.N. headquarters in Jerusalem. Two days later the IDF recaptured that building and occupied the Old City as well as the West Bank.[25]

Shortly after the end of the war, with the consolidation of IDF control in east Jerusalem, the Knesset amended the *Law and Administration Ordinance* by adding to it Section 11B, stating: "The law, jurisdiction and administration of the State shall extend to any area of Eretz Israel [Land of Israel] designated by the Government by decree."[26] The amendment came into effect on the day of its enactment – 27 June 1967 – and on the following day the government promulgated an order extending

---

[21] Whiteman, *op. cit.*, p. 1164.

[22] *Ibid.*, pp. 1165-1166.

[23] *Ibid.*, pp. 1166-1167.

[24] Hassan Bin Talal (*supra*, note 4), p. 12.

[25] U. Benziman, *Jerusalem – City Without a Wall*, 1973, p. 11 (Hebrew); U. Narkiss, *The Liberation of Jerusalem*, 1983, pp. 97-99.

[26] *Laws of the State of Israel*, Vol. 21, 5727-1966/67, pp. 75-76; Lapidoth & Hirsch, *The Jerusalem Question* (*supra*, note 16), p. 167.

Israeli law, jurisdiction, and administration to east Jerusalem (see Map 3).[27] The Knesset also amended the *Municipalities Ordinance*,[28] empowering the Minister of the Interior to enlarge the area of a municipality to include any area designated under the newly adopted Section 11B of the *Law and Administration Ordinance*. That order was duly promulgated.[29] Also on 27 June the Knesset enacted the *Protection of the Holy Places Law, 1967*, assuring freedom of access to the holy places and stipulating severe criminal sanctions against anyone desecrating or otherwise violating a sacred site.[30]

The U.N. objected to these measures. On 4 July 1967 the General Assembly was convened in emergency session and adopted Resolution 2253 (ES-V), expressing deep concern at Israel's measures to alter the status of Jerusalem, declaring them null and void, and calling on Israel to rescind them.[31] This was followed on 14 July by Resolution 2254 (ES-V), reiterating the main points of the previous resolution and expressing regret at Israel's failure to obey it.[32] In November 1967 the Security Council adopted Resolution 242, emphasizing "the inadmissibility of the acquisition of territory by war" and that a "just and lasting peace" in the Middle East should include "[w]ithdrawal of Israel armed forces from territories occupied in the recent conflict; ..."[33] The resolution does not refer explicitly to Jerusalem or state that Israel must withdraw from the city. Security Council Resolution 252 of 21 May 1968 recalled the above General Assembly resolutions and deplored the failure of Israel to comply with them. The resolution declared all the legislative and administrative measures and actions taken by Israel to change Jerusalem's legal status invalid and unable to alter the city's status.[34] Israel was again censured by the Security Council by Resolution 267 of 3 July 1969 for not carrying out the resolutions of the General Assembly and the Security Council; again the Israeli legislative and administrative measures were declared invalid and Israel was called upon to rescind them.[35]

---

[27] The details of the new boundary are contained in the *Law and Administration Order* (No. 1), 5727-1967, *Collection of Regulations (Subsidiary legislation)*, 5727-1966/67, no. 2064, 28 June 1967, p. 2690.

[28] *Laws of the State of Israel*, Vol. 21, 5727-1966/67, pp. 75-76; Lapidoth & Hirsch, *The Jerusalem Question* (*supra*, note 16), p. 167.

[29] *Collection of Regulations (Subsidiary legislation)*, 5727-1966/67, no. 2065, 28 June 1967, p. 2697 (Hebrew).

[30] *Laws of the State of Israel*, Vol. 21, 5727-1966/67, p. 76; Lapidoth & Hirsch, *The Jerusalem Question* (*supra*, note 16), p. 169.

[31] G.A. RES. 2253 (ES-V), UN *GAOR*, Resolutions adopted by the General Assembly during its Fifth Emergency Session 17-18 September 1967, Supp. 1, at UN Doc. A/6798 (1967).

[32] G.A. RES. 2254 (ES-V), *ibid*.

[33] S.C. RES. 242, *Official Records of the Security Council*, Twenty-Second Year, Resolutions and Decisions, 1382nd Meeting, 22 November 1967.

[34] S.C. RES. 252, *ibid.*, Twenty-Third Year, 1426th Meeting, 21 May 1968.

[35] S.C. RES. 267, *ibid.*, Twenty-Fourth Year, Resolutions and Decisions of the Security Council 1969, at 3-4 Doc. S/INF/24/Rev. 1 (1970).

8   *The Legal Status of Jerusalem*

Map 3
Jerusalem Municipal Area, 1967 (unofficial map)

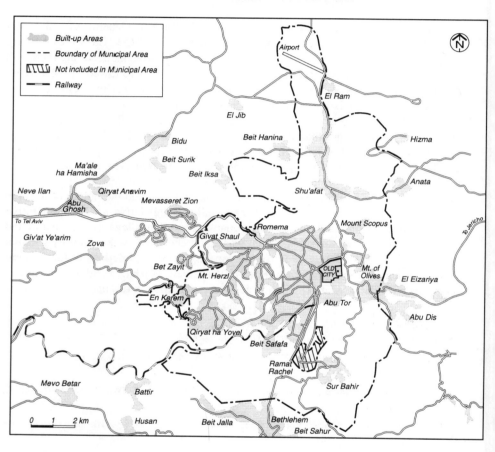

The Camp David agreements of 1978 between Israel and Egypt were silent as regards the status of Jerusalem. The parties clarified their conflicting positions on the subject in letters to the President of the United States delivered proximate to the signing of the agreements. The letter of Egypt's President Anwar al-Sadat stated: " 1. Arab Jerusalem is an integral part of the West Bank. ... 2. Arab Jerusalem should be under Arab sovereignty. 3. The Palestinian inhabitants of Arab Jerusalem are entitled to exercise their legitimate national rights, being part of the Palestinian People in the West Bank. 4. Relevant Security Council Resolutions, particularly Resolutions 242 and 267, must be applied with regard to Jerusalem. All measures taken by Israel to alter the status of the City are null and void and should be rescinded."[36] The letter of Israeli Prime Minister Menachem Begin stated that "[o]n 28 June 1967 – Israel's Parliament (The Knesset) promulgated and adopted a law to the effect: 'The Government is empowered by a decree to apply the law, the jurisdiction and administration of the State to any part of Eretz Israel (land of Israel – Palestine), as stated in that decree.' On the basis of this Law, the Government of Israel decreed in July 1967 that Jerusalem is one city, indivisible, the Capital of the State of Israel."[37] President Jimmy Carter affirmed that "[t]he position of the United States on Jerusalem remains as stated by Ambassador Goldberg in the United Nations General Assembly on July 14, 1967, and subsequently by Ambassador Yost in the United Nations Security Council on July 1, 1969."[38] The legal effect of these letters was to preserve rights and claims and to demarcate the area of dispute.

During the subsequent negotiations between Egypt and Israel on the autonomy regime for the West Bank and the Gaza Strip (1979-1982) the question of Jerusalem's future was a major stumbling block. The Egyptian government held that the jurisdiction of the Palestinian Self-Governing Authority will encompass "all of the Palestinian territories occupied after 5 June 1967," including east Jerusalem. Egypt claimed that Israel's decision to annex east Jerusalem is null and void and must be terminated. The relevant resolutions of the Security Council should be implemented, and especially Resolutions 242 and 267 on Jerusalem, which is an integral part of the West Bank.[39] Rejecting this position, the Israeli delegates argued that the Camp David agreements deliberately made no reference to Jerusalem, and stressed that Jerusalem is the capital of Israel, indivisible, and is not a subject for discussion or negotiation.[40]

---

[36] Lapidoth & Hirsch, *The Jerusalem Question* (*supra*, note 16), p. 299.

[37] *Ibid.*, p. 300.

[38] *Ibid.* On the position of the United States, see *infra*, this chapter, and Ch. 2.

[39] Lapidoth & Hirsch, *The Arab-Israel Conflict* (*supra*, note 1), p.211; M. Gemer, *The Negotiations on Establishing the Autonomy Regime (April 1979-October 1980) – Principal Documents*, 1981, p. 41, and see also pp. 29, 66 (Hebrew).

[40] See Israel's comments on the Egyptian model during a meeting of the Israeli, Egyptian, and American delegations to the working groups of the autonomy talks: the main points were made by Mr. Chaim Kubersky, the head of the Israeli delegation to the working groups, on 29 January 1980; from *Speaking of Autonomy*, Information Center, 1981, pp. 12, 13. See also Gemer, *op. cit.*, pp. 29, 45, 66; and A. Shalev, *The Autonomy Regime – The Problems and Possible Solutions*, 1979, p. 127 (Hebrew).

On 30 July 1980 the Knesset enacted the *Basic Law: Jerusalem, Capital of Israel*, of which Article 1 states that "Jerusalem, complete and united, is the capital of Israel." According to Article 2, "Jerusalem is the seat of the President of the State, the Knesset, the Government and the Supreme Court."[41] The law did not change the city's legal status; its importance lies in its declarative effect. Still, the reaction of the international community was negative. The Security Council adopted Resolution 478 censuring the new legislation and declaring it "a violation of international law." The resolution added that "all legislative and administrative measures" taken by Israel "which have altered, or purport to alter" the city's status "are null and void and must be rescinded forthwith." Finally, all states having diplomatic missions in Jerusalem were called on to remove them from the city.[42] The General Assembly passed a similar resolution, censuring Israel for enacting the law, asserting that it was in breach of international law, and declaring null and void all the legislative and administrative steps taken by Israel to alter the city's status.[43] Following the Security Council resolution, all the states that maintained diplomatic missions in Jerusalem transferred them to Tel Aviv.[44] El Salvador and Costa Rica moved their embassies back to west Jerusalem in April 1984.[45]

The peace initiative of U.S. President Ronald Reagan, announced on 1 September 1982, stated that "Jerusalem must remain undivided, but its final status should be decided through negotiations." At the same time, the United States supported the participation of the Palestinian inhabitants of east Jerusalem in the elections to the self-governing authority which was to be established in the West Bank and the Gaza Strip.[46]

A resolution adopted on 6 September 1982 by the Arab summit meeting, held at Fez, Morocco, declared that Israel must withdraw from all the territories it had occupied in 1967, including "Arab Jerusalem." The conference also called for the establishment of a Palestinian state with Jerusalem as its capital.[47] A similar approach was taken in the declaration of the Palestine Liberation Organization (PLO) in Algiers

---

[41] *Laws of the State of Israel*, Vol. 34, 5740-1979/80, p. 209; Lapidoth & Hirsch, *The Jerusalem Question* (*supra*, note 16), p. 322.

[42] S.C. RES. 478, *Official Records of the Security Council*, Twenty-Second Year, Resolutions and Decisions, 20 August 1980.

[43] G.A. RES. 35/169 (E), *Resolutions and Decisions Adopted by the General Assembly*, During the First Part of its Thirty-Fifth Session, 1980.

[44] The following states had maintained diplomatic missions in Jerusalem until then: Bolivia, Central African Republic, Colombia, Congo (Brazzaville), Congo (Kinshasa), Costa Rica, Dahomey, Dominican Republic, Ecuador, Gabon, Guatemala, Ivory Coast, Madagascar, The Netherlands, Nigeria, Panama, Upper Volta, Uruguay, and Venezuela.

[45] P. Malanczuk, "Jerusalem," in: R. Bernhardt (ed.), *Encyclopedia of Public International Law*, vol. 12, pp. 184, 192.

[46] Lapidoth & Hirsch, *The Arab-Israel Conflict* (*supra*, note 1), p. 287.

[47] *Ibid.*, p. 238.

on 15 November 1988 (the "declaration of independence"). In it the PLO reiterated its position that Israel must withdraw from "Arab Jerusalem" – the capital of the future Palestinian state. In the meantime "the occupied Palestine territories," including Jerusalem, should be placed under U.N. supervision for a limited period.[48]

Jerusalem is not mentioned in the May 1989 Peace Initiative of the Government of Israel[49] which recommended a number of steps to advance the peace process: continuing and expanding the Camp David process; establishing peaceful relations with the Arab states; an international effort to solve the problem of the residents of the Arab refugee camps in Judea, Samaria, and the Gaza district; and holding elections in the West Bank and Gaza to choose delegates who would negotiate with Israel on an interim settlement, to be followed by a permanent solution. One reason this proposal ran aground was disagreement over the participation of east Jerusalem personalities in the pre-elections negotiations. The Israeli government objected to this for fear it might be construed as an Israeli readiness to cede east Jerusalem. However, Israel's interlocutors from Judea and Samaria and the Gaza Strip and the Government of Egypt insisted on the participation of east Jerusalem representatives in order to emphasize that these neighborhoods were part of the West Bank, hence the interim agreement should apply to them.

In 1990 the Jerusalem issue made the headlines in two contexts. In March, U.S. President George Bush stated that in his view the Jewish quarters in the city's eastern section were in effect settlements.[50] The background to this declaration was related to the large-scale immigration to Israel from the Soviet Union: President Bush insisted that, as a condition for receiving loan guarantees from the Administration for the absorption of these immigrants, Israel undertake not to settle the new immigrants in settlements in the West Bank and Gaza Strip. The same condition, Bush said, should apply to the post-1967 Jewish quarters in Jerusalem. The President's statement generated an angry reaction in Israel and among American Jewry, and led the Congress to pass a joint resolution recognizing Jerusalem as the capital of Israel.[51] However, this was a type of resolution which was not binding on the President.

Jerusalem made the headlines again in October 1990, when Muslim worshippers on the Temple Mount, having received erroneous information that the Jewish group known as the Temple Mount Faithful was about to come to the site in order to lay the foundation stone for the Third Temple, threw stones at Jewish worshippers by the Western Wall, below. In the violent clash that developed between the police and the Muslims on the Temple Mount, eighteen people were killed. An official Israeli commission investigated the tragic event, and submitted proposals for new security

---

[48] English translation published in U.N. Doc. A/43/827, S/20278, 18 November 1988; also reproduced in 27 *International Legal Materials* 1661 (1988).

[49] Lapidoth & Hirsch, *The Arab-Israel Conflict* (*supra*, note 1), p. 357.

[50] *American Foreign Policy: Current Documents*, 1990, p. 567.

[51] Lapidoth & Hirsch, *The Jerusalem Question* (*supra*, note 16), p. 450.

arrangements on the Temple Mount. The Security Council condemned Israel and imputed the entire responsibility for the incident to Israel.[52]

October 1991 saw the convening of the Madrid Conference for Peace in the Middle East, followed by the start of negotiations between Israel and its neighbors. The issue of Jerusalem was particularly relevant to the negotiations between Israel and the Palestinians (who were part of a joint delegation with Jordan). According to the invitation to the peace conference issued by the United States and the Soviet Union,[53] the negotiations with the Palestinians would, in the initial phase, deal with the establishment of a self-governing authority for a five-year interim period, with the permanent status negotiations to begin in the third year of the interim arrangement.

Seeking to prevent an infringement of Israel's rights in Jerusalem, the Israeli government demanded that the city not be discussed in the negotiations and that the Palestinian delegation not include representatives from Jerusalem. The Palestinians, for their part, insisted that east Jerusalem residents take part in the talks, that east Jerusalem be included in the self-governing regime, and that Israel withdraw completely from the eastern part of the city.

Neither in the invitation nor in the letter of assurances from the U.S. to Israel was Jerusalem mentioned, though the letter stated that "no party in the process will have to sit [at the negotiations] with anyone it does not want to sit with." The subject was, however, mentioned in the letter of assurances to the Palestinians, in which the United States declared that the composition of their delegation would not prejudice their claims to Jerusalem. The Administration added that the city should never be redivided and that its final status should be determined in negotiations. The United States declared that it did not recognize Israel's annexation of the eastern sector, nor the extension of Jerusalem's municipal boundaries. Moreover, the Arab residents of east Jerusalem should be able to participate by voting in the elections for an interim self-governing authority.

As noted above, Israel took a radically different position. Nevertheless, prior to the ninth round of talks (May 1993) Israel agreed to the participation of Faisal al-Husseini, a resident of east Jerusalem, in the Palestinian delegation, and expressed readiness to allow the Palestinians of east Jerusalem to vote in the elections to the self-governing authority.

In May 1993, the municipal boundaries of Jerusalem were extended (see Map 4) to increase possibilities for developing the city. The extension was toward the west.

On 13 September 1993 representatives of the State of Israel and the Palestine Liberation Organization signed the "Declaration of Principles on Interim Self-

---

[52] U.N. Security Council Resolution 672, 12 October 1990; Lapidoth & Hirsch, *The Arab-Israel Conflict* (*supra*, note 1) p. 375.

[53] *Ibid.*, p. 384.

Government Arrangements."[54] Jerusalem is mentioned in this document in three contexts: the jurisdiction of the Council of the self-governing authority,[55] the elections to that Council and the negotiations on the permanent settlement.

The Agreed Minutes to Article IV appended to the Declaration state that: "Jurisdiction of the Council will cover West Bank and Gaza Strip territory, except for issues that will be negotiated in the permanent status negotiations: Jerusalem, settlements, military locations, and Israelis."[56] This article, together with Articles IV and V(3) of the Declaration make it clear that, at least for the five-year interim period, the elected Council of the self-governing authority will not have jurisdiction in Jerusalem. As for the relationship between the interim arrangements and the permanent settlement, Article V(4) states: "The two parties agree that the outcome of the permanent status negotiations should not be prejudiced or preempted by agreements reached for the interim period."[57]

As to the elections to the Council, Article III(1) notes that they will be "direct, free and general political elections." The parties will negotiate on the modalities and conditions of the elections with the goal of holding them "not later than nine months after the entry into force of this Declaration of Principles" (which, according to Article XVII(1), occurred one month after the signing). According to Article 1 of Annex I ("Protocol on the Mode and Conditions of Elections"), "Palestinians of Jerusalem who live there will have the right to participate in the election process, according to an agreement between the two sides." A key question here is whether east Jerusalem Arabs will only be eligible to vote or also stand for election to the Council.[58] As already noted, in May 1993 the Israeli government expressed readiness to let them take part as voters only. This issue will have to be negotiated before the parties reach an agreement on holding elections.

---

[54] 32 *International Legal Materials* 1525 (1993).

[55] Article 1 of the Declaration defines the "Council" as "the elected Council, ... for the Palestinian people in the West Bank and the Gaza Strip."

[56] *Ibid*.

[57] *Ibid*.

[58] On this issue, see D. Housen-Couriel and M. Hirsch, *East Jeruslaem and the Elections Intended to Be Held in Judea, Samaria, and the Gaza Strip According to the Peace Initiative of the Government of Israel of May 1989*, 1992, pp. 4-10 (Hebrew).

Map 4

Jerusalem Municipal Area, 1993 (unofficial map)

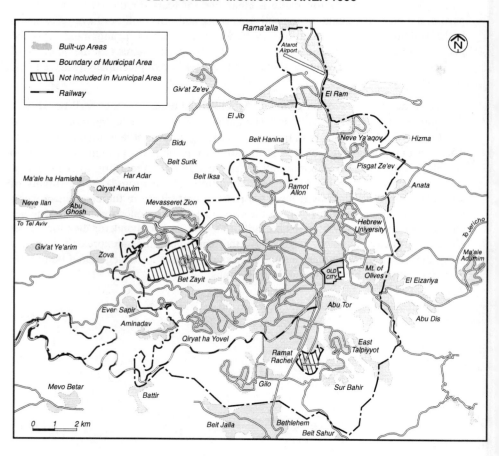

B. Opinions on the Legal Status of Jerusalem According to International Law

States and scholars alike are divided over the legal status of Jerusalem under international law; some positions derive from their espousers' ideological-political approach to the Arab-Israeli conflict. In the following section we shall survey briefly the main positions without taking a stand on their validity. A discussion on the city's legal status must differentiate between west and east Jerusalem, owing to the historical circumstances that brought about Israeli control in the latter. It should be pointed out that the cardinal dispute revolves around the rights of the State of Israel in east Jerusalem, whereas broader agreement exists regarding west Jerusalem, at least with respect to the future control of Israel over this part of the city (though not with regard to sovereignty).

(1) West Jerusalem

As noted above, on 29 November 1947 the United Nations General Assembly adopted the "Partition Resolution" which recommended that the entire city be a separate entity (*corpus separatum*) under an international regime to be administered under the auspices of the U.N.[59] The representatives of the Jewish community accepted this plan,[60] on the assumption that the Arabs would do likewise. However, both the representatives of the Palestine Arabs and the Arab states rejected the plan and claimed that it was illegal.[61] They attacked the Jewish community in the country, and laid siege to west Jerusalem. At the end of the 1948 war, Israel was in control of the city's western section. What, then, is Israel's status in west Jerusalem? Two main answers have been adduced: (a) Israel has sovereignty in this area; and (b) sovereignty lies with the Palestinian people or is suspended.

(a) Sovereignty of the State of Israel

This is the approach adopted by Israel and various international jurists, the most prominent being Elihu Lauterpacht.[62] It holds that the Partition Resolution (calling

---

[59] See *supra*, note 2.

[60] *U.N. Official Records of the Second Session of the General Assembly*, Ad Hoc Committee on the Palestinian Question, 1947, pp. 12, 15-17.

[61] On the position of the Muslim Supreme Council, see *ibid.*, pp. 5, 10-11. On the reaction of the Arab states to the Partition Resolution, see: *U.N. Official Records of the Second Session of the General Assembly*, Plenary Meetings, 1947, vol. 2, pp. 1425-1427. For the arguments of Arab jurists regarding the illegality of the Partition Resolution in general, see: "The Palestine Question," Seminar of Arab Jurists on Palestine, Algiers, July 22-27, 1967, reprinted in J.N. Moore, *The Arab-Israeli Conflict*, 1974, vol. 1, pp. 311-328. Regarding the arrangement proposed by the General Assembly for Jerusalem in particular, *ibid.*, pp. 349-356.

[62] Lauterpacht (supra, note 19), p. 1. The approach of Blum and Schwebel is discussed *infra* in the survey of the status of east Jerusalem.

for the city's internationalization) was merely a recommendation, like most General Assembly resolutions. The General Assembly can only recommend a solution which, if accepted by the parties to a conflict, may constitute the basis for an agreement between them.[63] Between 1947 and 1952 the principal U.N. institutions discussed on several occasions the proposal to establish an international regime in the city, but the fact that this subject did not subsequently appear on the organization's agenda until 1967 shows that the U.N. effectively acquiesced in the demise of the concept.[64] The termination of the British Mandate created a vacuum in sovereignty, which could be filled only by an entity that acted lawfully.[65] Immediately after the British evacuation the armies of Egypt, Iraq, Jordan, Lebanon, and Syria invaded Israel with the goal of resisting by force the realization of the Partition Resolution. These actions constituted a gross violation of the rules of international law prohibiting the use of force.[66] In the face of the invasion, Israel had the right to defend itself according to international law. Israel's consolidation of its hold in west Jerusalem while acting in self-defense filled the vacuum in sovereignty and accorded Israel sovereignty in that part of the city.[67] According to this opinion, the U.N. institutions too acquiesced in this conclusion.[68]

A similar view was espoused by M.I. Gruhin, who believes that with the termination of the British Mandate a situation of "limited *terra nullius*" (an area to a limited degree without a sovereign) was created in Jerusalem. In that situation Jordan and Israel could acquire sovereignty in the city through effectively taking possession. The armistice agreement between them precluded their acquisition of sovereignty in the city as long as that agreement remained in force. Upon its termination in the 1967 Six-Day War, Israel acquired sovereignty in Jerusalem by means of effective possession.[69]

In 1986 Professor Anthony Cassese, who supports the Palestinians' right to self-determination, published an article in the *Palestine Yearbook of International Law* detailing his objections to Lauterpacht's analysis.[70] However, he suggested that Israel's

---

[63] *Ibid.*, pp. 16-18.

[64] *Ibid.*, pp. 23-26.

[65] *Ibid.*, pp. 40-42.

[66] *Ibid.*, p. 43.

[67] *Ibid.*, pp. 44-45.

[68] *Ibid.*, p. 46.

[69] M.I. Gruhin, "Jerusalem: Legal and Political Dimensions in a Search for Peace," 12 *Case Western Journal of International Law* 169 (1980), pp. 205-207. On the reasons that the armistice agreement precluded the acquisition of sovereignty by the two states and the reasons for its termination in 1967, see *infra*, in the discussion on the status of east Jerusalem, in the section describing the position according to which sovereignty accrues to Israel.

[70] A. Cassese, "Legal Considerations on the International Status of Jerusalem," *The Palestine Yearbook of International Law*, vol. 3 (1986), pp. 13, 23-28.

sovereignty in west Jerusalem should be recognized for three main reasons: (a) the 1949 Israel-Jordan armistice line basically parallels the demographic division between Jews and Arabs in the city; (b) following the Six-Day War the U.N. called on Israel to withdraw from territories it had captured in that war, hence it can be inferred that the U.N. might be ready to accept that *de facto* control over western Jerusalem be turned into sovereign rights proper; and (c) the letter by Egypt's President Anwar al-Sadat in the context of the Camp David agreements[71] rejected Israel's claims to east Jerusalem but accepted implicitly Israeli control over the city's western areas.[72]

(b) Sovereignty of the Palestinian People or Suspended Sovereignty

According to Henry Cattan, already in the Mandate period sovereignty in Jerusalem, as in the rest of Palestine, accrued to the Palestinian people.[73] The Partition Resolution, which affirmed the principle of internationalization, is still in force and Israel is committed to implement it because of undertakings it gave to the U.N. in 1948 and 1949.[74] The Partition Resolution did not divest the Palestinians of their sovereignty over the whole city since it assigned to the U.N. Trusteeship Council merely an administrative role. Even if the General Assembly had intended to transfer sovereignty over the city, it was not authorized to do so.[75] Israeli control in west Jerusalem since 1948 was illegal and most states have not recognized its sovereignty there.[76] International law does not recognize the acquisition of a sovereign right by the use of force, and Israel's status in the New City is only that of an occupying power.[77]

A similar viewpoint, albeit less clear, was expressed by Jordan's Crown Prince Hassan Bin Talal, in a book published in 1979, according to which sovereignty in the city was "in suspense" pending the outcome of a comprehensive solution.[78] Israel, the Prince argued, had taken on itself (in a letter of 15 May 1948 from its Foreign Minister to the U.N.) to implement unilaterally the Partition Resolution as it referred

---

[71] See note 36.

[72] Cassese (*supra*, note 70), p. 38.

[73] H. Cattan, *Jerusalem*, 1981, pp. 104, 107; *idem*, "Sovereignty over Palestine," in: Moore (*supra*, note 61), vol. 1, pp. 191, 193-204; H. Cattan, *The Palestine Question*, 1988, pp. 324-326.

[74] Cattan, *Jerusalem*, pp. 105-107. Cattan refers here to a letter sent by the Foreign Minister of Israel's Provisional Government on 15 May 1948 to the U.N. Secretary-General and to remarks made by the Israeli representative to the U.N. during the deliberations on Israel's admission to the U.N., which in his view constitute a unilateral Israeli commitment to implement the arrangements stipulated in the Partition Resolution regarding Jerusalem. In his 1988 book *The Palestine Question*, Cattan also quotes the speech delivered by the representative of the Jewish Agency (Moshe Shertok) to the General Assembly on 27 April 1948. *Ibid.*, pp. 328-329.

[75] Cattan, *Jerusalem* (*supra*, note 73), pp. 107-108.

[76] *Ibid.*, pp. 107, 110-111.

[77] *Ibid.*, p. 121.

[78] Talal (*supra*, note 4), p. 25.

to Jerusalem. Israel's seizure of the western part of the city in 1948 did not grant it sovereignty because according to international law self-defense is not a method of acquiring title to territory; Israel's status in the city is that of a military occupant.[79] Nor do the resolutions passed by the U.N. after the 1967 War attest that the organization has recognized implicitly Israel's sovereignty in west Jerusalem, and most states have refused to recognize any such Israeli claim.[80] G.I.A.D. Draper also argues that Israel did not acquire sovereignty in west Jerusalem in 1948 (nor did Jordan in east Jerusalem), because the international community had intended to establish in the city an international regime under U.N. administration. Both then and now, sovereignty has remained suspended and Israel's status in the city is that of a military occupant.[81]

(2) East Jeruslem

As already mentioned, the Jordanian Army captured east Jerusalem in the 1948 War and administered it until 1950 under a military government. In 1950 the Jordanian National Assembly, which was composed of representatives from both banks of the Jordan, decided to unify the two areas under King Abdullah.[82] When the Six-Day War erupted the Jordanian Army shelled west Jerusalem and advanced toward its outlying neighborhoods, capturing Government House. Two days later the IDF occupied east Jerusalem.[83] Shortly after the war Israel enacted several laws that united the two parts of the city.[84] Three main approaches have been adduced regarding the legal status of east Jerusalem: (a) sovereignty accrues to Israel; (b) sovereignty accrues to Jordan and Israel is holding the area as an occupying power (which does not confer sovereign title); and (c) sovereignty accrues to the Palestinian people.

(a) Sovereignty of the State of Israel

This approach has been mainly presented in articles by Stephen Schwebel, Elihu Lauterpacht, and Yehuda Z. Blum. It holds that with the termination of the British Mandate in Palestine a vacuum was created in sovereignty, which could be filled only in pursuance of a lawful action. Jordan did not acquire legal sovereignty because its occupation of the Old City entirely lacked legal justification.[85] The armistice

---

[79] *Ibid.*, pp. 19-22, 25.

[80] *Ibid.*, pp. 26-27, 30, 39.

[81] G.I.A.D. Draper, "The Status of Jerusalem as a Question of International Law," in: H. Kochler (ed.), *The Legal Aspects of the Palestine Problem with Special Regard to the Question of Jerusalem*, 1980, pp. 154, 162-163.

[82] See *supra*, notes 20-24.

[83] See *supra*, note 25.

[84] See *supra*, notes 26-29.

[85] Lauterpacht (*supra*, note 19), p. 47; S.M. Schwebel, "What Weight to Conquest?" 64 *American Journal of International Law* (1970), pp. 344, 346.

lines that were delineated in the 1949 agreement between Israel and Jordan, which divided the city, were not intended to be final borders. The armistice agreement stated explicitly that its provisions would not prejudice the rights and claims of the two parties.[86] The annexation of east Jerusalem (together with the West Bank) in 1950 to the Kingdom of Jordan constituted a violation of international law and was therefore totally invalid.[87] The provisions of the armistice agreement remained in force until the Six-Day War. Jordan violated the agreement materially by its act of aggression against Israel at the beginning of the 1967 war. This gave Israel the right to consider the agreement as terminated, and it so declared.[88] Israel captured the eastern part of the city in June 1967 in the course of a lawful act of self-defense (after being attacked by Jordan) and acquired sovereign title there.[89] The (minor) difference between Lauterpacht's position and that taken by Blum and Schwebel is that Lauterpacht holds that Israel seized east Jerusalem legally and therefore had the right to fill the *vacuum in sovereignty*,[90] whereas Blum and Schwebel examine the post-1967 legal situation by *comparing* the rights of Israel and Jordan to east Jerusalem and concluding that Israel acquired sovereignty in the area since it has a better title in that territory.[91]

(b) Sovereignty of Jordan (Israel as an occupying power)

In a series of articles published by Yoram Dinstein of Tel Aviv University in 1971 he explained that in the Six-Day War Israel had acted in lawful self-defense and that in the course of doing so had captured east Jerusalem. Dinstein, however, maintains that military occupation does not grant legal title over the occupied area.[92] But the fact that international law does not grant Israel title to east Jerusalem does not mean it has there no right whatsoever. As long as the situation of military occupation continues (including ceasefire periods), Israel does have the right of possession. This situation can continue indefinitely, until a peace treaty is concluded with Jordan.[93] The document that determines Jordan's status following the 1948 war is the armistice

---

[86] See Article II(2) of the Jordan-Israel Armistice Agreement, *supra*, note 8; Y.Z. Blum, "Zion Has Been Redeemed in Accordance with International Law," *Hapraklit* 27 (1971), pp. 315, 320 (Hebrew).

[87] *Ibid.*, p. 319.

[88] *Ibid.*, p. 320.

[89] Lauterpacht (*supra*, note 19), p. 48; Blum (*supra*, note 86), p. 320; Schwebel (*supra*, note 85), p. 346; and see also Y.Z. Blum, "East Jerusalem Is Not Occupied Territory," *Hapraklit* 28 (1972), p. 183 (Hebrew).

[90] Lauterpacht (*supra*, note 19), p. 48.

[91] Schwebel (*supra*, note 85), p. 346; Blum (*supra*, note 86), p. 320; the latter's position is also set forth in Y.Z. Blum, *The Juridical Status of Jerusalem*, 1974, p. 5.

[92] Y. Dinstein, "Zion Shall Be Redeemed in International Law," *Hapraklit* 27 (1971), p. 5 (Hebrew).

[93] Y. Dinstein, " 'And She Was Not Redeemed,' or 'Not Demonstrations But Deeds,' " *Hapraklit* 27 (1971), pp. 519, 521 (Hebrew).

20 *The Legal Status of Jerusalem*

agreement.[94] In that agreement Jordan and Israel affirmed each other's control according to the lines established in the document, and Jordanian control of east Jerusalem was recognized by Israel.[95] These and other articles[96] suggest that in Dinstein's view sovereignty in east Jerusalem accrued to Jordan.

On 31 July 1988 King Hussein of Jordan delivered a speech declaring the dismantling of the legal and administrative links between Jordan and the West Bank (including Jerusalem).[97] This development, which has not yet been addressed publicly by the other authors cited in this chapter, did not lead Dinstein to change his mind. In a published interview he maintained that Hussein's speech had no relevance to title in the West Bank and Jerusalem.[98]

(c) Sovereignty of the Palestinian People or Suspended Sovereignty

As explained above in the discussion on west Jerusalem, H. Cattan holds that sovereignty over all of Palestine, including Jerusalem, accrued to the Palestinian people already in the Mandate period, and that this situation remained unchanged after the Partition Resolution, the 1948 War, and the Six-Day War.[99] As for the steps taken by Jordan in 1950 by which it annexed east Jerusalem,[100] Cattan believes that they did not impair the sovereignty of the Palestinian people over that part of the city. This is so because the decision by the Jordanian parliament of 24 April 1950 stated that the rights of the Palestinians would be reserved and the unification would not prejudice their rights in the final settlement of the Palestine question.[101] In Cattan's view, the steps taken by Israel after the Six-Day War are an attempt to annex east Jerusalem,[102] and U.N. institutions have declared a number of times that those measures violate international law and have no legal validity.[103] International law does not permit the acquisition of territory through the use of force, and the international community has refused to recognize Israel's annexation of east Jerusalem.[104]

---

[94] Y. Dinstein, "A Reply to Mr. Dawiq," *Hapraklit* 27 (1971), pp. 292, 293 (Hebrew).

[95] Dinstein (*supra*, note 93), p. 521.

[96] See especially Y. Dinstein, "Autonomy," in: Y. Dinstein (ed.), *Models of Autonomy*, 1981, pp. 291, 300.

[97] The text of King Hussein's speech was published in 27 *International Legal Materials* 1673 (1988).

[98] Y. Dinstein, "Israel Cannot Annex the Territories According to International Law," *Ha'aretz*, 4 August 1988, p. 1 (Hebrew).

[99] See notes 73-77.

[100] See notes 20-24.

[101] Cattan, *Jerusalem* (*supra*, note 73), p. 64.

[102] H. Cattan, *Palestine and International Law*, 1973, p. 71.

[103] *Ibid.*, pp. 139-141.

[104] Cattan, *Jerusalem* (*supra*, note 73), pp. 111-121.

Thomas and Sally Mallison also maintain that sovereignty in east Jerusalem accrues to the Palestinian people. In their view the Palestinian people has the right of self-determination, which includes the right to sovereignty (it is not quite clear whether this right applies to all the territories allocated to the Arab state in the Partition Resolution or only to the territories seized by Israel in the Six-Day War, although the second alternative would appear to be more in line with the authors' opinion).[105] The Partition Resolution, which is still in force,[106] enables both the Palestinian people and the Jewish people to implement the right of self-determination. A Palestinian state should be established in the area of the British Mandate lying outside pre-1967 Israel, with minor modifications, and following an interim stage east Jerusalem should be transferred to the control of that Palestinian state.[107]

Crown Prince Hassan Bin Talal maintained, in a book published in 1979, that Jordan did not acquire sovereignty over east Jerusalem between 1948 and 1967 and that its status in the city was that of a military occupant.[108] Israel's military occupation in 1967 did not grant it sovereign title, an attitude affirmed by the U.N. in many resolutions.[109] Israel's status in east Jerusalem is that of a military occupant. The legislation enacted by Israel after the Six-Day War constitutes indirect or implicit annexation, in violation of international law.[110] The international community did not recognize Israeli sovereignty over east Jerusalem and the U.N. did not abandon the internationalization plan. Sovereignty in the city remains suspended.[111] G.I.A.D. Draper took an almost identical stand.[112]

---

[105] W.T. Mallison & S.V. Mallison, *The Palestine Problem in International Law and World Order*, 1986, pp. 197-201.

[106] *Ibid.*, pp. 171-173.

[107] *Ibid.*, pp. 206, 233; S.V. Mallison & W.T. Mallison, "The Status of Jerusalem as a Question of International Law," in: H. Kochler (ed.), *The Legal Aspects of the Palestine Problem*, 1980, pp. 98, 110-112. Echoes of the opinion that sovereignty in Jerusalem accrues to the Palestinians are also found in M. Van Dusen, "Jerusalem, the Occupied Territories and the Refugees," in: M. Khadduri (ed.), *Major Middle Eastern Problems in International Law*, 1978, p. 51. A similar position, supporting the sovereignty of the Palestinian people in east Jerusalem (but which is not based on the Partition Resolution), is found in J. Quigley, "Old Jerusalem: Whose to Govern?" 20 *Denver Journal of International Law & Policy* (1991), pp. 145, 164-166.

[108] Talal (*supra*, note 4), p. 27.

[109] *Ibid.*, pp. 29-30.

[110] *Ibid.*, pp. 39-40.

[111] *Ibid.*, pp. 30-31.

[112] Draper (*supra*, note 81), pp. 162-163.

C. The Legal Status of Jerusalem According to Israeli Law

Thus far we have examined Jerusalem's status according to international law, and we turn now to survey its status in accordance with Israeli law. As described above, following the Six-Day War Israel enacted legislation resulting in the application of its law, jurisdiction, and administration in east Jerusalem.[113] The legal significance of these enactments was considered in several decisions handed down by Israeli courts, and the conclusion arising from them is that east Jerusalem is today part of the State of Israel.

A first hint of this trend was apparent in an *obiter dictum* uttered by Justice Agranat in a High Court of Justice case, *Ben Dov vs. Minister of Religious Affairs*, from which it could be deduced that the court considered east Jerusalem to be part of Israel.[114] The question of east Jerusalem's status arose more blatantly in a judgment delivered by the High Court of Justice in the case of *Hanzalis vs. Court of the Greek Orthodox Patriarchate*.[115] The case concerned a decision rendered by the court of that church, which has its seat in east Jerusalem, and which ruled that it had jurisdiction to consider a last will in violation of the Israeli succession law. The High Court quashed the church court's decision, and in a separate opinion Justice Halevy expressed his view that from the day the above-mentioned legislation was enacted, "united Jerusalem constitutes an integral part of Israel."[116]

The most important decision regarding the status of east Jerusalem according to Israeli law was given in 1970 by the Supreme Court in the case of *Ruidi and Maches vs. Military Court of Hebron.*[117] The two petitioners in this case were charged in the Hebron Court with exporting antiquities without a permit from the West Bank to their shop in east Jerusalem, violating the applicable Jordanian Law.[118] The cardinal question before the court was whether east Jerusalem was "abroad" *vis-à-vis* the West Bank; if so, the transfer of the antiquities was an unlawful "export." The court ruled that the indictment had been properly submitted since east Jerusalem was in fact "abroad" *vis-à-vis* the West Bank. Justice Y. Kahan stated: "...As far as I am concerned, there is no need for any certificate from the Foreign Minister or from any administrative authority to determine that east Jerusalem... was annexed to the State

---

[113] See notes 26-29.

[114] H.C. [High Court of Justice] 223/67, *Ben Dov vs. Minister of Religious Affairs*, 1968(1) *P.D.* 440 (Hebrew); Lapidoth & Hirsch, *The Jerusalem Question* (*supra*, note 16), p. 487.

[115] H.C. [High Court of Justice] 171/68, *Hanzalis vs. Court of the Greek Orthodox Patriarchate*, 1969(1) *P.D.* 419 (Hebrew); Lapidoth & Hirsch, *The Jerusalem Question* (*supra*, note 16), p. 489.

[116] *Ibid.*, p. 269.

[117] H.C. [High Court of Justice] 283/69, *Ruidi and Maches vs. Military Court of Hebron*, 1970(2) *P.D.* 419 (Hebrew); Lapidoth & Hirsch, *The Jerusalem Question* (*supra*, note 16), p. 502.

[118] *Ibid.*, pp. 421-422.

of Israel and constitutes part of its territory... by means of these two enactments... and consequently this area constitutes part of the territory of Israel..."[119]

This judgment provoked contradictory articles by Yoram Dinstein and Yehuda Z. Blum. Dinstein criticized the court's decision, arguing that if a statute is ambivalent and its content does not obligate a different interpretation, it should be construed in a way compatible with international law. Thus the 1967 law should be interpreted in a manner that would prevent a clash with international law. "This interpretation is both possible and practical, if one recognizes that the application of the law, jursidiction, and administration of Israel over east Jerusalem does not constitute an annexation."[120] Dinstein expressed the opinion that international law does not permit Israel to annex east Jerusalem and that Israel is a belligerent occupant in that area.[121]

Blum responded with a critique of Dinstein.[122] He agreed with Dinstein that the term "annexation" was inappropriate to describe the results of the Israeli legislation enacted in June 1967. His reason, however, was that the application of Israeli law to parts of the Land of Israel was not annexation of foreign territory, but its liberation from foreign rule. Jordan, Blum maintained, did not have sovereignty over east Jerusalem before the war, and the application of Israeli law there was essentially no different from its application to other areas of the Land of Israel which were not to be within the boundaries of Israel under the Partition Resolution.[123]

It is important to point out that from the point of view of internal Israeli law this dispute is not of great importance. As Amnon Rubinstein notes: "East Jerusalem has to all intents and purposes become part of the territory of the State. The status of east Jerusalem today is no different from the status of west Jerusalem and other territories that were incorporated into the State after the 1948 war."[124] This position was reaffirmed by the District Court of Jerusalem in the case of *Attorney General vs. Yoel Davis*.[125] Here the court considered a request by the Attorney General to extradite Davis to the United States in accordance with the extradition treaty between the two states. Article 1 of that treaty states that "Each Contracting Party agrees... to deliver up persons

---

[119] *Ibid.*, pp. 422-423.

[120] Dinstein (*supra*, note 92), p. 7.

[121] *Ibid.*, pp. 7-8. For Dinstein's view of the status of east Jerusalem, see notes 92-98.

[122] Blum (*supra*, note 86), p. 315.

[123] *Ibid.*, pp. 317-318; on Blum's position regarding the status of east Jerusalem according to international law, see notes 86-89.

[124] A. Rubinstein, *The Constitutional Law of Israel*, 3rd ed., 1991, p. 68 (Hebrew). In practice, Israel granted certain concessions to the residents of east Jerusalem, such as in the realm of education. See Legal and Administrative Matters (Regulation) Law, 1970, *Laws of the State of Israel*, vol. 24, 5730-1969/70, pp. 144-152; Lapidoth & Hirsch, *The Jerusalem Question* (*supra*, note 16), p. 242.

[125] *Attorney General vs. Yoel Davis*, 1989 (3) P.M. 336 (Hebrew); Lapidoth & Hirsch, *The Jerusalem Question* (*supra*, note 16), p. 535.

found in its territory who have been charged..."[126] Davis's lawyer argued that the treaty was inapplicable to his client because he lived in the Old City of Jerusalem, where indeed the arrest had been made and the extradition request delivered.[127] Judge Zemach rejected this argument, since both the United States and Israel accepted that the treaty applied to an individual being sought by the authorities who was living in east Jerusalem. The judge was able to glean the opinion of the United States from the extradition request itself (which noted the individual's place of residence in the Old City),[128] and as for Israel, he quoted the above-mentioned judgments on the status of Jerusalem and stated: "Not only the law of the State, but also its jurisdiction and administration apply in east Jerusalem. Consequently, that area constitutes part of the territory of Israel."[129]

---

[126] *Ibid.*, p. 338.

[127] *Ibid.*

[128] *Ibid.*, p. 339.

[129] *Ibid.*, p. 342.

Chapter Two

PROPOSALS AND POSITIONS CONCERNING THE FUTURE OF JERUSALEM

1. The Sykes-Picot Agreement

Date: The agreement was included in a letter of 16 May 1916 from Britain's Foreign Secretary, Sir Edward Grey, to the French Ambassador in London, Paul Cambon.

Source: J.N. Moore (ed.), *The Arab-Israeli Conflict: Readings and Documents; Abridged and Revised Edition*, Princeton University Press, Princeton, New Jersey, 1977, p. 880.

Background to the provisions of the agreement on Palestine: Y. Minerbi, *The Vatican, the Holy Land, and Zionism*, Ben-Zvi Institute, Jerusalem, 1985, pp. 21-28 (Hebrew).
D. Fromkin, *A Peace to End All Peace: The Fall of the Ottoman Empire and the Creation of the Modern Middle East*, Avon Books, New York, 1989, pp. 188-193.

Background to the agreement: Negotiations on the future of the Ottoman Empire began in November 1915 between Britain and France. In early 1916 their representatives, Sir Mark Sykes and Charles Georges-Picot (officials in the Foreign Service of Britain and France, respectively), reached an agreement on the future of the Middle East after World War I. As for Palestine, the two sides agreed that the area in the country's center would be subject to an international administration. In later years, as circumstances had changed, British policy makers came to believe that the internationalization arrangement was not in line with British interests in the Middle East and the agreement remained unimplemented.

National Aspirations

Article 3 of the agreement states that "in the brown area there shall be established an international administration, the form of which is to be decided upon after consultation with Russia, and subsequently in consultation with the other Allies, and the representatives of the Shereef of Mecca." According to the map attached to the agreement, the "brown area" included much of Palestine, with the exception of Haifa and Acre.

2. The British Mandate for Palestine

Date: 24 July 1922

Source: League of Nations Official Journal, August 1922, pp. 1007-1012.
A. Ginio, "Plans for the Solution of the Jerusalem Problem," in: J.L. Kraemer (ed.), *Jerusalem: Problems and Prospects*, Praeger, N.Y., 1980, pp. 41, 43-44.

Background: The Terms of the Mandate vested in Britain powers of administration in the area of Palestine under the supervision of the League of Nations (see *Mandate* in the Lexicon, Ch. 4). The Terms of the Mandate agreed upon by the Council of the League of Nations and by Britain, stemmed from the political results of World War I and reflected arrangements which had been agreed upon by the European powers (especially Britain and France) during the war. The Mandate did not refer explicitly to Jerusalem but only to the Holy Places.

National Aspirations

1. Britain was designated as the administering power of the territory of the Mandate under the supervision of the League of Nations.

2. The question of sovereignty over Palestine's territory was not explicitly determined in the Mandate (see Lexicon, Ch. 4), but Article 3 stated that the Mandatory power should "encourage local autonomy." The Mandatory power was also to create conditions which would "secure the establishment of the Jewish national home" and the "development of self-governing institutions."

Holy Places

1. Britain was made responsible for the Holy Places in Palestine and for "preserving existing rights" at those sites (see *Holy Places* and *Status quo* in the Lexicon, Ch. 4).

2. The Mandatory power would secure free access to the Holy Places, subject to the requirements of public order and decorum.

3. The Mandatory power would ensure the free exercise of worship at the Holy Places, subject to the requirements of public order and morals.

4. Britain was prohibited to interfere with "the fabric of the management of purely Moslem sacred shrines, the immunities of which are guaranteed."

5. Britain was to appoint a "special Commission" to "study, define and determine the rights and claims in connection with the Holy Places," in order to facilitate the making of decisions on these questions. The method of the Commission's nomination, its composition, and its functions were to be submitted for the approval of the Council of the League of Nations.

3. Proposal of Dr. Chaim Arlosoroff

Date: January 1932

Source: Letter from Dr. Chaim Arlosoroff to Sir Herbert Samuel, 7 January 1932 (Central Zionist Archives).
Letter from Dr. Chaim Arlosoroff to Major J.E.F. Campbell, Southern District Commissioner, 19 January 1932 (Central Zionist Archives).
Letter from Sir Herbert Samuel to Dr. Chaim Arlosoroff, 21 January 1932 (Central Zionist Archives).

Background: The proposal was put forward by Dr. Chaim Arlosoroff, head of the Jewish Agency's Political Department, in a letter to Sir Herbert Samuel (then an official in the British Home Office). The plan was formulated following talks between Arlosoroff and the British Commissioner for the Southern District of Palestine, Major J.E.F. Campbell. In his reply Samuel emphasized that he was expressing his personal opinion only (since the "matter rests with the Colonial Office"). According to Samuel, the creation of two municipal authorities "in immediate proximity to each other would almost be to invite friction," although this might be "the only means of avoiding greater evils."

National Aspirations

The underlying premise was apparently that Jerusalem, like the rest of Palestine, would remain under a British Mandate.

Municipal Administration

1. The city would be divided into two boroughs: one Jewish and one Arab.
2. The Jewish borough (Jerusalem West) would include the new sections of the city and its population would be predominantly Jewish. The Arab borough would comprise mainly the Old City (where 5,000 Jews lived at that time) and the Talpi'ot neighborhood, and its population would be predominantly Arab.
3. Each borough would have its own council, with certain "special rating powers."
4. The "united Municipal Council of Jerusalem would... retain a coordinating and controlling authority."

4. The Peel Commission Report

Date: The report was signed on 22 June 1937 and made public on 7 July 1937.

Source: Excerpts from the Report of the Palestine Royal Commission (The Peel Commission), 22 June 1937, in: J.N. Moore (ed.), *The Arab-Israeli Conflict, vol. III: Documents*, Princeton University Press, Princeton, New Jersey, 1974, p. 150.
H.E. Bovis, *The Jerusalem Question*, Hoover Institution Press, Stanford University, California, 1971, pp. 21-25.

Background: The Royal Commission was established by the British government following the riots that broke out in Palestine in April 1936. It was chaired by Earl Peel, former Secretary of State for India. The Commission heard testimonies from November 1936 to February 1937, both in Palestine and elsewhere in the region. The report was published on 7 July 1937, and on the same day the British government declared that it adopted its conclusions and would take the necessary steps for its implementation.

National Aspirations

1. The commission recommended the termination of the British Mandate in its current form and the establishment of two independent states, a Jewish and an Arab one, in the territory of the Mandate.
2. An enclave, to include Jerusalem, Bethlehem, Nazareth, the Sea of Galilee, and a corridor from Jerusalem to the Mediterranean Sea would remain under a British Mandate.
3. The purpose of the Mandate in those areas would not be to bring about future self-government but to ensure the protection of the Holy Places.

Holy Places

1. The Mandatory would guarantee free access to the Holy Places.
2. The Mandatory would preserve the existing rights at the Holy Places (see *Status quo* in the Lexicon, Ch. 4).
3. Britain should also be responsible for "the protection of religious endowments and of such buildings, monuments and places in the Arab and the Jewish States as are sacred to the Jews and the Arabs respectively."

5. Proposal of the Jewish Agency

Date: The report of the Woodhead Commission, in which the Jewish Agency's proposal appeared, was published in October 1938.

Source: Palestine Partition Commission Report, Cmd. 5854, H.M. Stationery Office, London, 1938, p. 73.
J. Le Morzellec, *La question de Jérusalem devant l'Organisation des Nations Unies*, Etablissements Emile Bruylant, Bruxelles, 1979, p. 50.

Background: In its concluding report, the Woodhead Commission proposed three alternatives for the partition of Mandatory Palestine – all of them leaving Jerusalem under a British Mandate. The proposal set forth below is described in the report as emanating from a "Jewish source." It is clear from other sources that the proposal was that of the Jewish Agency, which submitted a memorandum to the commission. In that document, the Jewish Agency opposed the inclusion of all of Jerusalem within the area of the British Mandate as proposed by the commission. The commission did not accept the Jewish Agency's position due to its assessment that the Muslims and the Christians would object to the inclusion of part of Jerusalem within the Jewish state and because of administrative problems entailed in implementing the proposal.

National Aspirations

1. The Old City and the areas to its north and south, which were populated primarily by Muslims and Christians, would remain under a British Mandate.

2. The "new Jewish Jerusalem," including the quarters to the west of the Old City along the road to Ein Karim, the Mekor Hayyim and Ramat Rahel neighborhoods, and the area of the Hebrew University, should be included in the Jewish state. According to the report, the population of those areas was predominantly Jewish (71,000 out of 74,500).

3. A corridor would be created between the Jewish area in Jerusalem and the Jewish state in the maritime plain.

6. Report of Sir William Fitzgerald

Date: 28 August 1945

Source: Report by Sir William Fitzgerald on the Local Administration of Jerusalem, 28 August 1945, Government Printer, Palestine.
A. Ginio, "Plans for the Solution of the Jerusalem Problem," in: J.L. Kraemer (ed.), *Jerusalem: Problems and Prospects*, Praeger, N.Y., 1980, pp. 41, 54-56.

Background: Sir William Fitzgerald, the Chief Justice of the Supreme Court of Palestine, was appointed by the High Commissioner for Palestine on 11 July 1945 to investigate, report, and make recommendations regarding the municipal administration of Jerusalem. Fitzgerald was given this task in the wake of a crisis in the functioning of the Jerusalem Municipal Council and the appointment of six British officials to run City Hall.

National Aspirations

Britain would continue to administer Palestine (including Jerusalem) as the Mandatory power, but significant changes would be introduced into the municipal structure of Jerusalem, modelled on the administration of the city of London.

Holy Places

1. All matters directly affecting the Holy Places "should be subject to the control of the Administrative Council" (see below).

2. Any dispute as to whether a particular site is a Holy Place "should be referred to the High Commissioner-in-Council."

3. Any question about whether a particular matter affects a Holy Place would be determined by the Administrative Council.

4. The Administrative Council may prevent the carrying through of certain projects and schemes affecting Holy Places.

5. The Administrative Council would maintain the *status quo* with regard to the Holy Places (see *Status quo* in Lexicon, Ch. 4).

Municipal Administration

1. The city would be divided into two boroughs, one Jewish and one Arab, each to be managed by a borough council, subject to certain supervisory powers vested in the Administrative Council (see below). The declared purpose was to grant the boroughs "the greatest possible measure of autonomy."

2. The municipal boundaries should be extended, with the areas outside the boroughs to be administered directly by the Administrative Council.
3. The borough councils would be elected by "taxpayers who habitually reside in the borough."
4. At its first meeting each borough council should elect its own mayor, subject to the veto of the High Commissioner.
5. The powers delegated to the borough councils would include rating, education, health, social services, and sewage (pipes in the borough).
6. The chairman of the Administrative Council should be appointed by the High Commissioner. The members of the Council should consist of four persons from each borough to be elected annually by the borough councils from among their councillors. Two additional council members – who "should be neither Jews nor Arabs" – would be nominated by the High Commissioner. The Government of Palestine should pay the salary of the "Administrator" (as the chairman of the Administrative Council would be titled).
7. The Administrative Council would have important powers regarding the Holy Places (see above), authority to approve town planning in the boroughs, allocation of water to the boroughs, and maintenance of the main sewerage system.
8. The activities of the Administrative Council for the boroughs would be financed by the borough councils, on the basis of precepts for payment to be issued by the Administrative Council.

7. The Morrison-Grady Committee Report

Date: The report was submitted on 25 July 1946 and made public on 30 July, 1946.

Source: A. Ginio, "Plans for the Solution of the Jerusalem Problem," in: J.L. Kraemer (ed.), *Jerusalem: Problems and Prospects*, Praeger, N.Y., 1980, pp. 41, 56-57.
H.E. Bovis, *The Jerusalem Question*, Hoover Institution Press, Stanford University, California, 1971, pp. 39-40.
H.M. Sachar, *A History of Israel*, Knopf, N.Y., 1979, pp. 270-272.

Background: Herbert Morrison (of Britain) and Henry Grady (of the United States) headed the joint committee which was asked to propose detailed steps to implement the recommendations of the Anglo-American Committee of Inquiry, submitted in May 1946 (proposing that that the British Mandate in Palestine become a U.N.-supervised trusteeship). Nevertheless, several elements of the Morrison-Grady Report contradicted the conclusions of the Anglo-American Committee. The British Cabinet immediately adopted the proposed plan, but both representatives of the Jewish community and leaders of Arab institutions in Palestine rejected it. On 12 August 1946 U.S. President Harry Truman informed the Prime Minister of Britain Clement Attlee that the United States would not support the plan.

National Aspirations

1. The British Mandate would be replaced by a trusteeship under U.N. supervision, with Palestine to be cantonized into two autonomous provinces (one Arab and one Jewish), and two zones (District of Jerusalem and District of the Negev) under direct rule of the Central Government.

2. The Central Government would be headed by the British High Commissioner.

3. The Jewish province would comprise the Jordan Valley starting north of Beit She'an, the coastal plain between Acre and Wadi Rubin, and a corridor running from those two areas to Afula. The Arab province would comprise the rest of the country other than the two districts to be controlled by the Central Government. The Negev District would include the entire area south of Beersheba, and the Jerusalem District would also include Bethlehem, both to be under the control of the Central Government.

4. Each province would elect its own "Legislative Chamber," while the "Chief Minister" and the cabinet in each province would be appointed by the British High Commissioner.

5. All powers of defense, foreign relations, customs and excise, police, courts, and communications would be exercised by the Central Government.

Holy Places

A principal task of the (British) Central Government in the Jerusalem District would be to protect the interests of the three religions at the Holy Places.

Municipal Administration

1. The majority of the Jerusalem District Council's members would be elected by the inhabitants, but certain members would be nominated by the High Commissioner.
2. The powers of the Jerusalem District Council would be similar to those vested in a municipal council.

8. Proposal of the Minority of UNSCOP

Date: The report was submitted to the U.N. General Assembly on 31 August 1947.

Source: United Nations Special Committee on Palestine, Report to the General Assembly, vol. 1, *Official Records of the Second Session of the General Assembly*, Supp. No. 11, pp. 59-63.
H.E. Bovis, *The Jerusalem Question*, Hoover Institution Press, Stanford University, California, 1971, pp. 41-43.

Background: On 2 April 1947 Britain referred the Palestine question to the U.N. General Assembly. At a special meeting of the General Assembly on 28 April, convened at the request of Britain, the British delegate stated that although his government would accept the General Assembly's recommendation, it could not accept responsibility for implementing a resolution which would not be accepted by the Jews and the Arabs. On 15 May 1947 the General Assembly established a special committee (United Nations Special Committee on Palestine – UNSCOP) which on 31 August submitted a report to the General Assembly including majority and minority opinions. The minority proposal (supported by India, Iran, and Yugoslavia) was not accepted by the General Assembly (the majority opinion, which was accepted with minor modifications, is described below; see "The Partition Resolution.")

National Aspirations

1. An independent federal state would be established, composed of two autonomous districts (one Jewish and one Arab) under the supervision of a central federal government. Jerusalem would be the capital of the federal state.
2. The government of each district would be vested with powers regarding education, local taxation, right of residence, licensing of businesses, approval of land transactions, immigration, settlement, police and punishment of offenders, social services and institutions, housing, public health, local roads, agriculture, and local industry.

Holy Places

1. The federal constitution would include provisions to guarantee:
    (a) The sacred character of the Holy Places.
    (b) Free access to the Holy Places based on the existing rights and subject to the requirements of public order.
    (c) Freedom of worship at the Holy Places, subject to the requirements of public order.

(d) Preservation of the existing rights of the religious communities at the Holy Places (see *Satus quo* in the Lexicon, Ch. 4).
(e) Should urgent repairs be required at a Holy Place, the federal government would ask one of the religious communities to carry out the work. If no action were taken within a reasonable time, the central government would carry out the repairs.
(f) No taxes would be levied on Holy Places that were exempt from taxation on the day independence was granted.

2. An impartial system for the settlement of disputes regarding the Holy Places.

3. The U.N. would establish a permanent international body for the supervision and protection of the Holy Places in Palestine. This body:
   (a) Would comprise three U.N.-appointed members and one representative from each recognized faith with an interest in the Holy Places;
   (b) Would be responsible for protecting the Holy Places in Palestine, subject to the preservation of existing rights; and
   (c) Would be the representative institution *vis-à-vis* the federal government with respect to the Holy Places and would prepare reports for the U.N. on such matters.

Municipal Administration

1. Jerusalem, the capital of the federal state, would comprise two separate municipalities: one Arab, with authority over the city's Arab sections, including the Old City; and one Jewish, with authority over areas which are inhabited predominantly by Jews.

2. The two municipalities would have the powers of a local administration in the areas under their control and would also participate in joint institutions of self-government, provided equitable representation were assured to the followers of the faiths.

3. The two municipalities would jointly provide common services such as sewerage, garbage collection, fire protection, water supply, local transport, telephone, and telegraph.

9. The Resolution on the Future Government of Palestine (The "Partition Resolution") of the U.N. General Assembly (Resolution 181 [II])

Date: 29 November 1947

Source: G.A. RES. 181 (II), 29 November 1947, *Official Records of the Second Session of the General Assembly, Resolutions*, 16 September-29 November 1947, p. 131.

Background: In this resolution the General Assembly adopted the majority recommendation of UNSCOP (see preceding document on UNSCOP) with minor modifications: Jaffa, Beersheba, and a strip adjacent to the Egyptian border would be part of the proposed Arab state (instead of the Jewish state, as recommended by the UNSCOP majority). The resolution, passed by a majority of 33 to 13, recommended the partition of Palestine into two independent states, one Jewish and one Arab, to be bound by an economic union, and the establishment of a *corpus separatum* of Jerusalem.

National Aspirations

1. Jerusalem would be considered a separate entity (*corpus separatum*) under an international regime, to be administered by the U.N. ("internationalization").

2. Additional areas would be added to the city, so that its new borders would include: Abu Dis in the east, Bethlehem in the south, Ein Karim in the west, and Shu'fat in the north.

3. The city would be demilitarized and neutral (on both terms, see Lexicon, Ch. 4).

4. The city would be included in the "Economic Union of Palestine" encompassing both the Jewish and the Arab state.

5. The inhabitants of both states would be guaranteed freedom of entry and residence in Jerusalem, "subject to considerations of security, and of economic welfare."

6. All residents of the city would *ipso facto* become "citizens of the City of Jerusalem unless they opt for citizenship of the State of which they have been citizens."

7. Jerusalem would have an "independent judiciary system," to which all residents of the city would be subject.

8. Arabic and Hebrew shall be the official languages of the city.

9. After ten years of U.N. administration, the inhabitants would be consulted by a referendum on "possible modifications" of the regime of the city.

Holy Places

1. The existing rights at the Holy Places would be preserved (see *Status quo* in Lexicon, Ch. 4).
2. Freedom of access to and worship at the Holy Places would be secured "in conformity with existing rights" and subject to the requirements of public order.
3. Nothing would be done to impair the sacred character of the Holy Places.
4. Should the Governor of the city conclude that a Holy Place needed urgent repair, he could call on the "community or communities concerned" to execute the repair work, and if this were not accomplished within a reasonable time the Governor himself could have the work done.
5. No taxes would be levied on Holy Places that were exempt from taxation "on the date of the creation of the City."
6. The protection of the Holy Places would be "a special concern of the Governor."
7. With respect to Holy Places outside Jerusalem, The Governor would decide, on the grounds of the powers granted to him by the constitutions of the two states (the Jewish and Arab states to be established), whether the provisions of those constitutions regarding the Holy Places were "being properly applied and respected."
8. "The Governor shall also be empowered to make decisions on the basis of existing rights in cases of disputes which may arise between the different religious communities" regarding the Holy Places "in any part of Palestine."

Municipal Administration

1. "A Governor of the City of Jerusalem shall be appointed by the [U.N.] Trusteeship Council."
2. The Governor would represent the U.N. in the city and "exercise on [its] behalf all powers of administration, including the conduct of external affairs."
3. "The existing local autonomous units in the territory of the city (villages, townships and municipalities) shall enjoy wide powers of local government and administration."
4. The Governor would submit to the Trusteeship Council "a plan for the establishment of special town units" encompassing the "Jewish and Arab sections of new Jerusalem."
5. The Governor would establish a "special police force" – its personnel to be "recruited outside of Palestine" – to help maintain public order and protect the Holy Places.

6. The city's "Legislative Council," to be popularly elected, would have "powers of legislation and taxation." However, its legislative authority would not "conflict or interfere" with the provisions of the "Statute of the City" (to be elaborated and approved by the Trusteeship Council).

7. The Governor would have veto power over "bills inconsistent with the provisions" of the Statute, as well as the power "to promulgate temporary ordinances in case the [Legislative] Council fails to adopt in time a bill deemed essential to the normal functioning of the administration."

10. Proposal of the Archbishop of Canterbury

Date: 31 October 1949

Source: "The Future of Jerusalem," *GAOR*, 5th Sess., 1950, Supp. 9 (A/1286).
A. Ginio, "Plans for the Solution of the Jerusalem Problem," in: J.L. Kraemer (ed.), *Jerusalem: Problems and Prospects*, Praeger, N.Y., 1980, pp. 41, 74.
H.E. Bovis, *The Jerusalem Question*, Hoover Institution Press, Stanford University, California, 1971, pp. 65-66.

Background: The Archbishop of Canterbury submitted this plan to the U.N. as a private memorandum. Its main points, with their emphasis on territorial internationalization, conflicted with the position adopted by most Protestant bodies of the period, which advocated the city's functional internationalization (on this term, see the Lexicon, Ch. 4).

National Aspirations

1. "[T]he large Jewish residential area in the north and west" (the area that lies "to the north and west of a line beginning from the junction of the Nablus Road with St. Paul's Road and running south-west along St. Paul's road, then west along the Street of the Prophets and then south along King George Avenue as far as Terra Sancta College") should be "incorporated in the Israeli State."

2. The rest of the area which was assigned to the international enclave – the *corpus separatum* under the U.N. Partition Plan – should "remain under international authority, but without any division into zones."

3. "Facilities should be given for the return of Jews to the former Jewish quarter [in the Old City]."

Holy Places

In the framework of "the international enclave in Jerusalem it will be easy to arrange some degree of international supervision of Nazareth or of any other Holy Place outside Jerusalem as a safeguard against any possible misuse of these Holy Places."

11. U.N. Trusteeship Council: A Draft Statute for Jerusalem

Date: The proposal was approved by the U.N. Trusteeship Council on 4 April 1950.

Source: GAOR, 5th Sess., 1950, Supp. 9 (A/1286), Annex 2, pp. 19-27.

Background: U.N. General Assembly Resolution 181 (II) – the "Partition Resolution" (described in detail above) – recommended that Jerusalem be an entity separate (*corpus separatum*) from the two states that were supposed to be established in the territory of the British Mandate. The resolution assigned the Trusteeship Council the task of administering the city on behalf of the U.N. and requested it to draw up a detailed statute to that end. General Assembly Resolution 303 (IV) of 9 December 1949 requested the Trusteeship Council to complete the draft statute for Jerusalem.

National Aspirations

1. The City of Jerusalem, within the boundaries delineated in the Partition Resolution, would be a separate area (*corpus separatum*) and be administered by the Trusteeship Council on behalf of the U.N.
2. The city would be declared neutral and be demilitarized.
3. Freedom of entry into and exit from the city "shall be ensured to all foreign pilgrims and visitors without distinction as to nationality or faith," subject "to the requirements of public order, public morals and public health."
4. *Executive authority* – The Trusteeship Council would appoint a Governor for the city. The Governor would:
   (a) Represent the U.N. in the City.
   (b) Exercise executive authority in the City and act as the chief administration officer.
   (c) Act according "to the provisions of the Statute and to the instructions of the Trusteeship Council."
   (d) Be responsible for organizing and directing the police.
   (e) Be authorized, in a period of emergency, to take measures contrary to any legislation in force.
   (f) Be responsible for the City's "external affairs."
5. *Legislative authority* would be vested in a "Legislative Council," or in the Governor in special cases:
   (a) The Legislative Council would consist of twenty-five representatives, popularly elected, and no more than fifteen additional members to be appointed by "the Heads of the principal religious communities."
   (b) The twenty-five representatives would be elected by four "electoral colleges" – Christian, Jewish, Muslim and one composed of residents "who declare that they do not wish to register with any of the other three colleges." The

first three colleges would each elect eight members to the Legislative Council, and the fourth – one member.
(c) An equal number of members would be appointed by each religious community.
(d) The Legislative Council would serve a four-year term, which the Governor could prolong by one year.
(e) "A bill adopted by the Legislative Council shall become law only upon promulgation by the Governor." The latter would have the right to "disapprove" a bill which is in conflict with the provisions of the Statute, liable to "impede the Administration of the City or inflict undue hardship on any section of the inhabitants of the City."
(f) At any time when there is no Legislative Council, the Governor would be able to "legislate by order," although the newly elected Legislative Council could amend or repeal such laws.
(g) "When the Legislative Council is in session but fails to adopt in time a bill deemed essential to the normal functioning of the Administration the Governor may make temporary orders."
6. An independent *judicial system* would be established, consisting of several instances:
(a) Judges of the Supreme Court to be appointed by the Trusteeship Council.
(b) The Statute would "prevail over any legislation or administrative act" in cases brought before the courts of the City.
(c) Legislation or administrative acts declared by the Supreme Court to be "incompatible" with the provisions of the Statute would be "void and of no effect."

Holy Places (including religious buildings and sites)

1. The Governor would be responsible for protecting the Holy Places.

2. The Governor would decide whether any site not previously regarded as a Holy Place should be granted that status.

3. Disputes between religious communities regarding Holy Places would be settled by the Governor.

4. Should the Governor deem that a particular Holy Place "is in need of urgent repairs," he may request the religious community concerned to make the repairs. If the community fails to comply "within a reasonable time," the Governor may arrange for the work to be done at the City's expense, the costs later to be recovered from the community concerned.

5. Holy Places that were exempt from taxation on 29 November 1947 would remain exempt. No change in taxation would be made which would place the "owners or occupiers" of Holy Places "in a position less favorable" than they enjoyed on the above date.

6. The Governor would ensure respect for the property rights of "churches, missions and other religious or charitable agencies."
7. The Governor would ensure the preservation of existing rights at the Holy Places and act to prevent their impairment.
8. "Subject to the requirements of public order, public morals and public health," the Governor would guarantee "free access" to the Holy Places and "free exercise of worship" at them.
9. The Governor would ensure that Holy Places "are preserved."
10. He would be responsible for ensuring that the Holy Places were not desecrated.

Municipal Administration

1. The existing autonomous units and those to be established would enjoy "wide powers of local government and administration."
2. Following consultation with the Legislative Council, the Governor would submit to the Trusteeship Council "a plan for dividing the City into local autonomous units."
3. Likewise, and following consultation with the Legislative Council, the Governor would submit to the Trusteeship Council a plan "for the allocation of powers between the City authorities and the authorities of those autonomous units."

12. Proposal by the Government of Israel

Date: 26 May 1950

Source: U.N. General Assembly Official Records, Fifth Session, Supp. No. 9 (A/1286), p. 29.

Background: On 26 May 1950 the Government of Israel submitted a memorandum to the Trusteeship Council proposing arrangements for the Holy Places in Jerusalem. The Israeli proposal was a response to the draft Statute for Jerusalem adopted by the Trusteeship Council in April 1950 (see preceding document); an accompanying letter explained Israel's objections to the provisions of the Statute. Israel's position was that the U.N. should focus its attention exclusively on the Holy Places (most of which were at that time under Jordanian control) and that only for them should a special regime be established.

Holy Places

1. A statute, acceptable to all the parties concerned, would be drawn up to determine the powers of the U.N. at the Holy Places.

2. To fulfill its tasks at the Holy Places, the U.N. would appoint a representative body. This representative would be an independent authority and his authority would emanate from the U.N. General Assembly, independently of any government.

3. The delegate's main tasks with respect to the Holy Places would be:
    (a) To supervise and protect them.
    (b) To settle disputes between the religious communities regarding rights at Holy Places.
    (c) To preserve existing rights at the Holy Places.
    (d) To execute repairs at them.
    (e) To ensure tax exemption for them.
    (f) To supervise free access and pilgrimage to the Holy Places, subject to the requiremens of public order.
    (g) To prepare reports for the U.N. on the above subjects.

4. The definition of a "Holy Place" would be as determined and applied at the time of the termination of the British Mandate for Palestine. All the parties concerned would negotiate on the definition and location of the Holy Places at which the U.N. representative would be active.

5. The U.N. representative would also be authorized to negotiate with other states regarding protection of the Holy Places outside Jerusalem.

6. The states concerned would issue a declaration with assurances:
    (a) To respect human rights, especially freedom of worship and education.
    (b) To respect the immunity and sanctity of the Holy Places.
    (c) To maintain free access to the Holy Places in their territory by all, and permit pilgrimage to them.
    (d) To preserve and maintain the existing rights of the churches and religious institutions in their territory, especially those relevant to the Holy Places.
    (e) Not to levy taxes on the Holy Places that were exempt from taxation on the day of the termination of the British Mandate.
    (f) To cooperate in good faith with the U.N. representative in the execution of all his tasks.

13. Proposal Submitted by Sweden

Date: The proposal was submitted to the U.N. General Assembly on 5 December 1950.

Source: U.N. Doc. A/AC.38/L.63 (5 December 1950).

Background: Since it had proved impossible to implement the U.N. General Assembly's "Partition Resolution" (see above) of 29 November 1947, several countries submitted draft resolutions to the General Assembly on the Jerusalem question. The Swedish proposal resembled others – such as those put forward by Bolivia, Holland, and Cuba – that advocated functional internationalization (see Lexicon, Ch. 4) of the Holy Places. Sweden's proposal, however, attracted special attention because of its greater detail.

National Aspirations

1. The boundaries of Jerusalem would be those stipulated in the Partition Resolution.

2. Control and jurisdiction in each part of Jerusalem would be exercised by Israel and Jordan, respectively, subject to the powers of the U.N. Commissioner in the area.

3. The U.N. Commissioner would be empowered to employ guards to perform his functions in the Jerusalem area and to assure his personal security. At the Commissioner's request "the governments in the Jerusalem area shall... direct their respective police forces to assist the Commissioner in the performance of his duties."

4. "The governments of the States administering the Jerusalem area shall gradually reduce their armed forces in that area in conformity with article VII of the General Armistice Agreement between [Jordan and Israel] of 3 April 1949."

5. Any dispute between the Commissioner and either Israel or Jordan "concerning the interpretation or implementation of this resolution... which is not settled by negotiation, shall be referred for final decision to an *ad hoc* tribunal of arbitrators, one each to be nominated by the Kingdom of Jordan, the State of Israel, and the U.N. Secretary-General."

Holy Places

1. The proposed arrangements would not apply to Muslim Holy Places situated in territory controlled by Jordan or to Jewish Holy Places located in territory under Israeli control.

2. The Holy Places in the entire area of the former British Mandate for Palestine "shall be preserved and no act shall be permitted which may in any way impair their sacred character."

3. "Rights, immunities and privileges of religious denominations" and religious institutions with respect to the Holy Places "shall be preserved as they existed on 14 May 1948."

4. The U.N. Commissioner would be responsible to the General Assembly, and among his tasks would be:
   (a) To draw up an "authoritative list" of Holy Places according to the situation which existed on 14 May 1948. Claims that a site which was not considered a Holy Place on that date should now have that status conferred on it would be "referred to the arbitral tribunal" noted above if the government concerned refused to accept the Commissioner's positive recommendation.
   (b) To settle disputes between the religious communities regarding the Holy Places according to the existing rights.
   (c) "To request the governments in the Jerusalem area to modify, defer or suspend" laws, ordinances, regulations, and administrative acts which "impair the protection of and free access to Holy Places, or the rights, immunities and privileges referred to [above]."
   (d) To request the governments concerned to take the necessary measures for the maintenance of public security at the Holy Places in order to ensure their protection, free access to them, and "the safeguarding of the rights, immunities and privileges concerned."
   (e) To ensure that the governments concerned carry into effect "without delay" such requests by the Commissioner. "If a government objects to a request made by the Commissioner under this article," the matter would be referred to the "arbitral tribunal" mentioned above.
   (f) Should the Governor deem that a particular Holy Place "is in need of urgent repair," he may call upon the religious community concerned to carry out the repair. If the work is not carried out "within a reasonable time," the Governor may arrange for repairs to be carried out or completed, and the "expenses incurred shall be borne by the religious denominations or bodies concerned."

14. Proposal by Professor Benjamin Akzin

Date: 8 June 1967

Source: Photocopy of the original document (Hebrew).

Background: Benjamin Akzin was Professor of Public Law and Political Science at the Hebrew University of Jerusalem, Dean of the Faculty of Law at that institution, and the first Rector of Haifa University. This proposal was drafted during the 1967 Six-Day War. (For details of the situation at that time, see background to Prof. Avigdor Levontin's proposal, on p. 48.)

National Aspirations

Sovereignty in east Jerusalem should be vested in Israel.

Holy Places

1. "Quasi-internationalization" arrangements would be introduced for the Holy Places in the Old City. This arrangement might also be considered for certain Holy Places in the new city (such as the Dormition Church and Mount Zion).

2. An inter-religious committee would be established and would be vested with certain powers at the Holy Places.

3. The committee could consist of representatives of: the Chief Rabbis of Israel, the Council of Qadis in Israel, the Pope, the Greek Orthodox Church, the Archbishop of Canterbury, the association of other Protestant churches (*sic*), the Armenian Church, and the Ethiopian Church.

4. Its chairman would be Israel's Minister of Religious Affairs.

5. It would have no armed forces at its disposal – police or other.

6. The guards at the Holy Places would be appointed by each religious community, subject to approval by the Minister of Religious Affairs of Israel.

7. The possibility may be considered to exempt the committee and its personnel from direct taxation, granting it partial relief from customs duties, and permitting it to issue special stamps for use at the Holy Places.

15. Proposal by Professor Avigdor Levontin

Date: 10 June 1967

Source: Memorandum drawn up by Professor Levontin, of the Hebrew University of Jerusalem.
U. Benziman, *Jerusalem: City Without a Wall*, Schocken, Jerusalem and Tel Aviv, 1973, p. 282 (Hebrew).

Background: Immediately after Israeli forces entered east Jerusalem, Professor Avigdor Levontin of the Hebrew University was asked, within the framework of a special project group set up by the Israel National Academy of Sciences, to put forward ideas for a political solution to the status of Jerusalem. Levontin submitted his "Memorandum on Jerusalem" on 10 June 1967. The expectation was that the government would within days declare the complete unification of Jerusalem and annexation of all city territories to Israel. Clearly, this might cause difficulties with the Christian world, and even more so spark a confrontation with the Muslim world (where it was already possible to discern incipient signs that Islam was readying for a *jihad* – holy war – to liberate its Holy Places), and also feed extremist moods in the Jewish world, notably a desire to replace the Muslim shrines on the Temple Mount with a rebuilt Temple.

When the memorandum was written the area in question, including the immediate surroundings of the Western Wall, was very different from what it is today. The large suburbs, which were partly intended to encircle east Jerusalem, had not yet been started, nor the expanded institutional rebuilding on Mount Scopus, nor the new housing projects such as Ma'aleh Adumim on the road to the Dead Sea. Moreover, before the far-reaching extension of the municipal boundaries, the area of Jerusalem to which the memorandum related (and with the annexation of which the memorandum dealt) was far smaller than today's city.

Similarly, the international situation was radically different. Before the 1973 War, the Lebanon War, the Intifada, and the Scud missile attacks on Israel in the Gulf War, Israel's active ability to force others in the region to take account of its will appeared far greater, as did its passive capacity to retain what it held in disregard of the will of others.

Nor had Islamic fundamentalism become a force to reckon with. Before the Khomeini era the prospects for the participation of certain Muslim groups in the International Muslim Council (referred to hereafter) did not seem as remote as they now do.

National Aspirations

The memorandum recommended that the authorities consider:

1. Annexing all parts of Jerusalem (according to its boundaries then) to Israel.

2. Viewing "Jordanian Jerusalem" as two separate parts: (a) the area outside the walled city; (b) the area within the walls (the "Old City"). The first was peredominantly secular and free of potent emotional associations. The second was suffused with sacred and historical associations – this being the "Jerusalem" that evoked fierce passions and political entanglements.

3. Declaring that the Government of Israel had decided to preserve the *status quo* in the walled city – not only ensuring freedom of worship and equal access to members of all faiths, but also preserving the distinctive character of the area. The idea was that the general rules of town planning and building would not apply to this part of Jerusalem. Instead, special regulations would be enacted, under which the Old City would become a kind of historical reserve, "international" in character if not in juridical status. This did not seem unattainable, because the walled city was even then less Arab and less homogeneous than the extramural area (as for the Jewish Quarter, see below).

Holy Places

1. There would be an International Muslim Council, associated with the Ministry for Religious Affairs, for shrines and sites sacred to Islam. An effort would be made to secure the participation of non-Arab Muslim representatives (e.g., from Iran, Turkey, and East Africa), as well as Israeli Muslims. Similarly, an International Christian Council would be set up for shrines and sites sacred to Christianity. Both bodies would have powers of deliberation and recommendation.

2. No international council was required for the Jewish Quarter in the Old City, including the Western Wall (as it then was), since the State of Israel itself was the custodian of the Jewish national-religious interest.

Municipal Administration

1. The Ministry for Religious Affairs would bear administrative responsibility for the Old City (with the possible exception of the Jewish Quarter: see below), and serve as the authorized channel for external communication, although it would in fact be reinforced by the Ministry of Foreign Affairs and otherwise.

2. Urban service for the Old City would be provided by the Municipality of Jerusalem.

3. The Jewish Quarter (including the Western Wall, as it then was) could be brought directly under the jurisdiction of the Municipality of Jerusalem, similarly to extramural "Jordanian Jerusalem." Alternatively, it could be placed under a regime similar to that of the other quarters of the Old City, but without an international council.

Note: Professor Levontin considers the above proposal as entirely superseded by the flow of events, although the Memorandum may retain some historical or suggestive interest.

16. Proposal by the Government of Israel after the Six-Day War

Date: 1967-1969

Source: U. Benziman, *Jerusalem: City Without a Wall*, 1973, Schocken, Jerusalem and Tel Aviv, pp. 110-114, 275 (Hebrew).
S. Berkovitz, "The Juridical Status of the Holy Places," Ph.D. diss., The Hebrew University of Jerusalem, 1978, pp. 204-208, 323-326 (Hebrew).
Vienna Convention on Diplomatic Relations, 500 *United Nations Treaty Series* 95, 1961.
Security Council Official Records, 1969, S/9537, p. 148.

Background: Following the 1967 Six-Day War, Israel proposed that the Holy Places in the Jerusalem area be granted the status of diplomatic missions. The subject was discussed between representatives of Israel and Vatican emissaries, and a draft agreement to this effect was drawn up. The proposed arrangement was also intended to alter the custodial areas of the Christian denominations at the Holy Places and to recognize the Pope as the representative of all the Christian communities in the city. However, the Pope finally declined to sign the agreement, claiming it would be construed as Vatican recognition of Israeli control of both parts of Jerusalem.

National Aspirations

Israel would retain sovereignty over the city (conferring diplomatic immunity on a specific site does not affect sovereignty).

Holy Places

1. The Holy Places in the Jerusalem area would be granted a status similar to that of diplomatic missions.

2. Christian and Muslim clerics serving at the Holy Places would be granted a special status, similar to that of diplomatic representatives in Israel.

3. Jordan would be considered as the "sending State" of Muslim clerics, and the Vatican as the "sending State" of Christian clerics.

4. Each Holy Place would constitute a separate and distinct entity with respect to the above-mentioned immunities.

5. To clarify the essence of the proposal, we shall cite in brief several articles from the *Vienna Convention on Diplomatic Relations, 1961* (see also Lexicon in Ch. 4):

(a) "The premises of the [diplomatic] mission [for present purposes: the Holy Places] shall be inviolable. The agents of the receiving State [i.e., Israel] may not enter them, except with the consent of the head of the mission. The receiving State is under a special duty to take all appropriate steps to protect the premises of the mission against any intrusion or damage and to prevent any disturbance of the peace of the mission or impairment of its dignity. The premises of the mission, their furnishings and other property thereon and the means of transport of the mission shall be immune from search, requisition, attachment or execution."

(b) "The sending State [for present purposes: Jordan or the Vatican] and the head of the mission [Holy Place] shall be exempt from all national, regional or municipal dues and taxes in respect of the premises of the mission, whether owned or leased, other than such as represent payment for specific services rendered."

(c) "The archives and documents of the mission [Holy Place] shall be inviolable at any time and wherever they may be."

(d) "Subject to its laws and regulations concerning zones entry into which is prohibited or regulated for reasons of national security, the receiving State [Israel] shall ensure to all members of the mission freedom of movement and travel in its territory."

(e) "The receiving State [Israel] shall permit and protect free communication on the part of the mission for all official purposes."

(f) "The person of a diplomatic agent [the cleric serving at the Holy Place] shall be inviolable. He shall not be liable to any form of arrest or detention. The receiving State [Israel] shall treat him with due respect and shall take all appropriate steps to prevent any attack on his person, freedom or dignity."

(g) "A diplomatic agent [cleric] shall enjoy immunity from the criminal jurisdiction of the receiving State [Israel]."

(h) "A diplomatic agent [cleric] shall also enjoy immunity from civil jurisdiction, except in three cases: "a real action relating to private immovable property situated in the territory of the receiving State [Israel];" an action involving succession; and "an action relating to any professional or commercial activity exercised by the diplomatic agent in the receiving State outside his official functions."

(i) "The receiving State [Israel] may at any time... notify the sending State [Jordan or the Vatican]" that a member of the diplomatic mission is *persona non grata*; in such a case, "the sending State shall, as appropriate, either recall the person concerned or terminate his functions with the mission."

(j) A diplomatic agent [cleric] must respect the laws of the receiving State [Israel].

17. Proposal by Dr. Meron Benvenisti

Date: 2 July 1968

Source: The plan was published in the daily paper *Ma'ariv* on 4 May 1971 (Hebrew). U. Benziman, *Jerusalem: City Without a Wall,* 1973, Schocken, Jerusalem and Tel Aviv, p. 291 (Hebrew).

Background: The proposal was put forward at a meeting initiated by Ambassador Mordechai Gazit, at the time an advisor to the Minister of Foreign Affairs. Dr. Benvenisti was then advisor on east Jerusalem affairs to the Mayor of Jerusalem, but the proposal was submitted in his name alone.

Purpose

1. Creation of a unified municipal zone for the areas within the sphere of influence of metropolitan Jerusalem, to serve as a proper framework for the city's development.
2. Establishment of independent municipal units within the framework of the extended municipal area, with due attention to the types of settlement it contains (villages, small towns) and to the desire of the minorities for self-government (east Jerusalem).
3. An attempt to meet the Arabs' request for control in part of Jerusalem while ensuring Israeli sovereignty over the territory within the city's current boundaries.

Means

1. Delimiting municipal boundaries which would include terrritories under Israeli and Jordanian sovereignty, i.e., a bi-sovereign, uni-municipal city.
2. Establishing a joint umbrella-council (Greater Jerusalem Council) for five boroughs: Jewish Jerusalem, Arab Jerusalem, the villages, Bethlehem, and Beit Jalla.
3. Granting limited autonomy to the Arab Jerusalem borough and the villages sector, with some of the villages to be under Jordanian sovereignty.

Method

A) The area will be divided according to a map (unpublished), with the following specifications:

Jewish borough: The entire Jewish city as well as a strip between Sanhedriya and Mount Scopus, the Old City's Jewish and Armenian Quarters, the Mount of Olives, the City of David, East Talpiyot-Kibbutz Ramat Rachel area, Mar Elias Monastery-Beit Safafa area and Neve Ya'akov area. This territory ensures development and settlement possibilities for some 30,000 families (about 100,000 people). It includes no more than 9,000 Arabs and should be entirely under Israeli sovereignty.

Arab borough: The Old City's Muslim and Christian Quarters, Sheikh Jarrah, the American Colony, Wadi Joz, A-Tur, Shu'afat and urban Beit Hanina, Silwan – all currently under Israeli sovereignty – and Elazariyeh and Abu Dis, which are not under Israeli sovereignty.

Villages borough: The semi-agricultural villages around the city, some of which are under Israeli sovereignty – Issawiyeh, Sur Bakher, Um Tuba – while others are under Jordanian sovereignty: A-Ram, Anata, Kafr Aqab, Beit Hanina, Bir Naballa, Kalandiya, Judida.

Bethlehem borough: The entire municipal area of Bethlehem.

Beit Jalla borough: The entire municipal area of Beit Jalla.

Basic Data

Population of Greater Jerusalem	298,000	
Jerusalem residents under Israeli sovereignty	261,000	
Jerusalem residents under Jordanian sovereignty	37,000	

Population distribution by communities

Jews	195,000	(66%)
Muslims	77,000	(25%)
Christians	26,000	(9%)
Total	298,000	

Population distribution by boroughs

Jewish borough (incl. 8,500 Arabs)	203,000
Arab borough	61,000
Beit Jalla borough	5,500
Bethlehem borough	13,500
Villages borough	15,000
Total	298,000

Greater Jerusalem Council
51 members elected by boroughs as follows:

Jewish borough total	*33*
Jews	31
Armenians	1
Muslims	1
Arab borough total	*11*
Muslims	9
Christians	2
Bethlehem borough total	*3*
Christians	2
Muslims	1

Beit Jalla borough total	1
Christians	1
Villages borough total	3
Muslims	3
Distribution by communities	
Jews	31
Christians	6
Muslims	14
Total	51

The Greater Jerusalem Council will deal with the following subjects:
1. Preparation of town planning plans (to be approved by planning authorities of both states).
2. Coordination of the programs and operations of the boroughs.
3. Regional and rural development.
4. Economy and tourism.
5. Firefighting.
6. Regional sewerage.
7. Joint projects: removal and exploitation of sewerage and waste, electricity, Kalandiya airport, industrial parks.
8. Regional water projects and distribution of water.
9. Regional transportation.
10. Parks and historic buildings.
11. Housing.

To enhance its work, the Council will establish committees, some with the participation of public figures and professionals. The boroughs will finance the Council's operations by setting aside a certain percentage of their budgets. The governments will assist in the development budgets of the Council according to size of area, population, and type of project. Allocations will be transferred directly to the Council and not through the constituent boroughs.

The chairman of the Council will be elected by the Council members and will be one of the members.

The mayors will comprise the Council's executive committee.

The composition of the Financial Committee will be based on the representation of each borough.

The state authorities will have the power to annul any decision relating to their sovereign sphere. The name of the Greater Jerusalem Council (or G.J.C.) will appear together with the name of the local borough. For example: G.J.C.-Bethlehem borough, or G.J.C.-East Jerusalem borough.

Boroughs

There will be two types of boroughs:

Type A – Independent boroughs with full municipal powers: Bethlehem, Beit Jalla, and the Villages borough.

Type B – Dependent boroughs, in which decisions of the borough council will, in certain matters, be subject to approval by a joint council. These are: the borough of Arab Jerusalem and the borough of Jewish Jerusalem. In the dependent boroughs most of the administration will be unified.

From the aspect of sovereignty there will be two types of boroughs:

Type A – boroughs entirely under the sovereignty of one state: Bethlehem, Beit Jalla, and Jewish Jerusalem.

Type B – boroughs under the sovereignty of two states: the Villages and Arab Jerusalem.

Type A municipalities will be subject to the Municipalities Ordinance and to the procedures that prevail in the state in which they are located.

The Type B municipalities will function as specified in the sections on Villages borough and Arab Jerusalem borough:

Villages Borough

Each village will elect its own village committee, according to Jordanian or Israeli law respectively, depending on the sovereign power in the area where the village is located.

The Villages Council will be elected by the same method as are the regional councils in Israel. A committee composed of officials from the Israeli and Jordanian Interior Ministries will determine the powers of this council.

A joint committee will formulate taxation principles.

The Israeli and Jordanian governments will underwrite the municipality's development budgets.

Arab Jerusalem Borough

Its independent powers will cover the following areas:
1. Local town building committee (following approval of master plan).
2. Education (subject to Israeli or Jordanian law, depending on the respective sovereign power).
3. Public works, lighting, parks.
4. Transportation.
5. Public health.

6. Sanitation and hygiene.
7. Crafts, industry, kiosks, peddlers.
8. Public tenders and purchases.
9. Welfare.

The implementation of these powers will be restricted by the following procedures:

Six representatives from the Borough council will, together with the twenty-one Jewish members, constitute the Greater Jerusalem Council. This body will approve the budget for the entire city, following which the Arab Borough will be able to expend it according to its discretion.

Arab members will be coopted to joint statutory committees which are mandatory under Israeli law. After common principles are determined and coordinating bodies formed, these committees will transfer the powers detailed above, which refer to the Arab area, to the parallel committees of the Arab Borough.

Should differences arise between the borough councils, they will be referred for a decision to a committee composed of the mayor of Greater Jerusalem, one of his deputies, and the mayor of Arab Jerusalem. This committee's decisions will not require the approval of the municipal committee.

The municipal administration of the entire city will remain united, and a joint Personnel committee will be established. The Arab Borough will commission services and works within the framework of its approved budget. It will have the right to order services from commercial firms.

The Arab Borough will have a small professional administrative staff to commission services and works and to supervise their quality.

The election law, taxation, and bylaws will be in accordance with the Israeli law. Should Jordan insist that its law prevail in these spheres in the part of the city under its sovereignty, the residents of that area will elect a number of representatives (according to their proportion of the population) to the Arab council according to Jordanian law. In addition, taxes will be collected according to Jordanian law and transferred to the joint treasury.

Since part of Arab Jerusalem will be under Jordanian sovereignty (Elazariyeh, Abu Dis, and part of A-Tur), an arrangement will be introduced by which the Jordanian Interior Ministry will exercise a certain supervision (its scope to be determined in negotiations) over the operations of the Arab Borough.

The name of the Greater Jerusalem municipality will be the "Jerusalem Municipality," and in Arabic: "Baladiya Urshalim al-Quds."

The name of the Arab Jerusalem Borough will be "Baladit (or Amnat) al-Quds Ashraqiya," and in Hebrew: East Jerusalem Municipality.

The name of the Jewish Jerusalem Borough will be the "Jerusalem Municipality," and in Arabic: "Baladiya Urshalim."

18. Proposal by Prof. E. Lauterpacht, CBE, Q.C.

Date: 1968

Source: E. Lauterpacht, *Jerusalem and the Holy Places*, The Anglo-Israel Association, London, 1968 (reprinted 1980).

Background: Elihu Lauterpacht, CBE, Q.C., served as Lecturer and reader in international law at Cambridge University until 1988, and is currently the director of that institution's Research Centre for International Law. He has been involved in several of the most famous cases of international litigation.

National Aspirations

Sovereignty over the whole of Jerusalem is vested in Israel.

Holy Places

1. Israel will publish a unilateral Declaration (accompanied by a Statute) intended to create international obligations regarding the Holy Places (its main points are given below). Other states may accept this arrangement, and undertake neither to act nor to permit on their territories any action, contrary to the Declaration and Statute.

2. Disputes between the states that so affiliate themselves will be settled by the International Court of Justic.

3. The Statute will ensure complete freedom of attendance and worship at the Holy Places.

4. The Holy Places shall remain in the custody and subject to the jurisdiction of the religious communities concerned and the *status quo* that prevailed on the eve of Israel's establishment will be preserved.

5. The organization and conduct of services in each of the Holy Places shall be regulated exclusively by the personnel of those Places.

6. Disputes over rights at the Holy Places will be settled by a "Commissioner of the Holy Places," to be appointed by the U.N. Secretary-General with Israel's consent, or by some other special jurisdiction.

7. Israeli law will apply to all acts occurring in the Holy Places and the courts in Israel will have jurisdiction over such acts.

8. The religious communities will have jurisdiction over their personnel "in all matters which are traditionally the subject of regulation by the rules of the communities."

9. There will be a Council of the Holy Places, consisting of the heads of the communities interested in the Holy Places, to represent the collective view of these communities.

10. Differences regarding jurisdiction over personnel of the religious communities will be settled by the Commissioner of the Holy Places.

11. Representatives of Israeli public authorities will not enter the Holy Places without the consent of the religious community "in charge of such Holy Place," except in cases of emergency.

12. The religious communities will pay rates for services they receive from the Jerusalem Municipality.

13. All provisions of the arrangement are subject to the security interests of Israel, and for reasons of security the government of Israel may "restrict the liberties" stipulated above, subject to a right of complaint to the Commissioner.

19. Proposal by Professor S. Shepard Jones

Date: 1968

Source: S. Shepard Jones, "The Status of Jerusalem: Some National and International Aspects," 33 *Law and Contemporary Problems* 169, 1968.

Background: Professor Shepard Jones, at the time a lecturer at the University of North Carolina, published an article on the status of Jerusalem in international law in which he also suggested guidelines for a future settlement in the city.

National Aspirations

1. The walled city should be declared a separate area (*corpus separatum*) and would be subject to an international regime.
2. The parties to the dispute will negotiate the drafting of an international statute to apply in the area subject to the international regime.
3. The international community will recognize west Jerusalem as the capital of Israel.
4. These arrangements will be guaranteed by the "principal Powers."

Municipal Administration

1. The city would remain united, without restrictions on the movement of people and goods between its various parts.
2. The arrangements to be determined for the administration of the city will take into account the interests of all the inhabitants as well as of the Jewish, Christian, and Muslim communities.

20. The Rogers Plan (U.S. Secretary of State William Rogers)

Date: 9 December 1969

Source: Y. Lukacs (ed.), *Documents on the Israeli-Palestinian Conflict, 1967-1983*, Cambridge University Press, Cambridge, 1984, pp. 18-23.
W.B. Quandt, *Peace Process: America's Diplomacy and the Arab-Israeli Conflict since 1967*, The Brookings Institution, Washington D.C. and University of California Press, Berkeley and Los Angeles, 1993, pp. 75-85.

Background: The proposal was put forward by William Rogers, at the time Secretary of State of the U.S., at the height of the War of Attrition (the frequent local armed clashes) between Israel and Egypt along the Suez Canal, following the 1967 Six-Day War. Rogers' plan, which reflected the principles adopted by the U.S. Administration (in this case the Nixon Administration) for resolving the Arab-Israeli conflict, was rejected by both Egypt and Israel. However, the cease-fire proposal provided in the Rogers' Plan was agreed to by both Egypt and Israel and lasted until the 1973 War. One of the reasons for Israel's negative reaction was that the plan itself did not specify that Jerusalem would remain under Israeli rule.

National Aspirations

1. The United States "cannot accept unilateral actions by any party to decide the final status of the city."
2. Jerusalem's "final status can be determined only through the agreement of the parties concerned," primarily Jordan and Israel, "taking into account the interests of other countries in the area and the international community."
3. Jerusalem should remain unified.
4. "There should be open access to the unified city for persons of all faiths and nationalities."

Holy Places

The plan does not refer specifically to the Holy Places but does cite the need to ensure free access to the city and to "take into account the interests of all its inhabitants and of the Jewish, Islamic, and Christian communities" in the city's administration.

Municipal Administration

1. Jerusalem "should be a unified city within which there would no longer be restrictions on the movement of persons and goods."
2. "Arrangements for the administration of the city should take into account the interests of all its inhabitants and of the Jewish, Islamic, and Christian communities."

21. Proposal by Evan M. Wilson

Date: 1969

Source: E.M. Wilson, "The Internationalization of Jerusalem," 23 *Middle East Journal* 1, 1969.

Background: Evan M. Wilson held many posts in the American Foreign Service, of which the last prior to the writing of this article was Minister-Consul General in Jerusalem. Wilson's proposal is based on several underlying assumptions: the West Bank will revert to Arab rule; Jerusalem will not be physically redivided; the need to safeguard the interests of Israel, Jordan, and the inhabitants of the West Bank; free access to the city; recognition of the international community's interest in the city.

National Aspirations

1. Control over Jerusalem will be divided: (a) Israel to control the western city (all the areas under Israeli control until 1967 with the exception of Mount Zion); (b) Jordan to control the eastern part of the city; (c) internationalization of the Old City, Mount Scopus and the Mount of Olives as well as the area between these two mountains, and Government House (UNTSO headquarters).

2. "Supreme authority for the international sector would rest with the United Nations, which would appoint a Special Representative to embody its presence in the city."

3. Both Israel and Jordan would "benefit from the revenues from tourism in the international sector."

4. The parties would reach an agreement on "customs and currency matters and [on] the citizenship to be held by the residents of the [international] sector."

5. Freedom of movement would be guaranteed between the international zone and Israel, Jordan, and the West Bank.

6. "Day-to-day administration [of the international sector] would be in the hands of a City Council, elected by the residents of the sector," with the council also to "have supervision over municipal services for the sector."

Holy Places

1. Freedom of access to the Holy Places would be guaranteed "within the area proposed for internationalization in 1947" – i.e., in the area delimited in the U.N. General Assembly's Partition Plan.

2. The U.N. Special Representative "would be responsible for the protection of the Holy Places within the [international] sector and for this purpose would have some sort of police force."

3. "The actual maintenance of the Holy Places... would be in the hands of the different religious communities."

22. Proposal by Professor W. Michael Reisman

Date: The proposal was contained in a book published in 1970.

Source: W.M. Reisman, *The Art of the Possible: Diplomatic Alternatives in the Middle East*, Princeton University Press, Princeton, New Jersey, 1970, pp. 71-79.

Background: Professor Reisman is a lecturer in international law at Yale University. His plan seeks to combine limited Israeli sovereignty over Jerusalem with international supervision of the Holy Places and of the municipal administration. Reisman's justification for granting Israel sovereignty is that, whereas Islam and Christianity require free access to and protection of the Holy Places in Jerusalem, Judaism "requires its political control as the capital of the Jewish Commonwealth." The principle of international supervision in Jerusalem is desirable because this mode "would tend to neutralize the controversial political status" of the city while furnishing a good guarantee of unimpeded access to the Holy Places. The arrangement should be anchored in an "international statute for Jerusalem" which would be recognized by the U.N. The statute should be drafted by the "Four Power negotiators" with the participation of Israel, Jordan, "the Palestine Arabs, and the diverse religious groups concerned."

National Aspirations

1. Limited sovereignty over the city would be vested in Israel (the limitations concerning the Holy Places and the city's administration are detailed below).

2. A constitutional court ("a Jerusalem Administrative Tribunal") would be established to settle "disputes regarding the interpretation and application of the Statute. Appeal from its judgments would lie to the International Court of Justice through a request for an advisory opinion..."

Holy Places

1. The autonomous status of the Holy Places would be guaranteed.

2. Freedom of access to the Holy Places would be guaranteed to adherents of all faiths, including "unimpeded pilgrimage privileges," subject "only to conventional health measures."

3. Legislative competence over the Holy Places would be vested in an appointive Curia which is described below.

Municipal Administration

1. The rights of adherents of all faiths would be guaranteed in the municipal government.

2. "The mayor would be chosen by popular election of the inhabitants of Jerusalem and would serve as the executive of the city."
3. The council would be bicameral:
    (a) The representatives in one of the houses of the City Council, the "Curia," would be appointed "by all the religious sects in the city." Its legislative powers would encompass matters related to the Holy Places, and its consent would also be required "for those secular decisions made by the second house... affecting religious places or practices."
    (b) The second house – the "Senate" – would be "elected popularly on a proportional representation system, insuring representation of each ethnic and religious group in Jerusalem" (as long as the inhabitants preferred to identify themselves on ethnic lines). "The Senate would have jurisdiction over the mundane secular matters of any urban administration."
4. A mechanism would be established to settle "municipal disputes."

23. Proposal by Dr. Raphael Benkler

Date: 1972

Source: R. Benkler, "Proposals for Determining the Status of Jerusalem," *International Problems*, vol. 8, 1970, p. 8 (Hebrew).
R. Benkler, "The Peace of Jerusalem," *International Problems*, vol. 11, 1972, p. 11 (Hebrew).

Background: Dr. Raphael Benkler received his doctorate from the University of Paris for a dissertation on the unification of Jerusalem in international law. His proposal, which was an appendix to that dissertation, was submitted at the summer 1971 session of the International Academy for Peace which convened in Helsinki. Dr. Benkler emphasized that a basic condition for the success of his plan was the existence of a stable peace between the two peoples who live in Palestine.

National Aspirations

1. Jerusalem will be the capital of the two states: Israel and the Arab state (the latter would be "Palestine, Jordan or a federative union of Jordan-Palestine").

2. Jerusalem will be a free city open to the citizens of the two states.

3. The city will be demilitarized. Neither state will be permitted to maintain army units in Jerusalem, other than special guard units. Public order will be preserved by the local police of the boroughs.

4. The area of jurisdiction of the Jerusalem Municipality will be considerably extended, to create "Greater Jerusalem." The author does not elaborate on the city's territorial structure, using the boundaries of the Benvenisti proposal (see above). The guiding principle is that Israel would exercise sovereignty over all the areas included in the city in accordance with the Israeli unification legislation of June 1967, with possible slight modifications. Areas that will be under Arab sovereignty will be added to the city.

5. Some of the Islamic Holy Places, including the mosques on the Temple Mount, will be under Arab "quasi-sovereignty."

6. Direct access will be guaranteed from the Arab state to those Holy Places in Jerusalem which will be under Arab control.

7. All Jerusalem residents will be citizens of the State of Israel or of the Arab state to be established; dual citizenship will be excluded.

8. Every resident will bear the obligations of the state of which he is a citizen (e.g., military duty and taxation), and will benefit from the rights it confers.

9. The criminal jurisdiction of the relevant state will apply to Jerusalem according to the location where an offense is committed.

10. A common economic system will be maintained between Israel and the Arab state for the development of the joint capital. This will include the establishment of a uniform currency, or coordination regarding currency exchange rates.

Holy Places

1. Freedom of access to and worship at the Holy Places will be guaranteed to both peoples.
2. The Holy Places will be administered by the religious authorities of each site according to the *status quo*.
3. The two states will enact laws to implement this arrangement at the Holy Places, and empowering the boroughs and the umbrella-municipality to supervise the situation at and around the Holy Places.
4. Some of the Islamic Holy Places, including the mosques on the Temple Mount, will be placed under Arab "quasi-sovereignty."
5. Direct access will be guaranteed from the Arab state to the Holy Places that will be under Arab control.

Municipal Administration

1. Greater Jerusalem will include five boroughs: Arab; Jewish; Villages; Bethlehem; and Beit Jalla (the division follows the Benvenisti proposal).
2. The boroughs will deal with many subjects, excluding "central matters that the treatment by the umbrella-municipality would simplify and make more efficient."
3. The umbrella-municipality's tasks will include: preparation of a master plan; coordination of activities of the borough municipalities; a certain supervision of the borough municipalities; regional and rural development; economy and tourism; central services such as a regional sewerage system; coordination and command of firefighting operations; water projects; electricity; waste and garbage disposal; a city airport; industrial zones; transportation; housing; parks and historical buildings; supervision of activities at the Holy Places.
4. The umbrella-municipality ("Greater Jerusalem Council") will comprise representatives of the five borough municipalities in direct proportion to their population (the Council's structure corresponds with the Benvenisti plan).
5. The two states will enact a law concerning the approval of the city budget and allocation of funds to the umbrella-municipality, as well as the procedures for approving a master plan, coordinating the various statutes regarding municipal administration, and for emigration between the various boroughs. The law will vest in the Greater Jerusalem Council powers to collect taxes and enact municipal bylaws, as well as jurisdiction for the municipality's tribunals under these bylaws.

24. Proposals of Sen. Richard Nixon and Sen. J. William Fulbright

Date: Nixon – 24 June 1967; Fulbright – 7 July 1974.

Source: Ma'ariv, 25 June 1967, p. 3 (Hebrew) (Nixon).
Yediot Aharonot, 8 July 1974, p. 2 (Hebrew) (Fulbright).
S. Berkovitz, "The Juridical Status of the Holy Places," Ph.D. diss., The Hebrew University of Jerusalem, 1978, p. 316 (Hebrew).
M.H. Mendelson, "Diminutive States in the United Nations," 21 *International & Comparative Law Quarterly* 609, 1972.
J.H.M. Verzijl, *International Law in Historical Perspective,* Nijhoff, the Netherlands, 1969, vol. 2, p. 297.
B.J. Wersen, "Vatican City," *The New Encyclopedia Britannica, Macropedia,* vol. 19, 15th ed., Chicago, 1983, p. 36.
"Italy-The Holy See Agreement to Amend the 1929 Lateran Concordat, 18 February 1984," 24 *International Legal Materials* 1589, 1985.

Background: We have combined the proposals by Sen. (as he then was) Richard Nixon and Sen. J. William Fulbright because of their great similarity. During his visit to Israel after the Six-Day War, Nixon – who would be elected President of the United States in the following year – spoke of finding a formula according to which the Holy Places in the Old City could be placed under a Vatican-like regime which, nevertheless, would not prejudice Israeli sovereignty over united Jerusalem. Senator Fulbright, interviewed on the NBC-TV program "Meet the Press," stated that Jerusalem should be given a special status resembling that of the Vatican. Neither Nixon nor Fulbright elaborated their proposal. The following is a brief survey of the status of Vatican City (although clearly some details are irrelevant to Jerusalem) (see also Lexicon, Ch. 4).

Vatican City

Vatican City has an area of about 0.4 square km and a population of approximately 1,000. The Lateran Treaties between Italy and the Holy See of 11 February 1929 (one of which, the Concordat, was amended on 18 February 1984) determine the status of Vatican City in Italy. In the agreement Italy recognized the Holy See's complete, exclusive and absolute authority, and sovereignty over the city. A map attached to the agreement delineated the city's boundaries (St. Peter's Basilica and the adjoining areas). Italy undertook not to intervene in the activity of the Holy See and its institutions, while the Holy See promised freedom of access for the public to the Vatican's treasures. The Vatican renounced intervening in secular disputes among other states, though it could exert its moral influence, with the consent of all the parties involved in a particular conflict. Vatican City was recognized as a neutral and inviolable state. The agreement also recognized the Vatican's right to issue its own stamps and currency. Italy undertook to supply certain public services to the city (such as water, communications, and trains) and to exempt clerics in the service of the Holy See from military service. The Italian police may not enter places of worship without authorization of the person in charge of the building, other than in emergencies.

Under the Vatican statute, drafted by Pope Pius XI in 1929, the Pope is granted absolute legislative, jurisdictional, and executive powers in the city. Subsequent legislation established the legal system that applies in Vatican City and settled the citizenship question. Most of the residents are permanent employees of the Vatican. When a citizen of Vatican City leaves the city, his citizenship there is suspended and he resumes his former nationality. If his country of origin does not recognize dual citizenship, Italian nationality is automatically conferred.

Vatican City has three instances of independent courts, a "military" force of about 100 Swiss Guards, and its own banking system. The Italian police patrol the city and the Vatican authorities must extradite wanted criminals to Italy. The Holy See maintains extensive diplomatic relations with many states and is a member of some international organizations. International jurists are divided as to whether Vatican City constitutes a "state" according to the conditions prescribed by international law (population, territory, effective control, competence to enter into relations with other states).

25. Report by the Aspen Institute

Date: June 1975

Source: "Jerusalem: A Proposal for the Future of the City" (unpublished), Aspen Institute for Humanistic Studies, New York City, June 1975.

Background: An Aspen Institute working group analyzed the interests of the different actors regarding the future status of Jerusalem, examined a number of earlier proposals, and developed a new plan which, the team thought, might prove acceptable to all parties.

National Aspirations

1. It seems that according to the proposal, Israel would be vested with sovereignty over most of the city.

2. There would be a "small Moslem-Arab political authority around the El Aqsa Mosque."

3. The Temple Mount area would be an "Arab-Israeli condominium" (see Lexicon, Ch. 4), or an "international zone" (with preference for the condominium because of Israeli and Arab objections to an international regime).

4. (a) A special corridor between the Muslim Holy Places and the nearest Arab state (Jordan or some future closer Palestinian state) would be created for pilgrims; (b) it would be controlled by an international authority or by the condominium; (c) this "way of pilgrims" would be "discreetly walled along its flanks so as not to provide a security risk for Israel"; (d) and it would be policed by an "international authority."

5. "A major international project" would be launched "to make the Old City a preeminent center of Arab culture and Moslem spirituality."

6. (a) Certain areas in the Old City, adjacent to the Holy Places (the exact area to be determined by "factors of natural setting and administrative convenience"), would be placed under "minimal Arab-Moslem jurisdiction"; (b) this area might, in time, "be linked to a larger Arab borough in Jerusalem"; (c) no arms would be permitted in this area, the ban to be enforced by an international police body.

7. Jerusalem residents would have dual citizenship: "each person would be both a citizen of the single, undivided city" and also, according to individual choice, "either of Israel or of the adjacent Arab state." It would be possible, in "special circumstances," to be a citizen of both adjacent states.

Holy Places

1. (a) The Al-Aqsa mosque and its immediate surroundings would be under Muslim-Arab "political authority" (see "National Aspirations"); (b) "arms would not be permitted [in this area], except on the part of the local Moslem-Arab police force, as at present."

2. (a) The Temple Mount area would be under a condominium or an international zone (see "National Aspirations"); (b) responsibility for protecting and restoring the Dome of the Rock and the surrounding gardens "should be delegated to Arab-Moslem authorities"; (c) a special "international authority" would be responsible for "policing" this zone; (d) "archeological work would be under the direction of the international authority, and might be temporarily enjoined."

Municipal Administration

1. Jerusalem would remain unified.

2. The metropolitan area would be divided into five boroughs, "at least two of them to the East being largely Arab-Moslem in population."

3. The area of the Al-Aqsa mosque and the area under "minimal" Arab authority (see "National Aspirations") might be defined as a borough.

4. "The separate boroughs would be administratively as autonomous and strong in authority as sound governance warrants" (the model being London rather than New York).

5. The boroughs would be able to purchase their "necessary city services from city-wide services."

6. The "first officer" of the metropolitan city council would serve in rotation.

26. Report of the Brookings Institution

Date: December 1975

Source: The Brookings Institution, *Toward Peace in the Middle East: Report of a Study Group*, December 1975, The Brookings Institution, Washington, D.C., 1975. See also: W.B. Quandt, *Decade of Decisions*, University of California Press, Berkeley, 1977, pp. 290-291.

Background: The report was drawn up by a group of diplomats and academics who were invited in the summer of 1974 by the Brookings Institution in Washington to examine how the United States could assist in finding a "workable, fair, and enduring settlement" to the Arab-Israeli conflict. The Middle East Study Group was chaired by Roger Heyns of the American Council on Education. On many issues the report represents compromises "among the diverse views" of the group's members. The conclusions gained the support of Jimmy Carter, then a candidate for the U.S. presidency. The report offers no detailed solution for Jerusalem but recommends a number of principles which should be incorporated in any solution.

National Aspirations

1. Israel would withdraw in stages to the lines of 5 June 1967 "with only such modifications as are mutually accepted." The new borders will be "safeguarded by demilitarized zones supervised by UN forces."

2. The report notes that its principles could be met within a city "under Israeli sovereign jurisdiction," or "under divided sovereign jurisdiction between Israel and an Arab state," or "under either of these arrangements with an international authority in an agreed area," such as the Old City.

3. Palestinian self-determination would be provided, either as an independent state or as "a Palestinian entity voluntarily federated with Jordan."

Holy Places

1. Freedom of access to the Holy Places will be guaranteed.

2. Each Holy Place "should be under the custodianship of its own faith."

Municipal Administration

1. "There should be no barriers dividing the city which would prevent free circulation throughout it."

2. "Each national group within the city should, if it so desires, have substantial political autonomy within the area where it predominates."

27. The Allon Plan

Date: October 1976

Source: Y. Allon, "Israel: The Case for Defensible Borders," 55 *Foreign Affairs*, 1976 p. 38.
Y. Lukacs (ed.), *Documents on the Israeli-Palestinian Conflict, 1967-1983*, Cambridge University Press, Cambridge, 1984, pp. 98-105.
S. Hattis Rolef (ed.), *Political Dictionary of the State of Israel*, Macmillan Publishing Company, New York, 1987, p. 18.

Background: Yigal Allon held many senior positions in Israel's army and government until 1977. He drew up his plan when he was serving as Minister of Foreign Affairs. Although the Allon Plan was never adopted as official government policy, as long as Labor was in power (1977) most settlement activity in the territories seized by Israel in the Six-Day War took place within the parameters set by Allon. In 1973 the plan's principles were incoporated into the platform of the Labor Party.

National Aspirations

1. Israel would give up most of the territories seized in the Six-Day War, but will remain in security zones that would allow the army to ward off possible attacks by Arab states (no map was attached to the plan).

2. Areas in the West Bank and the Gaza Strip heavily populated by Arabs would be placed under Jordanian-Palestinian sovereignty.

3. Jerusalem would not be divided. The city, and the surrounding areas which are essential for its defense and for communicating with it, would remain under Israeli rule.

Holy Places

Representatives of the religious communities at the Holy Places would enjoy a special status.

Municipal Administration

The city's municipal structure would be based on subdistricts taking into account their ethnic and religious composition.

28. Proposal by Ambassador James George

Date: 1978

Source: J. George, "Jerusalem: The Holy City, A Religious Solution for a Political Problem," *International Persepctives*, March/April 1978, p. 18.

Background: James George served in the Canadian Department of External Affairs until 1977. His last post was Ambassador to Iran and Kuwait.

Holy Places

1. The Holy Places on and around the Temple Mount would be internationalized under a "religious regime composed of Jews, Moslems and Christians."
2. A supreme interfaith council would be established, with representatives from Judaism, Islam, and Christianity. This "Holy City Council" would be the highest authority in the international zone.
3. "The Holy City Council might have a consultative and coordinating role in regard to the other Holy Places" in Israel and the West Bank.
4. All decisions by the Council would have to be adopted unanimously.
5. "Unlimited access" to the Holy Places would be guaranteed, with the proviso that those entering the city from outside leave by the same way.

29. Proposal by Dr. Shmuel Berkovitz

Date: 1978

Source: S. Berkovitz, "The Juridical Status of the Holy Places," Ph.D. diss., The Hebrew University of Jerusalem, 1978, pp. 344-377.

Background: S. Berkovitz put forward his proposal, which focuses on the Holy Places, in his doctoral dissertation, prepared under the supervision of Professor R. Lapidoth and Professor Y. Engelrad. Some elements of the proposal resemble ideas adduced by Prof. E. Lauterpacht and by the Government of Israel in its post-1967 proposal, but Dr. Berkovitz's proposal is much more detailed.

National Aspirations

1. Jerusalem will remain complete and united under the sovereignty of the State of Israel.

2. (a) Israel will publish a unilateral declaration and adopt a Statute regarding the Holy Places. The declaration will bind Israel in its relations with states that will announce publicly their consent to the provisions of the Statute and will undertake to implement them with respect to Holy Places located in their own territory.
(b) The Statute will apply to the Holy Places in Jerusalem, with the exception of sites sacred to the Jews only, as specified in a list which will be prepared in consultation with the heads of the various religions and be attached to the Statute.

3. The Government of Israel will accept the jurisdiction of the International Court of Justice regarding any legal dispute with another state that accepts the Statute, provided that the other state also accepts the jurisdiction of the International Court on a mutual basis.

Holy Places

A. Supervisory mechanism

1. An international supervisory mechanism for the Holy Places will be established to oversee implementation of the Statute.

2. The mechanism will be headed by a special Commissioner to be appointed by the U.N. Secretary-General, subject to Israel's consent.

3. The Commissioner's tasks will be: (a) to settle disputes between religious communities regarding their rights at the Holy Places; (b) to revise the list of religious communities and of Holy Places with the consent of Israel's Minister of Religious Affairs, following consultation with the Holy Places Council (described

below); (c) to determine the arrangements for access to the Holy Places following consultation with representatives of the religious communities; (d) to approve the arrangements for worship at the Holy Places which were determined by representatives of the religious communities; (e) to issue orders regarding urgent repairs to the Holy Places; (f) to administer the Holy Places Council and to represent it *vis-à-vis* the State of Israel.

4. The staff of the supervisory mechanism will be appointed by the U.N. Secretary-General and receive their salary from the U.N.

5. The Commissioner and the other members of the staff of the supervisory mechanism will enjoy in Israel and in the occupied territories immunities and privileges, such as are granted usually to representatives of an international organization.

6. Every decision made by the Commissioner according to the provisions of the Statute will be final under Israeli law, and will be enforceable by the Israeli courts and execution offices.

B. Holy Places Council

7. A Holy Places Council will be established, composed of an equal number of representatives from each religion with rights at the Holy Places. Its chairman will be the Commissioner.

8. The tasks of the Holy Places Council will be: (a) to represent the religious communities in all matters regarding Holy Places; (b) to advise the Commissioner and the Minister of Religious Affairs on matters regulated by the Statute; (c) to carry out an advance inquiry into disputes between the communities regarding their rights at the Holy Places; if the communities are unable to reach agreement on how to resolve the dispute, it will be referred to the Commissioner for a decision.

9. The members of the Holy Places Council will have the same status as the clerics serving at the Holy Places according to the Statute (elaborated below).

10. Participation in Council discussions and voting on any matter or dispute involving religious communities will be limited to the representatives of the communities concerned.

11. In any vote held by the Council on an issue involving a number of religious communities, or on a dispute between them, each religion will have one vote, irrespective of the number of communities from that religion which are involved in the issue or dispute.

C. Status of the Holy Places

12. The Holy Places will be protected against any infringement of their integrity, honor, or sanctity.

13. The Holy Places and all the movables located thereon and belonging to these sites will be immune from any search, seizure or execution, other than cases in which the search and/or seizure are required to ensure public order and/or state security. The search or seizure permit will be issued by the chief of the Jerusalem Police.

14. Those possessing rights at Holy Places will be exempt from any taxation, fee, or other mandatory levy, with the exception of fees for services rendered.

D. The Temple Mount

15. The Holy Places on the Temple Mount to which the entry of Jews will be permitted by decision of the Chief Rabbinate, will be under the exclusive jurisdiction of the Ministry of Religious Affairs, which will be authorized to bar the entry of non-Jews to those places.

16. The Al-Aqsa mosque and the Dome of the Rock mosque will be under the exclusive jurisdiction of the Supreme Muslim Council.

17. The Temple Mount and its gates, with the exception of the places which Jews may enter and the above-mentioned mosques, will be jointly administered by the Ministry of Religious Affairs and the Supreme Muslim Council.

18. Entry to the Temple Mount through all the gates will be unimpeded and free of charge, subject to the provisions of the Statute.

E. Freedom of Access

19. Freedom of access to the Holy Places will be guaranteed to all faiths, subject to their existing rights at those sites.

20. Arrangements for access to the Holy Places will be determined by the Commissioner following consultation with representatives of the respective religious community for whom the site is holy.

21. The Government of Israel will ensure convenient access and departure routes to and from the Holy Places.

22. The Government of Israel may restrict or prohibit the entry or stay of any person at the Holy Places for reasons of security, public health, or any other essential public interest.

23. Representatives of Israeli authorities will not be permitted to enter the Holy Places without the prior permission of one of the heads of the religious communities that have rights at the particular site, unless such entry is essential for public peace and/or state security, its need having been confirmed in advance and in writing by the chief of the Jerusalem Police.

F. Freedom of Worship

24. Freedom of worship at the Holy Places will be guaranteed to the members of all the communities for whom the sites are sacred, subject to the existing rights of members of all the various faiths at those sites.

25. Arrangements for worship at the Holy Places will be determined by the representatives of the above communities and with the approval of the Commissioner.

G. Rights at the Holy Places

26. In this Statute the term "existing rights" will have the following meaning:
For places sacred to Christians, the rights that currently exist in fact at the Holy Places under the Ottoman *status quo* arrangement, and/or under later agreements between the Christian communities.
For the places sacred to both Jews and Muslims (such as the Temple Mount and the Western Wall), the rights that currently exist in fact, as determined by the Israeli authorities after June 1967.
For the other Holy Places, the rights that currently exist in fact according to long-established and accepted tradition.

27. The existing rights of the religious communities at the Holy Places will be preserved.

28. Should a question arise regarding the existence of a right accruing to a particular community, or should the right contradict the Statute, the matter will be decided by the Commissioner.

29. The Commissioner will settle any dispute between the religious communities regarding any rights at the Holy Places.

H. Administration

30. The administration and maintenance of the Holy Places will be entrusted to the various communities according to their existing rights at those places.

31. The authorized bodies of the communities will have exclusive jurisdiction over their personnel at the Holy Places in matters under their jurisdiction according to their laws and according to the *status quo*. In all other matters, the jurisdiction will be vested in the Israeli courts according to Israeli law.

32. Should a question arise regarding jurisdiction in a matter related to the Statute, it will be decided by the Minister of Religious Affairs of Israel.

33. In the absence of agreement between the religious communities regarding the execution of urgent repairs at a Holy Place, the repairs will be carried out according to the orders of the Commissioner, the expense to be borne by whom the Commissioner will decide.

I. Status of Clerics

34. The list of clerics intended to serve at the Holy Places will be transmitted in advance to the Minister of Religious Affairs of Israel. He may refuse to approve the service of a particular cleric at a Holy Place if he is convinced that the person endangers the security or safety of Israel, public order, or other vital interests of the State of Israel.

35. The clerics of the religious communities – with the exception of the Jewish clerics, serving at the Jewish Holy Places, who will be considered ordinary citizens of Israel – will enjoy privileges and personal immunities similar to those granted to diplomatic agents by the Vienna Convention on Diplomatic Relations, 1961, albeit without being considered diplomatic representatives of any state.

36. The Government of Israel will have the right to order the suspension of a cleric serving at a Holy Place, if the government is convinced that the individual's conduct endangers the security, peace, or public order, or that his conduct harms vital interests of the State of Israel.

J. Offenses and Torts

37. Every act or omission done at a Holy Place which, had it been committed elsewhere would have constituted a criminal offense or a civil wrong under Israeli law, will fall under the jurisdiction of the courts in Israel according to Israeli law.

38. The jurisdiction of the Israeli courts in civil matters relating to the Holy Places will be subject to the immunity of the clerics serving at those places.

39. Notwithstanding the above, if the adjudication of a civil dispute relating to a Holy Place involves a substantive determination between two or more religious communities regarding the rights of any religious community at any Holy Place, the matter will not come under the jurisdiction of the courts of Israel, but under that of the Commissioner, subject to prior inquiry by the Holy Places Council.

30. Proposal of Dr. Joëlle Le Morzellec

Date: 1979

Source: J. Le Morzellec, *La question de Jérusalem devant l'Organisation des Nations Unies*, Etablissements Emile Bruylant, Bruxelles, 1979, pp. 463-472.

Background: Joëlle Le Morzellec, holder of a doctorate in jurisprudence, set forth her proposal in a book that is based on her doctoral dissertation, which was submitted in 1976. The author is of the opinion that the problem of Jerusalem should be resolved in stages. In the final stage, an Israeli-Arab confederation – and afterward a federation – would be established with Jerusalem as its capital. Initially, the Arab boroughs should be granted municipal autonomy. Referring to the precedents of Greater London and Paris, the author proposes three parameters for municipal autonomy in Jerusalem: autonomy of the boroughs, joint administration of the common services, and the maintenance of a capital city.

National Aspirations

The author proposes that in the final stage Jerusalem will serve as the capital of an Arab-Israeli confederation, or federation.

Holy Places

1. Freedom of access and of worship at the Holy Places will be guaranteed to all.

2. The Holy Places will enjoy substantial immunity, to be assured by international guarantees.

Municipal Administration

Until the above-mentioned confederation is established, the following arrangements should be in effect as part of the municipal administration:

1. Jerusalem should be divided into boroughs in accordance with the dominant population in a specific area: Arab, Armenian, or Jewish.

2. A "Municipal Council of Jerusalem" should be established, to be composed of representatives who will be elected in the various boroughs. The number of representatives from each borough will be proportionate to the population of the boroughs.

3. The Municipal Council of Jerusalem will have powers in the realm of supplying general services to all the city's residents: overall planning, economic administration, roads, sewerage, firefighting, housing, water supply, defending the city, and preserving the cultural heritage.

4. The head of the Council, who will also serve as the mayor, will be an Israeli. He will be assisted by an Arab deputy mayor. The mayor and his deputy will be elected by the Municipal Council of Jerusalem.

5. Every decision will require the approval of the mayor and of the deputy mayor before it enters into force.

6. A sub-municipality (*municipalité déléguée*) will be established in each borough. It will consist of the borough head (*maire délégué*) and the Borough Council.

7. The borough head will be elected from and by the Borough Council. He will be responsible for the population administration and the police. With the assistance of the Borough Council, the borough head will supervise the daily management of the borough's affairs.

8. The Borough Council will consist of delegates who have been elected in the borough to the Municipal Council of Jerusalem and of about ten additional officials who will be responsible for social affairs, education, culture, and family matters within the borough.

9. The first instances of Israeli and Arab courts will have concurrent jurisdiction and defendants will be able to choose the court in which their case will be heard. Every appeal will be heard by a mixed tribunal, to be comprised of an equal number of Arab and Israeli judges and to be headed by an Arab or an Israeli judge, who will be designated by lot.

10. Every borough will have a staff of municipal workers and an appended municipality.

11. An Israeli police chief will be responsible for maintaining security and public order throughout the city. He will be assisted by an Arab deputy whose powers will extend mainly over the Arab boroughs.

31. Proposal by Lord Caradon

Date: 1980

Source: Lord Caradon, *The Future of Jerusalem: A Review of Proposals for the Future of the City*, Research Directorate, National Defense University, Washington, D.C., 1980.
"Why Palestinians See the Holy City as a Gateway to Peace," *The Times*, 7 January 1977.
"Jerusalem, Gateway to Peace," *The Washington Post*, 12 December 1977.

Background: Lord Caradon was an official in the British Mandatory administration in Palestine in the early 1930s and afterward held various positions in the British Foreign Service. In 1967, as British Ambassador to the United Nations, he actively participated in the formulation of Security Council Resolution 242.

National Aspirations

1. Sovereignty over west Jerusalem should be vested in Israel, while east Jerusalem should be under Arab sovereignty (apparently the author had in mind a Palestinian state which would encompass the West Bank and the Gaza Strip).

2. The boundary between the two parts of the city will be determined by the U.N. Security Council after it receives recommendations from a special Boundary Commission to be appointed by the Secretary-General.

3. The Boundary Commission would hear the arguments of the two parties regarding the location of the border and "would be instructed to make two main changes" in the pre-June 1967 line: (a) "the Jewish Quarter of the Old City and the Western Wall should be included on the Israeli side of the line"; (b) "an area of Mount Scopus including the Hebrew University should be Israeli territory connected with Israel by an open bridge."

4. There will be "no barriers" between the two parts of the city, and "no impediment to freedom of movement between them."

5. The entire city will be demilitarized.

6. The U.N. Secretary-General will "appoint a Commission of Cooperation to work out and put into effect practical plans for economic and financial cooperation."

7. The U.N. Secretary-General will appoint a High Commissioner "to be stationed in Jerusalem." He will represent the U.N., and "work with all concerned" to implement the plan.

Holy Places

The High Commissioner will ensure free access to the Holy Places.

32. Proposal by Ya'akov Hazan

Date: 1980

Source: Ya'akov Hazan's proposal was appended to the resolutions of the 8th Mapam (Israel United Workers Party) Conference, 1980.

Background: Ya'akov Hazan was a leader of the left-wing Hakibbutz Ha'artzi (one of the country's Kibbutz movements), of Hashomer Hatza'ir (the Young Guard movement) and of Mapam (United Workers Party). He was a member of the central institutions of the Histadrut Labor Federation and a Knesset Member from the parliament's inception in 1949 until 1974.

National Aspirations

1. Unified Jerusalem is the capital of the State of Israel.

2. The Arab inhabitants of Jerusalem will have the right to choose the nationality of either Israel or of the Arab state to Israel's east. Those opting for Arab nationality will retain all the civil rights in Israel, including the right to participate in the Knesset elections.

3. The Old City would be declared a City of Peace. Matters pertaining to the Old City's religious and cultural character would be administered by a Religious Council, composed of equal representation from the three faiths.

4. The civil-secular matters pertaining to the Old City would be administered by a special commission comprising Arab members according to their proportion in the population of Jerusalem, with the addition of a member from the Armenian community.

5. Major Islamic and Christian sites in the Old City would be granted extraterritorial status and be administered by the communities' representatives on the Religious Council (see below).

6. The Temple Mount would be granted extraterritorial status and would be administered by the Muslim representative on the Religious Council. The part of the Temple Mount where Jews are permitted to pray might be excluded from that area.

7. The State of Israel would be responsible for maintaining law and order in the Old City, including the extraterritorial religious sites.

Holy Places

1. The religious sites possessing extraterritorial status would be administered by representatives of the relevant faith on the Religious Council.

2. Freedom of access to the Temple Mount would be guaranteed for Muslim pilgrims from the entire world.

Municipal Administration

1. Jerusalem will be divided into boroughs, to be administered by elected representatives.
2. The division into boroughs would be implemented, among other criteria, according to demographic data.
3. The general administration of Greater Jerusalem would be entrusted to the Jerusalem City Hall.
4. The elected councils of the municipality and of the boroughs with an Arab majority will be ensured broad autonomy in social affairs, culture, education, and any other sphere which will not prejudice the overall planning of Jerusalem and the civil rights of all its inhabitants.
5. The condition for maintaining autonomy in education is: education for allegiance to the State of Israel, good citizenship, mutual tolerance, and increasing the cooperation between the two peoples.
6. Members of the Armenian faith will have the right to establish an autonomous communal-personal organization encompassing all the spheres of social life, culture, and education.

33. Proposal by Mark Gruhin

Date: 1980

Source: M.I. Gruhin, "Jerusalem: Legal and Political Dimensions in a Search for Peace," 12 *Case Western Reserve Journal of International Law* 169, 1980.

Background: Mark Gruhin wrote this article while he was a doctoral student at American University in Washington D.C. The author believes that sovereignty over the whole of Jerusalem has been vested in Israel since the Six-Day War. Nevertheless, Israel should agree to the solution proposed below.

National Aspirations

1. Israel will retain sovereignty over Jerusalem but will accept the limitations elaborated below.

2. Israel will grant all the Palestinian Arabs who desire to live in Jerusalem Israeli citizenship and rights of city residents identical to those granted to Jewish residents of the city.

3. Israel will agree to allow Jerusalem residents to hold dual nationality. The future representative of the Palestinians (Jordan, the PLO, or some other Arab state) will permit the Palestinians in Jerusalem to hold nationality of the Palestinian state as well.

4. Israel will allow the consul of the Palestinian state to reside in Jerusalem and to exercise jurisdiction over Palestinian citizens involved in civil disputes and criminal offences, but this only if the defendant/accused so desires.

Holy Places

1. Israel will accept an international supervision of the Holy Places.

2. The clerics who have custody of the Holy Places will be responsible for their maintenance and protection.

3. The Holy Places will enjoy special diplomatic immunity and will be exempted from national and municipal taxation.

4. Possibly the courts of each religion may be granted jurisdiction over religious disputes at the Holy Places.

5. Disputes between two religious communities will be settled by a special tribunal composed of representatives of all the religious communities.

Municipal Administration

1. Jerusalem will be divided into two electoral districts: one Israeli and one Arab (however, the city will not be divided into two boroughs – an idea the author opposes).
2. Residents of the districts will elect representatives to two legislative chambers.
3. Representatives to the first chamber will be elected by residents of the two districts in direct proportion to the number of inhabitants in each district. Representatives to the second chamber will be elected by the inhabitants of both districts and it will be composed of an equal number of Jews and Palestinians.
4. The number of elected representatives in the two chambers will be small so that the legislative mechanism can be effective.
5. The chambers shall create joint mechanisms for policing, firefighting, rescue crews, and unified systems to supply water and electricity.
6. The mayor will be elected by all the city's residents.
7. It will be the mayor's duty to implement all the above-mentioned legislative enactments, though he will have the right to veto such legislation.

34. Peace Plan by Crown Prince Fahd of Saudi Arabia

Date: 6 August 1981

Source: Y. Lukacs (ed.), *Documents on the Israeli-Palestinian Conflict, 1967-1983*, Cambridge University Press, Cambridge, 1984, pp. 236-237.

Background: The plan was formulated by Crown Prince (later King) Fahd of Saudi Arabia in reaction to the peace treaty between Egypt and Israel. The plan was rejected by Israel, Iraq, and Syria.

National Aspirations

1. Israel would withdraw from all the territories it occupied in the 1967 war, "including Arab Jerusalem."

2. Israel would dismantle all the settlements established on Arab land since 1967.

3. An independent Palestinian state, with Jerusalem as its capital, would be established.

4. The West Bank and the Gaza Strip would be placed "under the auspice of the U.N. for a period not exceeding several months."

Holy Places

"[A] guarantee of freedom of worship for all religions in the Holy Places."

35. Proposal by the Honourable Terence Prittie

Date: 1981

Source: T. Prittie, *Whose Jerusalem?*, Frederick Muller Ltd., London, 1981.

Background: In 1981 Terence Prittie, a British journalist, published a book on Jerusalem. The last chapter surveys several earlier proposals regarding the city's status, after which Prittie presents his own proposal. Some elements of the Prittie plan resemble the Benvenisti proposal (see above).

National Aspirations

1. A special regime based on "administrative sovereignty" would be established in the city, according to the municipal authorities broad municipal powers, similar to the situation that prevailed in West Berlin at the time (before the reunification of Germany).
2. Jerusalem would be the capital of Israel and of "a Palestinian entity, or of the Palestinian component in a Jordanian-Palestinian Federation."
3. Israel would be "both trustee and 'protecting power' for Jerusalem."
4. The Arabs of east Jerusalem would have "the right to Jordanian (or Palestinian) citizenship" and the "right to vote in elections in neighboring Arab countries."

Holy Places

1. There would be "total Muslim control of Muslim Holy Places," with "Muslim flags" flying over them.
2. Israel would draft a declaration (or a statute) guaranteeing the religious rights of Christians and Muslims in Jerusalem.

Municipal Administration

1. The city would be divided into boroughs, each of which would manage its own local affairs.
2. A joint authority of all the boroughs would be established, with the participation of Jews and Arabs "in proportion to their numbers" in the city.

36. Proposal by Professor Saul Cohen

Date: 1981

Source: S.B. Cohen, "Jerusalem's Unity and West Bank Autonomy – Paired Principles," 8 *Middle East Review* 27, 1981 (Nos. 3 and 4).

Background: When he wrote this article, Prof. Cohen was President of Queens College at City University of New York. He linked his proposal for a settlement in Jerusalem with the arrangement to be worked out for the West Bank. Israel, he thought, should agree to more significant concessions regarding autonomy in the West Bank, while the Arabs should be more forthcoming concerning the future status of Jerusalem.

National Aspirations

1. Sovereignty over all of Jerusalem would be vested in Israel, though its powers would be limited as explained below.

2. Jerusalem's Arab residents could either accept Israeli citizenship or become "Citizens of Jerusalem." They could also "hold dual citizenship with a West Bank entity."

3. "Geographical corridors" could be created between Jerusalem and the West Bank entity.

4. The Knesset would appoint a subcommittee on Jerusalem. Its functions would cover public security (army and police), social security, medical facilities, employment, financing of housing projects, industrial plants, transportation infrastructure, and construction of schools. Revenue would come from the "national taxation system."

5. Special "citizen-bodies" would be established to provide "ideological guidance" in the areas of education, culture, and religious matters. These bodies would be "appointed by [the] city as special delegations to national parliaments and world organizations." Their activity would be financed by "religious institutional taxes" and by donations.

Holy Places

1. Each religious community would safeguard its own Holy Places.

2. Bodies would be established to represent the Arab, Jewish, and Christian communities, "distinct from specific sovereign states."

3. These bodies would have "control of religious and certain cultural institutions, including extraterritorial enclaves within the Old City" (there is no further elaboration).

4. Israel would ensure freedom of access to the Holy Places.

Municipal Administration

1. *Municipal level:* (a) A "popularly elected municipal council, weighted by size of Communities"; (b) the mayor to be chosen in a "City-wide election"; (c) the City Council would have responsibility for firefighting, transportation, water supply, electricity, sanitation and sewerage facilities, road construction and maintenance, municipal control, development and maintenance of public buildings, land-use planning, and establishment of environmental quality standards; (d) these services are to be financed by the state.

2. *Boroughs:* (a) The administration of each borough to be elected in "direct elections within [the] community"; (b) the administration would issue building permits, enforce rules on land use and environmental quality, hire and administer school staff and direct the educational programs, and operate parks and recreational programs; (c) these activities are to be financed from "state support and community-levied real estate taxes."

3. *Neighborhoods:* (a) "administrative wards" would be established to deal with preschool education, culture and sports activities, and small parks; (b) financing would come from "community support."

4. *Metropolitan authorities:* (a) "Joint Israeli-Arab authorities" would be established to supervise transportation, waste disposal, recreation facilities, highways, building, and markets; (b) funding would come from "national support (Israel and West Bank)."

5. *City-regional authorities:* (a) An "administrative-territorial framework" authority would be created for "Arabs and Jews living within and outside Jerusalem"; (b) its boundaries would include "heavily populated areas of the West Bank" and the "Jewish-settled Jerusalem Corridor"; (c) Arabs and Jews would be equally represented on the authority; (d) the authority's functions would include "cross-border" spheres such as industrial development, agriculture, tourism, health facilities, recreation, settlement, transportation, labor exchange, and the supply of electricity and water; (e) funding to come from "national support (Israel and West Bank)."

37. Proposal by Dr. Henry Cattan

Date: 1981

Source: H. Cattan, *Jerusalem*, St. Martin's Press, New York, 1981, p. 143.

Background: Henry Cattan was a member of the delegation that represented the Palestinian Arabs at the U.N. before the establishment of Israel and a member of the Palestine National Council as well as of the Palestine Bar Association. He believes that sovereignty over Jerusalem, as over the entire former Palestine, is wielded by the Palestinians.

National Aspirations

1. The U.N. should take measures to stop the process of the "judaization" of Jerusalem, "to rescind Israel's unlawful actions which violate [the city's] status, and to preserve the religious and historic heritage of the world in the Holy City."

2. Such actions by the U.N. should include: (a) enforcement of General Assembly Resolution 181 (II) (the "Partition Resolution," see above); (b) "repatriation of the Palestinian refugees"; (c) rescinding of "all measures [taken by Israel] which have altered the administration, the demography and land ownership of Jerusalem"; (d) dismantling of all the "settlements" in Jerusalem and "withdrawal of the settlers that Israel brought to colonize Jerusalem."

3. To supervise the implementation of these steps, a "Temporary International Authority" would be established "under the authority of the Security Council or the General Assembly."

4. This Authority would also be authorized to administer the city during an interim period. After the implementation of the above-mentioned measures, it would be succeeded by a "Tripartite Communal Council" with equal partitipation of the Christian, Muslim, and Jewish communities.

5. This Council, too, "would be set up under the authority of the Security Council or the General Assembly," and it "would succeed to the Temporary International Authority."

6. The Tripartite Communal Council would administer the city "pending a final settlement of the problem of Jerusalem and the Palestine question."

7. Establishment of the Council "does not aim at prejudicing the future political structure for the administration of Jerusalem under a final settlement of the Palestine question." The administrative structure could be "modified, adjusted or abrogated in the light of the final settlement."

38. Proposal by Professor Gerald I.A.D. Draper, OBE

Date: 1981

Source: G.I.A.D. Draper, "The Status of Jerusalem as a Question of International Law,": in: H. Kochler (ed.), *The Legal Aspects of the Palestine Problem with Special Regard to the Question of Jerusalem*, Wilhelm Braunmuller, Wien 1981, p. 154.

Background: Professor Draper was a lecturer in international law at the European Studies Department of the University of Sussex, England. He also assisted Jordan's Crown Prince Hassan Bin Talal to write his book on Jerusalem (see Ch. 1). Draper believes that sovereignty over the city is wielded neither by Israel nor Jordan, since each acquired control by the use of force. "Territorial sovereignty is probably in suspense," and since 1967 Israel has "belligerent occupant status" in Jerusalem. Any settlement must take into account "the existing right of self-determination of the Palestinian people."

It should be emphasized that in his article Draper surveys three possible solutions for Jerusalem (internationalization, division, and partial internationalization) but does not explicitly align himself with any of them. Below we shall discuss the proposal that was elaborated most fully in Draper's article.

National Aspirations

1. The city might be divided into three parts: (a) "the Western City as the capital of Israel"; (b) "the Eastern City as capital of any new Arab State of Palestine that may eventually be created"; (c) "the Old (Walled) City placed under international control."

2. The inhabitants of the Old City "could claim Israeli or Palestinian citizenship, at volition."

39. Resolution of the Arab Summit Conference at Fez

Date: 6 September 1982

Source: R. Lapidoth & M. Hirsch (eds.), *The Arab-Israel Conflict and Its Resolution: Selected Documents*, Nijhoff Publishers, Dordrecht, 1992, p. 296.

Background: This plan was formulated by the Arab Summit Conference probably in reaction to the plan announced on 1 September 1982 by U.S. President Ronald Reagan. The resolution adopted at the summit meeting is based on the Fahd plan (see above), though with substantial modifications. Only the provisions concerning Jerusalem are mentioned here.

National Aspirations

1. Israel will withdraw "from all Arab territories occupied in 1967, including Arab Jerusalem."
2. A Palestinian state will be created "with Jerusalem as its capital."

Holy Places

Freedom of worship will be guaranteed "for all religions at the Holy Places."

40. Proposal by Justice Haim Cohn

Date: 1982

Source: "Draft Statute for the City of Jerusalem" by Haim Cohn (unpublished).

Background: The draft drawn up by Justice Haim Cohn, formerly of the Supreme Court of Israel, was commissioned by the Mayor of Jerusalem and presented at a closed meeting of the International Committee for Jerusalem.

National Aspirations

The proposal intimates (without saying so expressly) that territorial sovereignty over Jerusalem would be vested in Israel.

Holy Places

1. A "Council of Holy Places" will be established, to be "composed of all religious communities."

2. The Council will appoint a "Commissioner of Holy Places" to "preside over the Council." The Commissioner shall be a neutral person of international standing.

3. The Council will discuss reports prepared by the Commissioner on "any occurrence or complaint relating to Holy Places" and make recommendations which the Commissioner will bring before the City Council. "The quorum of the Council shall be the heads of or representatives of at least one Jewish, one Muslim, one Druze, and one Christian religious community."

4. Such Holy Places as were in the custody and under the jurisdiction of any specific religious community by law or custom shall remain so.

5. In cases of conflicting claims to a Holy Place, the contesting communities "shall exercise [control] jointly." If they cannot reach agreement on joint control, the Commissioner of Holy Places will direct them on how to implement such control in practice.

6. "Police forces, or government or borough inspectors or agents, shall not enter a Holy Place in the performance of their official duties save with the consent or at the invitation of" the religious community which has custody of the site, or "in circumstances of emergency."

7. The Holy Places will be exempted from all taxation – government, city, or borough – but the religious communities "may be charged for water, electricity and other services supplied to such Holy Places."

8. Freedom of access to and worship at the Holy Places will be guaranteed. Persons from abroad "wishing to enter Israel for the sole purpose of visiting a Holy Place

in Jerusalem" will be granted "pilgrims' visas entitling them to proceed to and stay in Jerusalem for a period of two weeks," whatever their nationality.

9. All matters relating to the Holy Places, other than criminal offenses, will be decided by the Commissioner of Holy Places, whose "decision shall be final." Criminal offenses "committed in, or in relation to, a Holy Place," will be dealt with by the Israeli courts.

10. "The religious communities shall have exclusive jurisdiction over their personnel in all matters, other than those criminal matters, which are lawfully and traditionally subject-matters of internal discipline." Disputes as to whether a case entails internal discipline "shall be determined by the Commissioner of Holy Places."

Municipal Administration

1. The City is to be divided into nine (or more) boroughs, each governed by a Borough Council elected in separate popular elections. The Council will elect from among its members a Borough Mayor (the proposal elaborates election procedures).

2. The boroughs will be autonomous. Autonomy is to extend to matters of education and culture, religious, social, health and other municipal services.

3. The boroughs shall be deemed to be incorporated into a Municipal Union within the meaning of existing Israeli law (i.e., an association of several neighboring townships for the promotion of common interests). Powers vested by law in a Municipal Union shall be exercised by the City Council.

4. The City Council shall be composed of three representatives of each Borough Council; the Commissioner of Holy Places; one representative each of the Chief Rabbinate of Israel, the Supreme Muslim Council, and the Christian religious communities; eleven representatives of pertinent Israeli government authorities; a "town planning expert appointed by the National Town Planning Council"; a representative of the Israeli Council of Higher Education; and a former Jerusalem City Mayor. The Council shall elect a City Mayor from among the Borough Mayors, to rotate at prescribed intervals.

5. Boroughs may levy taxes as approved and enacted by the City Council. There will be no direct taxation by the State of Israel. Expenditures of the City Council will be borne by the boroughs: there will be no taxation by the City Council.

6. Borough Councils shall be deemed Town Planning Commissions for their respective areas of jurisdiction, and the City Council shall act as District Town Planning Commission, within the meaning of Israeli Town Planning Law.

7. The judiciary shall remain an integral part of the Israeli Judiciary.

8. Except as provided for in the City Constitution (e.g., in matters of taxation and the Holy Places), Israeli law shall apply.

41. Proposal by Ambassador Gideon Rafael

Date: The proposal was published on 25 December 1983.

Source: G. Rafael, "Steps to Peace," *Jerusalem Post*, 25 December 1983, p. 8.

Background: Gideon Rafael held various posts in Israel's Foreign Service from 1948 until 1978, including *inter alia* Ambassador to Belgium and Luxemburg, Ambassador to Britain, and Director-General of the Ministry of Foreign Affairs from 1967 to 1971.

National Aspirations

1. (a) "Jordan, the West Bank and Gaza would join in a confederation, with a wide measure of autonomy granted to the West Bank Palestinians."
   (b) The "Jordanian-Palestinian Confederation" would conclude a treaty with Israel on "security arrangements, such as demilitarization and the presence of Israel defense positions for a given period."
   (c) "The autonomous [Palestinian] region and Israel would establish a number of joint bodies" for cooperation in various spheres.
   (d) Israel would conclude a number of agreements with "the Jordanian part of the confederation."

2. Jerusalem will remain unified and the capital of Israel.

3. Jerusalem "may become the seat of the common institutions" of the confederation (without prejudicing Israel's sovereignty over the city).

Holy Places

1. "A tripartite religious ecumenical authority, composed of universally renowned and respected personalities, could be established."

2. Its functions would be to safeguard "the rights of all religions, the freedom of worship and access to the Holy Places, and promoting cooperation and mutual respect between the various communities."

Municipal Administration

1. The city's ethnic communities would be granted a "wide measure of self-administration."

2. The city's administration would be "based on the borough system, and maximum coordination between the boroughs and the central municipality of Greater Jerusalem."

42. Proposal by Professor Antonio Cassese

Date: 1986

Source: A. Cassese, "Legal Considerations on the International Status of Jerusalem," 3 *The Palestine Yearbook of International Law* 3 (1986).

Background: Antonio Cassese is Professor of International Law at the University of Florence and at the European University Institute in Florence. In 1986/1987 he headed the "Steering Committee for Human Rights" of the Council of Europe. In 1989-1993 he was President of the Council of Europe "Committee for the Prevention of Torture." Since 1993 he has served as President of the International Tribunal which was established to try war criminals in the former Yugoslavia. Cassese bases his proposal on the existing legal situation, as he perceives it, in Jerusalem. He believes that Israel "undertook to refrain from seeking any settlement of the [Jerusalem] question without United Nations consent." Consequently, Israel may not unilaterally change the status of the city. Jordan, too, assented (implicitly) not to make changes in the city's status without U.N. consent. Neither Israel nor Jordan wields sovereignty over the city because both acquired territories in the city through the use of military force. "Israel only exercises *de facto* control over Jerusalem." The principle of self-determination requires that the Palestinian people share in the process of determining the future status of Jerusalem." (Cassese's reasons for suggesting that nevertheless sovereignty over west Jerusalem should be vested in Israel are explained in Ch. 1.)

National Aspirations

1. "Sovereign rights over western Jerusalem should be granted to Israel."

2. "Sovereign rights" in east Jerusalem "should be granted to the legitimate representative of the Palestinian people."

Holy Places

There must be "full enjoyment by everyone of the rights of access and worship in the Holy Places."

43. Proposal by Professor Thomas and Ms. Sally Mallison

Date: 1981, 1986

Source: W.T. Mallison & S. Mallison, *The Palestine Problem in International Law and World Order*, Longman, London, 1986, pp. 207-239.
idem, "The Jerusalem Problem in Public International Law: Juridical Status and a Start Toward Solution," in: H. Kochler (ed.), *The Legal Aspects of the Palestine Problem with Special Regard to the Question of Jerusalem*, Wilhelm Braunmuller, Wien 1981, p. 98.

Background: Thomas Mallison is Professor Emeritus of Law and former director of the Institute of International Law at George Washington University in Washington D.C. Sally Mallison is a researcher at the latter institute. After surveying a number of proposals for resolving the Jerusalem question, the Mallisons recommend the solution described below. The authors believe one can justify the city's partition in light of the absence of protests and the silence of the international community after 1967, as well as in light of the claims asserted by Israel and Jordan to the parts of the city they had controlled before the Six-Day War.

National Aspirations

1. Israel will withdraw to the pre-June 1967 lines, retaining control over west Jerusalem.

2. The city's eastern part will be transferred directly to Arab control or "returned to the United Nations to act as a temporary trustee for Palestinian and other Arab interests pending a more permanent solution."

3. The permanent solution should be "either the *corpus separatum* for all or part of Jerusalem or a more permanent division of the City between a Palestinian State and the State of Israel."

Holy Places

1. The Holy Places will enjoy suitable protection.

2. Freedom of access to the Holy Places will be guaranteed.

44. Proposal by Dr. Walid Khalidi

Date: 1978, 1988

Source: W. Khalidi, "Thinking the Unthinkable: A Sovereign Palestinian State," 56 *Foreign Affairs* 695, 1978.
idem, "Toward Peace in the Holy Land," 66 *Foreign Affairs* 71, 1988.

Background: Walid Khalidi was Professor of Political Studies at the American University of Beirut until 1982 and currently is a Research Fellow at the Harvard Center for International Affairs. In the past he was a member of the Palestine National Council and carried out various political missions for the Palestine Liberation Organization.

National Aspirations

1. East Jerusalem will be the capital of "Arab Palestine," and west Jerusalem of Israel.
2. The two states would agree to arrangements for "freedom of movement and residence between two capitals."
3. Both parts of the city would be "demilitarized in part or wholly except for essential internal security forces."

Holy Places

1. Extraterritorial status would be granted to the Holy Places of Judaism in east Jerusalem, and freedom of access to them should be guaranteed.
2. An "interfaith council" would be set up, composed of senior representatives of Christianity, Judaism and Islam. The council will be chaired by a representative of the U.N. or by rotating chairmanship among the members.
3. The council "could oversee the special interests, Holy Places and institutions of each religion and act as an arbitration and conciliation body for disputes or claims arising with regard to them."

Municipal Administration

1. Two "separate municipalities of each sovereign state" would provide services to the city's residents.
2. "A joint inter-state great municipal council could operate and supervise certain essential common services."

45. Proposal by David Ish-Shalom

Date: 1987

Source: D. Ish-Shalom, *The Dread and the Hope*, Keshet Publishers, Jerusalem, 1987 (Hebrew); *idem*, "To Forgo the Dreams," *Ha'aretz*, 1 July 1993, p. B-4.

Background: David Ish-Shalom is an Israeli businessman who is active in the "East to Peace" movement and in the "Committee for an Israeli-Palestinian Dialogue."

National Aspirations

1. Unified Jerusalem will remain the capital of Israel.
2. Overall strategic control in Jerusalem will remain in Israel's hands.
3. The new Jewish neighborhoods in east Jerusalem will remain under Israeli sovereignty.
4. Jerusalem will be the symbolic and administrative capital of the demilitarized Palestinian entity (to be established in the West Bank and the Gaza Strip). This Palestinian capital will be located in the Muslim Quarter of the Old City (and perhaps in other quarters, as agreed by the parties). The symbolic capital will be modeled on the Vatican City. The offices of the Palestinian institutions will be located in the Palestinian capital.
5. Palestinian police forces will maintain law and public order in the above-mentioned symbolic and administrative capital, while Israeli forces will safeguard the area around.
6. All the Arab residents of east Jerusalem will be citizens of the Palestinian entity and have the right to vote for and be elected to its institutions.

Holy Places

1. The Islamic Holy Places will be administered by the Palestinian supreme institutions.
2. A Palestinian and/or Islamic flag will fly above the Islamic Holy Places.

46. Proposal by Dr. Grant Littke

Date: 1988

Source: G. Littke, "The Jerusalem Dispute: Settlement Proposals and Prospects," *Middle East Focus* 11, Summer 1988.

Background: At the time he wrote this article, Grant Littke was a senior doctoral candidate in the Department of Political Science and a research assistant at the Center for International and Strategic Studies at York University in Toronto, Canada. He is currently a Visiting Instructor at James Madison College, Michigan State University.

National Aspirations

1. Jerusalem will be the capital of Israel and of the future Palestinian state.
2. Neither Israel nor the Palestinian entity "would exercise complete sovereignty over the city," nor would sovereignty be vested in "an outside power." The two national entities "would, in a sense, share sovereignty over Jerusalem."
3. The city will be divided into a Jewish borough and an Arab borough.
4. Jerusalem will remain physically undivided, with freedom of movement guaranteed for all residents throughout the city.

Holy Places

1. "Some form of internationalization" of the holy sites will be established.
2. The "local religious authorities" will "retain administrative control" at their holy sites, subject to the supervision of an external body to be appointed by the U.N.
3. The U.N.-appointed body will ensure "unhindered access" to the holy sites and preservation of their sanctity.
4. Any change in the *status quo* of a holy site will be subject to the approval of the U.N.-appointed body, "and any violation of sanctity would be subject to its sanction."

Municipal Administration

1. Two "national boroughs" – one Jewish and one Arab – will be created, "defined according to the location of Arab and Jewish neighborhoods."
2. Each borough's powers will be vested in a council.
3. "A single municipal council" comprising representatives from the two boroughs would be established.
4. That council would provide "basic" and "city-wide services" and would "coordinate the activities of the two borough councils."

47. Proposal by John V. Whitbeck

Date: The proposal was first published on 14 April 1989.

Source: J.V. Whitbeck, "The Road to Peace Starts in Jerusalem," *Middle East International*, 14 April 1989.
idem, "Time to Reappraise the Middle East Peace Process," *Middle East International*, 19 March 1993.
idem, "And the Israeli Shall Live with the Palestinian," *Ha'aretz*, 6 October 1991, p. B-4 (Hebrew).
idem, "The Road to Peace Starts in Jerusalem: The Condominium Solution," *Middle East Insight*, September/October 1994.
idem, "The Road to Peace Starts in Jerusalem: The Condominium Solution," *Middle East Policy*, December 1994.

Background: John Whitbeck is a Paris-based international lawyer. His proposal regarding the future of Jerusalem is part of a general plan to resolve the Arab-Israeli conflict, according to which a confederation encompassing Israel and the Palestinian state would be established in the "Holy Land."

National Aspirations

1. Jerusalem will be the joint and undivided capital of both states. "The city would be a Condominium of Israel and Palestine."
2. Israeli government offices will be in the city's western sector and Palestinian government offices in the eastern sector. Municipal offices will be located in both areas.
3. The city could be fully demilitarized.
4. Supervision of persons or goods entering one state from the other should take place at the city's exit points rather than its entry points.
5. Appropriate rules concerning the applicable law (e.g., in personal, contractual and criminal cases) will be determined by legal experts of both parties in accordance with the subject matter, the parties involved and the district in which the issue or dispute arises.

Municipal Administration

1. The city will be "administered by an umbrella municipal council and local district councils."
2. A borough system modeled on the French-style *arrondissements* "could bring municipal government closer to the different communities in the city."

3. The proposal suggests "division of authorities" between the umbrella municipal council and the district councils. It would be desirable to employ "the European Union's principle of subsidiarity, to devolve as many aspects of municipal governance as possible to the district council level, reserving to the umbrella municipal council only those major matters that can only be administered efficiently at a city-wide level."

48. Proposal by Raphael Cidor

Date: The proposal was contained in a letter from the author to a resident of Jenin of September 1989.

Source: Author's letter, unpublished.

Background: Raphael Cidor is a journalist with Israel Radio. He calls his proposal "Guidelines for a Peace Treaty Between the State of Israel and a Future Independent Palestinian State." It was contained in a letter to a resident ("Hassan") of the West Bank city of Jenin whom he met two months after the Six-Day War and again twelve years later. Cidor's proposal was discussed in the first months of 1989 in the framework of meetings between Israeli and Palestinian politicians, journalists and intellectuals.

National Aspirations

1. Israel would recognize the right of the Palestinian people to independence in a sovereign state (following an interim period of self-government). The Palestinian state will extend from the 1967 borders in the west – with adjustments to be determined in negotiations – to the borders of Syria, Iraq, and Saudi Arabia: i.e., it will include both the Kingdom of Jordan and the Gaza Strip in the framework of a confederal merger under an Islamic constitutional monarchy or an Islamic parliamentary democracy.
2. Representatives of the Palestinian people will recognize the State of Israel's right to independent and sovereign existence.
3. The border between the two states will be open to the movement of people and goods.
4. Jerusalem will be the joint, united capital of the State of Israel and of Palestine, the seat of the parliaments and governments of the two states, and a spiritual center for Jews, Muslims, and Christians.
5. No international boundary will divide Jerusalem.

Holy Places

1. The authorized religious institutions of each faith will be entrusted with safeguarding its own Holy Places.
2. Freedom of access to the Holy Places will be guaranteed.

Municipal Administration

1. Israel and the Palestinian state will delegate their powers in their respective sections of Jerusalem to the capital's municipal institutions.
2. The mayor will be Jewish and his two deputies will be a Muslim and a Christian; all three will be elected in general municipal elections.
3. Jerusalem will be divided into boroughs, each with its own council.
4. The borough councils will elect from among their members the central City Council (other than the mayor and his deputies).
5. Enforcement of law and order will be entrusted to a special police force comprised of members of all the city's communities.

49. Proposal by Professor Gidon Gottlieb

Date: The proposal was published in the winter of 1989.

Source: G. Gottlieb, "Israel and the Palestinians," 67 *Foreign Affairs*, Fall 1989, p. 109.

Background: Gidon Gottlieb is Professor of International Law and Diplomacy at the University of Chicago and head of the Middle East Peace Project of the Council on Foreign Relations in New York.

National Aspirations

1. A confederation of peoples between the Palestinians, Israel and Jordan should be established. It would combine elements of both "separation" and "association." The "separation" features will protect the security and national character of the Jewish and Arab polities; "association" will allow practical problems such as trade and water resources to be addressed. These arrangements would be based on a variety of layered functional boundary and demarcation lines to govern security, holy sites and other concerns.

2. Jerusalem would remain the capital of Israel and might also become the "capital of the joint confederation" (a "capitals district").

3. "Jerusalem would remain an undivided city" with a complex regime deconstructing principles of temporal and spiritual sovereignty to safeguard the walled city and the character of the holy places.

4. The municipal boundaries "could well be enlarged," enabling the confederative institutions to be located in Jerusalem "together with [their] Israeli, Jordanian and Palestinian representatives."

50. Proposal by Shmuel Toledano

Date: The proposal was published in early 1991.

Source: "Peace in Stages," 1991 (Hebrew).

Background: The proposal was formulated by S. Toledano, a former Advisor to three Prime Ministers of Israel on Arab Affairs. It was supported by the Council of "Peace in Stages," whose members include ninety Israeli officers in the reserves with the rank of colonel and above, seventy professors, eighteen former ambassadors, as well as Arab and Jewish personalities.

The plan called for the Cabinet and Knesset to take the decision that Israel will be ready to withdraw from the West Bank and the Gaza Strip, with minor border modifications, after five years, and to delcare that it would not object to the establishment of a Palestinian state. The plan is conditional on an end to Palestinian terrorism and the Intifada, and on the renunciation by the Palestine Liberation Organization of the "right of return" as well as on its recognition of Israel – these steps to be taken during the five-year period. The Arab states would terminate the state of war. In the event of a significant threat to Israel from the east, the Israeli army would have the right to enter the Palestinian state during its first decade of existence.

National Aspirations

Sovereignty over Jerusalem would be vested in Israel.

Holy Places

The Holy Places would be administered by a representative from the faith or each of the faiths for whom the site is sacred.

Municipal Administration

Separate municipal elections will be held in the city's western and eastern parts respectively.

51. Proposal by Professor Daniel Elazar

Date: The proposal, published in 1991, is based on a plan first put forward in 1967.

Source: D.J. Elazar, *Two Peoples–One Land: Federal Solutions for Israel, the Palestinians, and Jordan*, University Press of America, Lanham, New York, London, 1991, pp. 147-174.

Background: Daniel Elazar is Professor of Political Science at Bar-Ilan University in Ramat Gan and the director of the Jerusalem Center for Public Affairs. Professor Elazar has written extensively on federal structures, and in the above-mentioned book he analyzes eleven possible structures of this kind which might serve as the basis for a settlement of the conflict involving Israel, Jordan, and the Palestinians. In the chapter on Jerusalem the author surveys a number of alternative mechanisms for municipal administration in cities with a heterogeneous population; any of them, or a combination of some of them, might be adopted in the future for Jerusalem.

National Aspirations

Daniel Elazar assumes that Jerusalem will remain unified, with Israel exercising exclusive control in most of the city, and perhaps jointly with another body at certain sites or in certain areas.

Municipal Administration

The alternatives presented in the study (any of which or a combination of which could be adopted) are:

1. "City-county arrangements": If a "county system" were instituted as part of a federal solution to the Arab-Israeli conflict, present-day Jerusalem could be "reconstituted as a county possessing full municipal powers," with "territories within it being given municipal status." As for the "links between the county and the municipalities within it," these could be "hierarchical, federal, contractual, or some combination of all three."

2. "Federated municipalities": This would entail the creation of a system of boroughs (possibly on the London model) with a division of powers between the boroughs and the umbrella-municipality, or a federation of a number of municipalities situated within a certain area.

3. "Neighborhood district programs": In this alternative neighborhood offices are set up "to manage special interest programs, to mobilize support for them, and/or to absorb public responses." These mechanisms enable the city administration to react more effectively to requests by borough residents and to supply various

resources (such as funds and personnel) in response to the feedback it receives from the neighborhood administrations.

4. "Functional programs": This alternative refers to the augmentation of "existing general-purpose local governments" by means of "special purpose authorities and departments." This may also occur among several local administrations (e.g., a number of cities). The new arrangements may be designed "to serve specific geographic areas," or cater to a particular population group with special needs (e.g., drainage, education, or neighborhood renewal).

5. "Extralocal models": Of the many models which are subsumed under this category, two are relevant to Jerusalem: (a) "Consociational arrangements," which are informal intercommunal arrangements that evolve over time among different ethnic, religious, and/or ideological groups, and "reflect fundamental commitment to structural pluralism" (examples are arrangements regarding "percentages of representation" for a particular group on national or municipal bodies, or for "separate spheres of influence"); (b) "capital districts" which in some countries are "set aside with special arrangements for their governance," which may be control by the national government, while in federal states (e.g., Australia, United States) they may be organized as "federal districts."

52. Proposal by Palestinian and Israeli Peace Activists

Date: The proposal was formulated at a meeting held from 15-19 July 1991, and was presented at a press conference on 16 July 1991.

Source: Framework for a Public Peace Process: Toward a Peaceful Israeli-Palestinian Relationship, Stanford Center on Conflict and Negotiation and the Beyond War Foundation, 1991.
Ha'aretz, 17 September 1991, p. A-2, and 24 September 1991, p. B-2 (Hebrew).

Background: The proposal was drawn up at a closed seminar held under the co-sponsorship of Stanford University's Center on Conflict and Negotiation and the Beyond War Foundation. The moderator was Dr. Harold Saunders, director of International Programs for The Kettering Foundation, and former U.S. Assistant Secretary of State under Dr. Henry Kissinger. Ten Israelis and Palestinians "actively involved in the search for peace" participated in the seminar. The Israeli side comprised Moshe Amirav, Giora Furman, Dr. Shlomo Elbaz, Dr. Galit Hasan-Rokem, and Lt. Colonel (Res.) Oded Megiddo; the Palestinian participants were Hanna Siniora, Dr. Bernard Sabella, Dr. Mamdouh al-Aker, and Dr. Rihab Essawi. A letter from Nabeel Shaath, chairman of the Political Committee of the Palestine National Council – who also took part in the conference – was appended to the proposal, stating that the Palestinian National Council accepted it as "a basis for future dialogue in the search for peace."

National Aspirations

1. Essentially, the proposal calls for the establishment of a Palestinian state alongside Israel in the pre-June 1967 borders with "a minimum of necessary modifications"; an end to "the state of war and all hostile activities" in the Middle East; comprehensive security arrangements for Israel and the Palestinian state; and reduction of arsenals, "including weapons of mass destruction."

2. After a five-year interim period following the signing of the peace agreement, the Palestinian part of Jerusalem will be the capital of the State of Palestine, and the Israeli part of Jerusalem will be the capital of Israel.

3. "Free movement through the city will be guaranteed to all citizens and visitors."

Holy Places

1. Freedom of access to the Holy Places will be guaranteed.

2. Freedom of worship at the Holy Places will be guaranteed.

Municipal Administration

1. The city will not be physically divided.
2. Each part of the city will have its own municipality.
3. "[A]n umbrella municipal council for metropolitan Jerusalem" will be set up, with "equal representation" for each of the two parts of the city.

53. Proposal by Dr. Sari Nusseibeh and Dr. Mark Heller

Date: The proposal is contained in a book published in 1991 (Hebrew) and 1993 (English).

Source: Mark A. Heller & Sari Nusseibeh, *No Trumpets, No Drums: A Two-State Settlement of the Israeli-Palestinian Conflict,* Hill and Wang, New York, 1993, pp. 114-124.

Background: The resolution of the Israeli-Palestinian conflict proposed in this book is the product of discussions held by the co-authors over a period of several months. The proposal is based on unity between all parts of the city, though the details are not always clear. This vagueness is not accidental, and the authors note that "What is now needed is a combination of clarity and obfuscation at different levels" (p. 120). Sari Nusseibeh is a lecturer in philosophy and the director of "MAQDES," a research center in east Jerusalem. He is a prominent figure among the Palestinian leadership in the territories. Mark Heller is a Senior Research Associate at the Jaffee Center for Strategic Studies at Tel Aviv University.

National Aspirations

1. The entire city will be demarcated by a marked, continuous border line that can serve a variety of purposes (such as specifying the limits of a "free-trade zone").

2. Within the city, intercommunal boundary lines will be drawn to "specify the municipal limits of the two sets of Jewish and Arab neighborhoods." In principle, "these lines will distinguish between the main Jewish and Arab population clusters." At the same time, they can help define the "communal standing of properties, burial grounds, or building complexes" that are situated on both sides of the intercommunal boundary lines.

3. These lines, although "sovereign lines," will in fact be "imaginary," since they will not impair the city's "continued physical and functional unity."

4. "Israel's Jerusalem" will be the capital of Israel, and "Palestine's Jerusalem will be its capital, housing the seat of its government."

5. Religious matters and questions of personal status "will continue to be regulated by the millet system of self-governing communal authorities established in Ottoman times."

6. For civil and criminal matters which are not addressed by municipal enactments, "Jews and Arabs will ordinarily be subject to Israeli and Palestinian law, respectively." Legal disputes and criminal cases involving members of the different communities will be decided by a "metropolitan code of laws" to be formulated

by "individuals seconded from the Israeli and Palestinian Justice Ministries." This code would also be applicable to "intercommunal traffic [and] commercial" cases.

7. Both Israeli and Palestinian currency could be legal tender in the city.

Municipal Administration

1. The above-mentioned boundary lines will "specify the municipal limits of the two sets of Jewish and Arab neighborhoods."
2. Two separate municipal councils and a roof municipality will be established.
3. Jerusalemites "will be able to express their separate sense of identity through the culture-specific activities of their council," in areas such as educational curricula at school and language of instruction, leisure and cultural activities, marking of holidays, and the distribution of various types of licenses and permits.
4. The budgets of the two municipal councils could be financed through "some proportion of property taxes," grants from the national governments, and private donations.
5. The roof municipality will be elected by all residents of Jerusalem, and the "neighborhoods or wards" will "send representatives to the metropolitan government."
6. The metropolitan government would supervise joint matters such as "water and sewage, roads and urban transportation, firefighting, sanitation, and traffic and tourist departments, and it should be administratively responsible for the Jerusalem police force."
7. The metropolitan government will regulate zoning with special reference to the demographic development.
8. Municipal courts can deal with cases covered by a joint code of laws.

54. Proposal by Professor Francis A. Boyle*

Date: 1992

Source: F. Boyle, "The Future Peace of Jerusalem," *The Arab-American News*, Vol. VII, No. 335, Detroit, Michigan, February 1-7 1992, p. 4.
idem, "The International Legal Right of the Palestinian People to Self-determination and an Independent State of Their Own," *The Scandinavian Journal of Development Alternatives*, Vol. XII, Nos. 2&3, June-September 1993, p. 29, at 40-42.

Background: Francis A. Boyle is Professor of International Law at the University of Illinois at Urbana-Champaign and served as a legal advisor to the PLO.

"The 1947 United Nations Partition Plan for the Mandate of Palestine called for the creation of an international trusteeship for the City of Jerusalem, that would be administered as a *corpus separatum* apart from both the Jewish State and the Arab State contemplated in there. Today, however, it would not be necessary to go so far as to establish a separate United Nations trusteeship for the City of Jerusalem alone under Chapter XII of the U.N. Charter. Rather, all that would need to be done is for the Israel army to withdraw from the City of Jerusalem and a United Nations peacekeeping force to be substituted in its place. This U.N. force would maintain security within the City of Jerusalem while the provision of basic services to the inhabitants could continue much as before.

The simple substitution of a U.N. peacekeeping force for the Israeli army would have the virtue of allowing both Israel and Palestine to continue making whatever claims to sovereignty they want with respect to the City of Jerusalem. Thus, Israel could continue to maintain that Jerusalem is the sovereign territory of Israel, its united capital, and shall remain as such, one and undivided, forever. The Israeli Knesset could remain where it is as a capital district, and the Israeli flag could be flown anywhere throughout the City of Jerusalem.

Likewise, the State of Palestine could maintain that Jerusalem is its sovereign territory and capital. Palestine would be entitled to construct a parliament building and capital district within East Jerusalem, perhaps on the Mount of Olives near where there is a Palestinian community center today. The Palestinian flag could also be flown anywhere within the territorial confines of the City of Jerusalem. Both Israel and Palestine would be entitled to maintain ceremonial honor guards, perhaps armed with revolvers, at their respective capital districts. But no armed troops from either Israel or Palestine would be permitted within Jerusalem.

---

* The text of this proposal was kindly provided by Prof. Boyle and we are grateful to him for doing so.

114 *Proposals and Positions*

The residents of Jerusalem would be citizens of either Israel, or Palestine, or both, depending upon the respective nationality laws of the two states involved. Residents of Jerusalem would be issued a United Nations identity card to that effect, which would give them and only them the right to reside within the City of Jerusalem. Nevertheless, all citizens of the State of Palestine would be entitled to enter Jerusalem through U.N. checkpoints at the eastern limits of the city. Likewise, all citizens of the State of Israel would be entitled to enter Jerusalem at U.N. checkpoints located at the western limits of the city. Yet, mutual rights of access for their respective citizens to the two states through Jerusalem would be subject to whatever arrangements could be negotiated between the government of Israel and the government of Palestine as part of an overall peace settlement.

In addition, both Israel and Palestine would have to provide assurances to the United Nations that foreign tourists and visitors would be allowed unimpeded access through their respective territories in order to visit the Holy Sites in the City of Jerusalem. Some type of U.N. transit visa issued by the U.N. peacekeeping force should be deemed to be sufficient for this purpose by both governments. Of course this right of the transit could not be exercised in a manner deleterious to the security interests of the two states.

Thus, daily life in Jerusalem would go on much as it did before. Jerusalem would remain a free, open, and undivided city for visitation and worship by people of all faiths from around the world. Neither Israel nor Palestine would have to surrender whatever rights, claims, or titles they might assert to the city. Security would be maintained by the United Nations peacekeeping force. And the City of Jerusalem would remain subject to this U.N. regime for the indefinite future..."

"There are many other historical precedents that could be drawn upon to produce a mutually acceptable arrangement for Jerusalem: e.g. the Free City of Danzig, Berlin, the Vatican City State, the District of Columbia, etc...."

55. Proposal by H.E. Ambassador Adnan Abu Odeh

Date: The proposal was published in April 1992.

Source: Adnan Abu Odeh, "Two Capitals in an Undivided Jerusalem," 70 *Foreign Affairs*, 1992, p. 183.

Background: Ambassador Adnan Abu Odeh is Permanent Representative of Jordan to the United Nations and former Chief of the Royal Hashemite Court of Jordan. He also held positions as Political Advisor to the King, Minister of Information and Culture, and Minister of the Occupied Territories. In this article Adnan Abu Odeh urges that the issue of Jerusalem not be postponed until the end of the negotiations between Israel and the Arab states. It should, rather, be addressed in the initial stages of the talks. The author does not elaborate on the proposed arrangement, since he is of the opinion that the "administrative details of the spiritual city of Jerusalem would be left to creative minds in negotiations."

National Aspirations

1. Mr. Abu Odeh suggests that only the walled city, where the holy places are located, and their immediate surroundings, inhabited for centuries by believers, is the "holy city". Therefore, "the walled city, the true and holy Jerusalem, would belong to no single nation or religion" and "no state would have political sovereignty over it." It would be called "Jerusalem" and "would be governed by a council representing the highest Muslim, Christian and Jewish religious authorities" (see elaboration in "Holy Places," below).

2. "The Arab part of the city" (the urban areas that stretch beyond the ancient walls to the east, northeast, and southeast) would be known as "Al-Quds" (the name used by Arabs and Muslims), over which the Palestinian flag would fly. The Arabs would be "Palestinian nationals and vote for their national institutions." As for "the Jewish settlements in Al-Quds, they would be subject to the same solution reached for the other settlements in the occupied territories."

3. The urban areas to the west, northwest, and southwest of the walled city would be known as "Yerushalaim" (the name used by Jews), over which the Israeli flag would fly.

4. The Jews residing in the walled city would be Israelis and vote, as now, in their national elections. The Arabs in the walled city will be Palestinian citizens and vote in their national elections.

Holy Places

1. The Old City is the holy part of Jerusalem and as such should be separated from the rest of the city: it would be a "spiritual basin" for Judaism, Christianity, and Islam.
2. No flag would fly over "the walled city of Jerusalem," which "would be open to all."
3. Each religious authority "would be responsible for running and maintaining the holy sites of its faith."

56. Proposal by Dr. Cecilia Albin, Moshe Amirav, and Hanna Siniora

Date: The complete proposal was published in winter 1991/2.

Source: C. Albin, M. Amirav & H. Siniora, "Jerusalem: An Undivided City as Dual Capital," Israeli-Palestinian Peace Research Project, Working Paper Series, No. 16, Harry S. Truman Research Institute for the Advancement of Peace, and the Arab Studies Society, Jerusalem, Winter 1991/2.
M. Amirav, "Blueprint for Jerusalem," *The Jerusalem Report*, 12 March 1992, p. 41.

Background: Cecilia Albin was at the time a doctoral student at Johns Hopkins University, Washington, D.C. Moshe Amirav was a representative of the Shinui party on the Jerusalem City Council and chairman of its Committee for East Jerusalem Affairs. Hanna Siniora was the editor of the east Jerusalem newspaper *Al-Fajr*. This proposal was published within the framework of a research project conducted by the Truman Institute to analyze a number of key issues involving the resolution of the Arab-Israeli and Palestinian-Israeli conflict. The authors begin with several basic assumptions, including: parity in the civil, political, and religious spheres between Jews and Arabs in Jerusalem; a functional division of powers between Jews and Arabs in the city; and the existence of two sovereign states, Israel and Palestine, with Jerusalem as the capital of each.

National Aspirations

1. The area of the city would be quadrupled "by adding an almost equal amount of territory from Israel and the West Bank." The new metropolis would include Ramallah in the north, Mevasseret Tzion in the west, Bethlehem in the south, and Ma'aleh Adumim in the east. With the new boundaries, Jerusalem would have a population of some 800,000, almost equally divided between Jews and Arabs.

2. The population balance would be maintained in the future by means of an immigration policy based on an annual increase of no more than 3 percent.

3. Metropolitan Jerusalem would be divided into twenty municipalities.

4. The governments of Israel and the Palestinian state "would still handle most matters normally vested in national authorities" (including national security, foreign affairs, and currencies). Some of the relevant authority would be transferred to the "Assembly of Metropolitan Jerusalem" and to the municipalities (see below, "Municipal Administration").

5. The currencies of both states would be "acceptable interchangeably" as tender throughout Metropolitan Jerusalem.

6. The two states would maintain jurisdictions to adjudicate in the metropolis. The "national courts" would deal with serious crimes (such as those involving threats to state security or to human life). "The area of the city in which serious crimes are committed – not the nationality of the person – would determine what jurisdiction will apply."

7. Israelis would continue to vote for the Knesset, while Palestinians would vote for the Palestinian parliament, "irrespective of where in the city they live."

8. "The citizenship of residents of Jerusalem would be determined by their own wishes rather than by the area of the city in which they happened to live."

9. The source of authority in the city "would ultimately lie in a Charter of Jerusalem" which would be adopted by both parliaments and become "part of a general peace treaty." The Charter provisions would comprise the arrangements elaborated in the proposal.

10. Metropolitan Jerusalem would be "one physically open area with no checkpoints or physical barriers" which would have precluded the free movement of persons and goods.

11. Three flags would fly over the city: the flag of Israel, of Palestine, and "the flag of Jerusalem." Each person could run up one of those flags, according to his choice (see below for special arrangements regarding the Holy Places).

12. A "special international fund for Jerusalem" would be established, its resources to be "devoted to supporting the objectives and policies of peace and coexistence in the city." The fund would also support projects "to improve and equate the standard of living in the two communities," initiatives to enhance Jerusalem's position as the center of a number of cultures, education and tourism projects, and efforts to raise the city's economic level.

Holy Places

1. The Old City "would form its own municipality" (like the other municipalities) and be run by a city council (see "Municipal Administration").

2. "Decisions regarding physical planning and development must be approved unanimously by the members of the city."

3. Each faith would have "full administrative power over its holy sites."

4. No flags would be flown at the holy sites.

Municipal Administration

1. The metropolitan area of Jerusalem would be divided into twenty municipalities, and it will be headed by the Assembly of Metropolitan Jerusalem.

2. The Assembly, the city's most important institution, "would run the affairs of the entire municipal area."

3. It would consist of representatives appointed by the governments of the two states and of one delegate from "each municipality within the metropolis of Jerusalem" (irrespective of the municipality's size).

4. The Assembly would elect its chairperson, "a position that rotated between Arab and Jew."

5. All its decisions would require a majority, with the representatives of the Israeli and Palestinian governments to have "the right to a veto."

6. The Assembly would have "total authority" in the metropolitan area with regard to central planning and development (including roads and transportation), water, energy, housing, waste disposal, and other issues affecting environmental quality.

7. The Assembly "would clear decisions made at the local municipal level."

8. It would provide funds for projects at the local municipal level and establish new neighborhoods "with a view to reaching a balance between Israeli and Palestinian neighborhoods in number and size."

9. It would "be responsible for establishing a single system of transport throughout the metropolitan area."

10. The Assembly would develop special sites for international institutions wishing to have their headquarters in the city, and existing sites for government agencies and religious institutions.

11. The Assembly would create and maintain a police force in Jerusalem, to include both Israelis and Palestinians. "The chief of police and other positions of authority would be shared between the two communities on a basis of equality."

12. Collection of property tax and value added tax would be the Assembly's responsibility and its "main source of income, supplemented by revenue from the two national governments and from a special Jerusalem Fund" (see above, "National Aspirations").

13. The Assembly would be "responsible for many social services," such as the operation of city schools and city hospitals.

14. It would "maintain a municipal court system for crimes of a less serious nature" (traffic violations, illegal construction, etc.).

15. The twenty municipalities – ten Israeli and ten Palestinian – would each be run by an elected city council.

16. The exact boundaries of the municipalities would be determined by Israeli and Palestinian town planners who "would respect current population patterns in Jerusalem as much as possible." Areas with a predominantly Jewish population

would become Israeli municipalities, and "the same would hold true for Palestinian municipalities."

17. "The inhabitants of each area would elect their own mayors for five-year terms."

18. Local affairs would continue to be run by the municipalities "in very much the same way as they [are] today," although "there would be contact and coordination with their respective national governments as well as [with] the Metropolitan Assembly."

19. The municipalities would derive their revenue from municipal taxes "and contributions from their national governments."

57. Proposal by the Israel/Palestine Center for Research and Information (IPCRI)

Date: The proposal was published in June 1994.

Source: G. Baskin (ed.), *New Thinking on the Future of Jerusalem: A Model for the Future of Jerusalem: Scattered Sovereignty*, IPCRI, Jerusalem, June 1994.
G. Baskin, *Jerusalem of Peace: Sovereignty and Territory in Jerusalem's Future*, IPCRI, Jerusalem, 1994.

Background: The Israel/Palestine Center for Research and Information is a public-policy think tank of Israelis and Palestinians who study and propose possible solutions for the issues in dispute between the two peoples. This was the third proposal published by IPCRI. It was formulated following discussions during 1992 of IPCRI's "Roundtable Forum on the Future of Jerusalem." The proposal calls for Israeli and Palestinian representatives to draw up a "Charter for Jerusalem" setting forth guidelines for the city's future. In a chapter titled "General Principles" the authors put forward "basic assumptions that must govern any settlement in respect of Jerusalem: (a) Jerusalem is the most focal city for both the Jewish and Palestinian peoples in terms of its significance for the development of their national identity. (b) A political solution for Jerusalem must guarantee that the city will be open and physically undivided. (c) Jerusalem as defined in any settlement must include the whole of the present area under the jurisdiction of the Jerusalem municipality together with certain adjacent areas which are organically linked to the city. (d) Any definitive solution to the future of the city must take account of the desire of both the Israeli and Palestinian peoples to see the city as their national capital."

The Introduction to the proposal notes that the solution should enable "each community to feel that its interests are safeguarded. This will necessarily mean that there must be an increase in the Palestinian presence so as to secure a population which reflects demographically and socially the importance which both Israelis and Palestinians attach to the city."

National Aspirations

1. The city will not be divided physically and will preserve its open character.

2. Separate areas will be created, based on the composition of the population, in which Israeli and Palestinian authorities respectively would be vested with sovereignty. "The two sovereigns in Jerusalem, Israel and Paletine, will be limited in their sovereignty." "It is suggested... that soverreinty over the Old City be entirely relinquished by both sides."

3. Each community will maintain its legal system "in those areas where it has a demographic majority" according to the boundaries between municipalities or

boroughs (see also "Municipal Administration"). "The area in which a crime is committed will determine which legal system exercises jurisdiction over the individual concerned." "Criminals will be brought to justice within the national courts of each side or in the Jerusalem Court of Justice (depending on the nature of the offence).'

4. In addition to their "national citizenship," the inhabitants of Jerusalem will also be "citizens of the City of Jerusalem," entitling them to "enjoyment of full human rights in whatever area of the City they reside and guarantee[ing] them freedom of conscience, religion and worship, language, education, speech and self-expression as well as ensuring that the personal status of the members of the various communities shall be respected."

5. Each national authority will have the right to fly its national flag "in those sections of the city over which their nationals have control." In addition, "the Jerusalem flag" will be flown on all public buildings "and made available to citizens to fly as they shall determine."

6. The city's official languages will be Arabic, Hebrew, and English.

7. Internal security will be maintained by "a joint-international force," the Jerusalem Police Force, to be composed of Israelis and Palestinians in equal number. The Israeli force will operate mainly in areas of the city with an Israeli population, while the Palestinian force will operate in those areas populated by Palestinians. Funding will be jointly provided by the Israelis and Palestinians.

8. The Charter should include "provision for adequate primary and secondary education for all of the residents of the city in the language of their choice"; students in Israeli schools will learn Arabic and those in Palestinian schools will learn Hebrew.

9. The Charter will include legal stipulations "to protect the environment from noise, water and air pollution." The Charter will also include "regulations on the use of appropriate materials for construction in sensitive areas."

10. (a) A "Jerusalem Court of Justice" will be established with "equal representation from the two communities." (b) The court will be empowered to rule on matters "relating to the international status of the city," and the "separate national courts" may also refer cases to it. Individual residents of the city could petition the court, and the Justices "will decide which cases it will hear." (c) To deal with possible cases in which the Justices might be divided "on national lines," the court could include, by mutual agreement, "three internationally respected individuals" to ensure that a decision would be reached.

11. Issues related to the overall planning of the city should be addressed "at an early stage" in discussions between the parties. Certain parts of the city would be designated "development areas" and others public parks. The Old City would be declared an area "in which no major development should take place without the agreement of the national authorities of the two parties (and of the international

community in matters relating to the Holy Places)." High-rises should be built "on the periphery of the city," and "adequate open space" should be provided. Disputes between the communities regarding the city's development should be referred to "appropriate arbitration."

12. "A deliberate attempt should be made to improve the demographic position of the Palestinians by allocating large areas for development" to the Palestinian community and by "encouraging Palestinian immigration" to the city up to parity between the two communities.

13. The city will be demilitarized: "no paramilitary formations should be permitted within its borders nor any military exercises or maneuvers."

Holy Places

The Israeli and Palestinian parliaments will enact a law including the following principles:

1. "The Holy Places, religious buildings and sites [hereafter: 'the Holy Places'] will not be under the national sovereignty of either Israel or Palestine." U.N. map no. 229 of the Holy Places, from November 1949, "will serve as the reference for the marking of Holy Places."

2. The administration of the Holy Places will remain as in 1994.

3. The existing rights at the Holy Places will be preserved.

4. Free access to and freedom of worship at the Holy Places shall be secured "in conformity with existing rights and subject to the requirements of public order and decorum."

5. The Israeli and Palestinian governments "will guarantee the protection of the Holy Places," *inter alia* against any act liable to harm them or "impair their sacred character."

6. No taxes will be levied from the Holy Places, and "no change in the incidence of taxation shall be made" which might discriminate between the owners or occupiers of the Holy Places.

7. "The right to worship in a Holy Place does not imply the right to claim ownership."

8. "The right of individual worship does not imply or guarantee the right of collective worship."

9. "The regulations prevailing in 1992 concerning collective worship will be maintained."

10. The two municipalities will establish a joint planning commission to coordinate between the various religious authorities

11. The Old City (defined as the area within the sixteenth century Turkish walls) has a particular significance. A "Planning Commission for the Old City" will be established, with Israeli and Palestinian participation as well as "individuals from the minority communities" that have ages-old connections with the Old City. The Commission would deal with issues such as tourism, the quality of life in the Old City, and the relations between its constituent communities.

Municipal Administration

Two alternative proposals are presented for the future administration of Jerusalem. Both call for the encouragement of local government at the neighborhood level and the establishment of neighborhood bodies based on the *minhalot* (neighborhood-based self-governing bodies) which exist today in certain areas of the city.

Alternative A

1. Two municipalities, one Israeli and one Palestinian, will be established.

2. Each will be elected separately by Israeli and Palestinian citizens, respectively.

3. "Non-resident citizens will vote in accordance with the makeup of the population of the area in which they live either for the Israeli or the Palestinian municipality."

4. "Each municipality will have jursidiction over its sector of the city on the basis of geographic delineations which will correspond to the demographic makeup of the area which it serves."

5. Each municipality will levy taxes separately from citizens under its jurisdiction, using its own criteria.

6. The two municipal authorities will appoint joint planning commissions to deal "with areas of mutual concern." The commissions will have the power to recommend a course of action and find agreed solutions. The commissions will deal with: government of the Holy Places (this commission will include representatives of the various denominations), government of the Old City, transportation, communications, electricity, waste disposal, water, development planning, tourism, initiating and supervising archaeological research, planning of recreational areas, and providing open spaces.

7. A "Mayors' forum" will be established to enhance cooperation between the two municipalities and provide an informal setting for discussions on "issues which concern the city as a whole and the work of the joint planning" commissions (see preceding paragraph). Issues which cannot be resolved by the commissions will be referred to the Mayor's forum, which "will then have to receive the support of the democratically elected municipal councils."

8. Consultations will be held on other issues largely controlled at the local level but requiring joint planning (such as social and health services).

9. If the execution of a specific project requires "joint expenditure by both municipalities," the rate of participation of each will be determined by a "formula which takes account of the relative financial position of the two municipalities."

Alternative B

1. The establishment of an "overall municipal authority controlled jointly by Israelis and Palestinians in accordance with the demographic makeup of the city and of individual boroughs (local area councils – Israeli and Palestinian, but not mixed) to which as many powers as possible should be devolved."

2. The boroughs will be responsible for education, local cultural and social services.

3. The borough councils would be elected "in accordance with the demographic makeup of the population resident in the borough" (Israeli citizens to vote in Israeli boroughs and the same principle applying to Palestinians).

4. The overall municipal authority will be responsible for all areas requiring consultation (as in Alternative A). The borough councils will be responsible for "education, local culture and social services." The division of powers between the overall authority and the borough councils might be based on the former Greater London Council model or on the existing division in New York.

5. The council of the municipality shall be elected in accordance with a formula which shall give each community an appropriate representation.

58. Position of the Palestine Liberation Organization

Period: 1988-1995

Source: " 'Declaration of Independence' and Political Communique" adopted by the Palestine National Council in Algiers on 15 November 1988, contained in: *U.N. Doc.* A/43/827, S/20278, 18 November 1988; and in 27 *International Legal Materials* 1661, 1988.
See also M. Klein, *Arab Positions on the Question of Jerusalem*, The Jerusalem Institute for Israel Studies, 1989 (Hebrew). More on the PLO's position can be gleaned from the "Proposal by Israeli and Palestinian Activists," 1991, which was endorsed by the Palestine National Council (surveyed above).

Background: The PLO's declared position on the solution of the Arab-Israeli conflict has undergone changes since the formulation of the Palestinian Covenant in 1968. However, the position on the future of Jerusalem remains essentially unchanged, though its context has been modified. The PLO's position was given prominent expression in the resolutions adopted by the Palestine National Council in November 1988 and in a speech by PLO Chairman Yassir Arafat to the U.N. General Assembly (meeting in Geneva) on 13 December 1988. The provisions relating to Jerusalem in the Israel-PLO Declaration of Principles of September 1993 have been described extensively in Chapter 1.

National Aspirations

1. Israel shall withdraw from all the territories it occupied in 1967, including Jerusalem.

2. Those territories, again including Jerusalem, will be placed under U.N. supervision for a specified period. (The demand for a U.N. supervision for an interim period is included in the 1988 Algiers Declaration but does not appear in the 1993 Declaration of Principles of the PLO and Israel.)

3. Jerusalem will serve as the capital of the Palestinian state (this probably refers to east Jerusalem only).

Holy Places

Freedom of access to, worship at, and the holding of religious ceremonies at the Holy Places in Palestine will be guaranteed to all faiths.

59. Position of the Vatican

Period: 1989-1995

Source: "The Holy See and the Middle East," address by Archbishop Renato R. Martino, *Middle East Colloquium*, Fordham University, 10 April 1989, reproduced in: R. Lapidoth & M. Hirsch (eds.), *The Jerusalem Question and Its Resolution: Selected Documents*, Nijhoff Pubishers, Dordrecht, 1994, p. 439.
R.P. Stevens, "The Vatican, the Catholic Church and Jerusalem," in: H. Kochler (ed.), *The Legal Aspects of the Palestine Problem with Special Regard to the Question of Jerusalem*, Wilhelm Braunmuller, Wien 1981, p. 172.
G.E. Irani, *The Papacy and the Middle East, 1962-1984*, University of Notre Dame Press, Notre Dame, Indiana, 1986, pp. 75-81.
S. Berkovitz, "The Juridical Status of the Holy Places," Ph.D. diss., The Hebrew University of Jerusalem, 1978, pp. 238-279 (Hebrew).

Background: The Vatican (see on the Vatican in detail in Chaps. 2 and 4) has a salient interest in Jerusalem, the city in which Jesus was crucified and interred, according to the Christian faith. There are numerous other Christian Holy Places in Jerusalem, and some 18,000 Catholics live in the City. Until the end of 1993 the Vatican did not formally recognize the State of Israel, though it maintained contacts with its representatives and the Pope received Israeli leaders. Spokesmen of the Holy See explained at the time that the reason for the Vatican's nonrecognition of Israel lay in the absence of a solution to questions relating to Palestinian rights, the status of Jerusalem, the country's borders, and "the situation of the Christian Church in the occupied territories and in Israel." Some mentioned another reason: fear for the Christian communities in the Arab states. The Pope on several occasions stated that the Palestinians should be granted a "homeland," but the meaning of this term was not clarified by his representatives. The Holy See did not recognize the Palestinian "state" that was proclaimed in November 1988, although the Pope several times received PLO Chairman Yassir Arafat. On 30 December 1993 representatives of the Vatican and Israel signed an agreement to establish formal relations. Upon the agreement's ratification and the start of its implementation, the parties established full diplomatic relations.

The Vatican's Position on Jerusalem

Already in the early twentieth century the Holy See articulated its objection to Jewish control over the Holy Places in Jerusalem and proposed the establishment of an international regime for the city. This position was significantly strengthened following the adoption by the U.N. General Assembly of the "Partition Resolution" in November 1947. The Vatican's support for internationalization was expressed by representatives of the Holy See in numerous forums until the Six-Day War. After

June 1967 various senior personalities in the Vatican stated that the Holy See no longer espoused internationalization of the entire city, though this approach was not expressed officially. Currently the Holy See apparently advocates a special status for the Old City, to be supported by international guarantees which would ensure the rights of the three monotheistic faiths as well as the political and religious rights of the city's communities.

In a speech delivered at Fordham University in April 1989, Archbishop Martino, at the time the Vatican's Permanent Observer at the U.N., elaborated on the Holy See's proposed solution for the *Old City* (only). The Old City must remain united and should be given a special status to be supported by international guarantees. The "special regime" would ensure equality of rights to the three faiths, including freedom of worship at and access to the Holy Places. In addition, privileges presently enjoyed by the religious communities should be safeguarded, this within the framework of the city's cultural and historical preservation. Arrangements should be introduced to ensure that the three religious communities in the city can continue to coexist peacefully. As for sovereignty, Archbishop Martino noted that the Holy See does not attribute major importance to this subject. The highest consideration should be to maintain the city's distinctive sacred and universal character. The question of sovereignty should be resolved on the basis of just principles to be contained in a peace treaty which would also uphold the international guarantees. The Archbishop also expressed opposition to the Basic Law: Jerusalem the Capital of Israel (1980), on the grounds that it violated international law and was founded on belligerent occupation without the consent of the parties involved or the U.N.

In a press conference held following the signing ceremony for the Israel-Vatican agreement of 30 December 1993, the Vatican's Undersecretary for Relations Between States, Msgr. Claudio Maria Celli, stated that a true solution for the status of Jerusalem requires an internationally recognized *status quo*, an "international umbrella" to safeguard the uniqueness of the Holy City, and international guarantees recognizing its significance for the three faiths. Msgr. Celli emphasized that the Holy See would not discuss sovereignty over Jerusalem, but arrangements which would enable international protection for its special situation.

60. Position of Egypt

Period: 1978-1995

Source: Letters accompanying "A Framework for Peace in the Middle East Agreed at Camp David," 1978 (the "Camp David Accords"), in: R. Lapidoth & M. Hirsch (eds.), *The Jerusalem Question and Its Resolution: Selected Documents*, Nijhoff Publishers, Dordrecht, 1994, p. 199.
M. Gemer, *The Negotiations on Establishing the Autonomy Regime (April 1979-October 1980) – Principal Documents*, Tel Aviv University, 1981, pp. 28, 41, 66 (Hebrew).
A. Shalev, *The Autonomy Regime – The Problems and Possible Solutions*, Tel Aviv University, 1979, p. 124 (Hebrew).
M. Klein, *Arab Positions on the Question of Jerusalem*, The Jerusalem Institute for Israel Studies, Jerusalem, 1989 (Hebrew).

Background: In letters accompanying the Camp David accords the leaders of Israel and Egypt outlined their respective positions on the status of Jerusalem. The Egyptian position, as it appears in the letter of President Sadat, was afterward also reflected in the negotiations on the autonomy regime and seems not to have changed substantively since then. The letter of Israel's Prime Minister Menachem Begin described the legislative measures enacted by Israel following the city's reunification in June 1967. It concluded: "Jerusalem is one city, indivisible, the Capital of the State of Israel." It should be emphasized that these letters are not binding on the other parties to the accord. Their purpose was to clarify positions and assert claims with a view toward future negotiations.

Position of Egypt Regarding Jerusalem

Two sovereign authorities will exist in Jerusalem: "Arab Jerusalem [probably meaning east Jerusalem] should be under Arab sovereignty." In addition, "Arab Jerusalem is an integral part of the West Bank," the "legal and historical Arab rights in the city must be respected and restored," and the autonomy agreement to be negotiated under the Camp David accord should apply there also. The Palestinians residing in "Arab Jerusalem are entitled to exercise their legitimate national rights, being part of the Palestinian People in the West Bank." Measures taken by Israel "to alter the status of the city" are invalid and "should be rescinded." The relevant Security Council resolutions, especially Resolutions 242 and 267, must be implemented.

"All peoples must have free access to the City and enjoy the free exercise of worship and the right to visit and transit to the Holy Places without distinction or discrimination." The Holy Places of each faith might be placed under the administration and control of its representatives.

"Essential functions in the City should be undivided." A "joint municipal council," with an equal number of Arab and Israeli members, can supervise the implementation of these functions. "In this way, the city shall be undivided."

61. Position of the Hamas

Period: 1988-1995

Source: Islamic Resistance Charter: Manifesto no. 28 of the Hamas Movement, 18 August 1988 (translation), in: Z. Schiff & E. Yaari, *Intifada*, Shocken Pub., Jerusalem and Tel Aviv, 1990, pp. 222-245, 351-371 (Hebrew)
M. Klein, *Arab Positions on the Question of Jerusalem*, The Jerusalem Institute for Israel Studies, 1989 (Hebrew).

Background: "Hamas" is an acronym for the Islamic Resistance Movement, a secret religious organization that grew out of the Muslim Brothers (an Islamic political movement founded in Egypt in 1929, which has branches in other countries and among the Palestinian population). Hamas began operating in the Gaza Strip in 1987 and extended its activity to the West Bank and east Jerusalem the following year. Hamas has a deep loathing of Zionism and rejects any possibility of dialogue with Israel.

The organization's basic position is that "The soil of Palestine is an Islamic *waqf* [religious trust] of the Muslims for all their generations" (Art. 11 of the Hamas Charter) and "To cede any piece of land of Palestine is to cede part of the faith" (Art. 13). Hamas attributes special importance to Jerusalem, since "It is first in the direction of prayer and third of the Holy Places, the place to which the Prophet was brought" (Art. 14). Therefore, "its liberation is a personal duty for all Muslims wherever they may be" (Art. 14).

Hamas calls for a *jihad* (holy war) against Israel to evict it from all of "Palestine" ("the liberation of Acre and Jaffa in addition to Gaza and Jenin – and then the liberation also of Jerusalem, the station on the journey of the Messenger of Allah to the very heart of Palestine" – Hamas Manifesto no. 28).

62. Position of the United States

Period 1947-1995

Source: S. Slonim, "The United States and the Status of Jerusalem," 19 *Israel Law Review* 179, 1984.
S.M. Averick, *U.S. Policy Toward Jerusalem the Capital of Israel*, AIPAC Papers on U.S.-Israel Relations, American-Israel Public Affairs Committee, Washington, D.C., 1984.
Hearing Before the Committee on Foreign Relations, United States Senate, Ninety-Eighth Congress, Second Session, S. 2031, U.S. Government Printing Office, Washington, D.C., 1984.
M. Kaufman, *America's Jerusalem Policy: 1947-1948*, The Institution of Contemporary Jewry, The Hebrew University of Jerusalem, 1985.
J. Boundreavit & Y. Salaam (eds.), *U.S. Official Statements: The Status of Jerusalem*, Institute for Palestine Studies, Washington, D.C., 1992.

Background: The importance of the position taken by the United States Administration on the future of Jerusalem stems in large measure from the major role played by the U.S. in the Arab-Israeli peace talks. The U.S. Administration has articulated positions on the status of Jerusalem since the early stages of the formulation of the UNSCOP proposal in 1947 (see above). The American position has undergone changes over the years. It was not always clear, and different members of the same Administration have on occasion made contradictory statements on the Jerusalem question.

Position of the United States

In 1947-1948 the United States advocated territorial internationalization of Jerusalem, a position reflected *inter alia* in its support for the November 1947 Partition Resolution of the U.N. General Assembly. Apparently the Administration took this position in order to ensure the status of the Holy Places and the international character of the city, which is sacred to Judaism, Islam, and Christianity. However, beginning in late 1948, various Administration officials suggested that internationalization was not a realistic solution (due to the U.N.'s limited ability to implement the plan on the scale required and to the objection by both Jordan and Israel). During this period some in the Administration supported – albeit not explicitly – functional internationalization of the Holy Places.

From 1949 (when the Israel-Jordan armistice agreement was concluded) and on the United States refused to recognize Israel's or Jordan's sovereignty over the parts of the city each had seized in the 1948 War. As a sign of its displeasure, the State Department that year forbade its representative in Israel to attend the first session of the Knesset to be convened in Jerusalem. Similarly, the United States did not move its embassy from Tel Aviv to Jerusalem. During the 1950s U.S. representatives stated on a number of occasions that a special international status should be established for Jerusalem, a status which would assure suitable protection of the Holy Places and be acceptable to Israel, Jordan, the U.N. (which has a special interest in the city's status), and the international community. Nevertheless, the United States has in fact recognized the applicability of Israeli law in the western part of the city.

Between 1967 and 1969 American representatives to international institutions stated that the city's status should be determined in negotiations between the parties within the framework of a comprehensive settlement of the Arab-Israeli conflict. Washington also rejected any unilateral measures by the parties, which could affect the city's future. Hence its opposition to the Knesset's legislation in June 1967 which formally united the city; such actions, the United States declared, could not alter the status of the city. The American position that the status of the Holy Places and free access to them must be guaranteed was given strong expression in a statement made on 14 July 1967 at the General Assembly by U.S. Ambassador to the U.N., Arthur Goldberg.

The year 1969 saw a significant change in U.S. policy on the status of Jerusalem. The new U.S. Ambassador to the U.N., Charles Yost, stated in the Security Council (1 July 1969) that east Jerusalem was "occupied territory" and hence subject to the laws of belligerent occupation laid down in the Fourth Geneva Convention of 1949. He added that the parties to the dispute have to resolve the dispute over Jerusalem, "and until it is resolved, ...they [should] take no action anywhere which could jeopardize its resolution."

The Camp David Accords of 1978 (which the President of the U.S. signed as a witness) do not mention Jerusalem, but in the accompanying letters the leaders of the signatories stated their positions on the status of the city. U.S. President Jimmy Carter wrote: "The position of the United States on Jerusalem remains as stated by Ambassador Goldberg in the United Nations General Assembly,... and subsequently by Ambassador Yost in the United Nations Security Council..." As noted above, Goldberg and Yost had expressed somewhat differing views regarding the city's status. At the end of 1978 sources in the Carter Administration asserted that the status of east Jerusalem differed from that of the rest of the West Bank. Nevertheless, Arab inhabitants of east Jerusalem who were not Israeli citizens should be allowed to vote in the election to the self-governing authority which was to be established in the West Bank according to the Camp David Accords – this, without prejudice to the question of the city's permanent status.

On 1 March 1980 the United States supported Security Council Resolution 465 which criticized Israel for its settlement policies in the territories and included a reference to Jerusalem as part of the occupied territories. Two days later the White House spokesman stated that U.S. support for this resolution had resulted from a "breakdown in communications" among Administration officials. The spokesman added that Jerusalem should remain undivided, with free access to the Holy Places for adherents of all faiths, and that its status should be determined in negotiations for a comprehensive peace settlement.

Similarly, President Ronald Reagan, in his peace plan announced on 1 September 1982, stated that "Jerusalem must remain undivided, but its final status should be decided through negotiations." "Talking Points" dispatched by the Administration to Middle East governments before the public announcement was made, stated that the United States would support the participation of the Palestinian inhabitants of east Jerusalem in elections to the self-governing authority in the West Bank in accordance with the Camp David Accords. In the years that followed, Secretary of State George Shultz stated a number of times that east Jerusalem is occupied territory. It is not clear whether the differences between the statements by the President (who did not describe east Jerusalem as occupied territory) and those by his Secretary of State resulted from a deliberate policy or from a lack of coordination within the Administration. Interestingly, the State Department itself, when asked to clarify its position on the city's status, was not always consistent: some of its official declarations did not include the view that east Jerusalem is occupied territory. In 1990 President Bush expressed a position according to which the Jewish suburbs in the eastern part of the city have a status similar to that of the Israeli settlements in the Occupied Territories. For the context in which this statement was made, see *supra*, Chapter 1.

63. Position of Jordan

Period: 1948-1995

Source: Resolutions concerning the annexation of the West Bank (including east Jerusalem) to the Kingdom of Transjordan, in: M. Whiteman, *Digest of International Law*, vol. 2, 1963, pp. 1164-1168.
King Hussein's plan for a federation, in: R. Lapidoth & M. Hirsch (eds.), *The Arab-Israel Conflict and Its Resolution: Selected Documents*, Nijhoff Publishers, Dordrecht, 1992, p. 143.
HRH Crown Prince Hassan bin Talal, *A Study on Jerusalem*, Longman, London, 1979, pp. 17-49.
The Agreement between Jordan and the Palestine Liberation Organization, 11 Feb. 1985, in: W.B. Quandt (ed.), *The Middle East: Ten Years After Camp David*, The Brookings Institution, Washington, D.C., 1988, p. 473.
King Hussein's statement concerning disengagement from the West Bank, 31 July 1988, 27 *International Legal Materials* 1637, 1988.
Treaty of Peace between the State of Israel and the Hashemite Kingdom of Jordan, 1994.

Background: The position of Jordan regarding the future of Jerusalem is of importance due to the former's close ties with east Jerusalem. Almost all the Arab residents of east Jerusalem still hold Jordanian citizenship and the government of Jordan has a considerable influence on the administration of the Muslim shrines on the Temple Mount and on the *Waqf* (Muslim religious endowment) authorities in east Jerusalem. The employees of the administration of the Temple Mount are officially appointed by the Jordanian Ministry of Islamic Endowment. The Waqf authorities administer some educational, religious, welfare and medical services in east Jerusalem.

Position of Jordan Regarding Jerusalem

The Jordanian position with regard to the status of Jerusalem has undergone several significant changes since 1948. As mentioned in Chap. 1, the Jordanian Army captured east Jerusalem and administered it until 1950 under a military government. Jordan considered itself to be sovereign in the West Bank (including east Jerusalem) following the resolutions adopted in 1950 by the Jordanian National Assembly – which was composed of representatives from both banks of the River Jordan – to unify the two banks under King Abdullah. In the Six-Day War, Israel seized the West Bank, including east Jerusalem. From 1967 until 1974 the government of Jordan demanded that Israel should withdraw from the West Bank and that Jordanian sovereignty would be restored in this area.

This attitude gradually changed since the early 70s, and particularly following the Arab Summit Conference at Rabat in 1974. That Conference decided, *inter alia*, to "affirm the right of the Palestinian people to establish an independent national authority under the command of the Palestine Liberation Organization... in any Palestinian territory that is liberated". In the period between 1972 and 1988 the Jordanian leaders explored the possibility of establishing a confederation or federation between the West Bank and Jordan, or some mode of an autonomy regime for the Palestinians in this area under the dominance of Jordan. Thus, for instance, King Hussein's plan for a federation of 15 March 1972 provided for the establishment of the "United Arab Kingdom" which would consist of two regions: "a. The Palestine region which will consist of the West Bank and any other Palestinian territories which are liberated and whose inhabitants desire to join it. b. The Jordan region which will consist of the East Bank." Under this plan, Jerusalem should "be the capital of the Palestine region." The Agreement between Jordan and the PLO of February 1985 provided for the implementation of the Palestinians' "inalienable right of self-determination... in the context of an Arab confederation, to be established between the two states of Jordan and Palestine."

In a book on Jerusalem published by Jordan's Crown Prince Hassan bin Talal, in 1979, the author contended that "since 1967 Israel has been in military occupation of the whole city" and that sovereignty over the city "was in obeyance."

On 31 July 1988 king Hussein delivered a speech declaring the dismantling of the legal and administrative links between Jordan and the West Bank. Following this declaration Jordanian officials nevertheless indicated that Jordan would continue to play its historical role as the guardian of the Islamic Holy Places in Jerusalem.

This policy found expression, *inter alia*, in the Jordan-Israel Joint Declaration ("The Washington Declaration") of 25 July 1994 and the Peace Treaty between the same States of 26 October 1994. Both texts provide that: "... Israel respects the present special role of the Hashemite Kingdom of Jordan in Muslim Holy shrines in Jerusalem. When negotiations on the permanent status [between Israel and the PLO] will take place, Israel will give high priority to the Jordanian historic role in these shrines" (Art. 9(3) of the Peace Treaty).

Some Palestinian personalities expressed their objection to this treaty provision and argued that it contradicts Israel's obligations under the 1993 Declaration of Principles between Israel and the PLO (see on that agreement in "The Position of the PLO"). The competition between Jordan and the Palestinians with regard to control over the Muslim Holy Places in Jerusalem intensified following the conclusion of the Peace Treaty between Israel and Jordan and has resulted in the appointment of two new competing Muftis for the Waqf in Jerusalem in the summer of 1994 (following the death of the single former Mufti who had been appointed by Jordan): one appointed by Jordan and the other by the Palestinians. According to press reports of November 1994, however, both parties seem to have agreed that Jordan would retain custody of the Holy Places until the Palestinians acquire control over the city in the framework of a permanent status to be negotiated later between the Palestinians and Israel (in accordance with the 1993 Declaration of Principles). Certain Muslim States, such as Saudi Arabia, support neither the Jordanian nor the Palestinian claim to custody of these Holy Places.

Chapter Three

COMPARATIVE ANALYSIS OF PROPOSALS AND POSITIONS ACCORDING TO SPECIFIC SUBJECTS

A. *General*

The preceding chapter described proposals made and positions adopted since 1916 by various individuals and institutions for a resolution of the Jerusalem question. The present chapter analyzes the ideas according to recurrent subjects. The analysis presents the principal alternatives that were proposed as a solution to the diverse aspects of the Jerusalem question. As in Chapter 2, the categories examined are: national aspirations, Holy Places, and municipal administration. For each subject the proposed solutions are analyzed and categorized according to criteria that are explained below.

Every general analysis does injustice to details. An analysis based on specific subjects naturally highlights major characteristics of many proposals, but subtle differences are necessarily neglected. Clearly, a thorough study of any of the subjects surveyed below must include a reading of the actual proposals, hence the many references to them which appear in the chapter. Some of the plans are vague about particular questions (in some cases deliberately, for political reasons, or due to a desire to leave room for flexibility in future negotiations). In such cases the present author was compelled to make generalizations and assumptions based on the details of the plans and their overall thrust. Finally, each proposal emphasizes a certain theme (sovereignty, Holy Places, or municipal administration), and one may find an interrelationship between the different elements of a proposal. For example, some authors suggested that sovereignty over the city should be granted to one of the parties involved in the conflict, and as compensation to grant broad internal autonomy to several neighborhoods of the municipality or to representatives of the religious communities in the administration of the Holy Places. We shall have occasion to remark on the relationship between the different elements contained in the proposals, but it should be emphasized that a correct understanding of the balance between the elements in each plan requires a reading of the full proposal in Chapter 2. This chapter, as already noted, will focus primarily on an analysis of each subject and less on the interrelationship between the subjects.

B. National Aspirations

The most controversial subject in a future settlement of the Jerusalem question is that of national aspirations. The crucial issue here is sovereignty over the city, but importance also attaches to arrangements concerning citizenship and the political rights of the inhabitants, the city's demilitarization and neutrality, as well as various forms of international supervision over the institutions that are to be entrusted with the city's administration.

During the period of the British Mandate in Palestine (see Ch. 1) it was proposed that Jerusalem should remain under a British Mandate in the future, with supervision by the League of Nations or the United Nations (Arlosoroff, 1932; Peel Commission, 1937; Fitzgerald, 1945; Morrison-Grady, 1946). This idea was abandoned following the termination of the British Mandate in Palestine and the establishment of the State of Israel.

A number of proposals endorse the currently existing situation in Jerusalem and advocate recognition of Israeli sovereignty in the entire city (Akzin, 1967; Levontin, 1967; State of Israel since 1967; Lauterpacht, 1968; Aspen Institute, 1975; Allon, 1976; Berkovitz, 1978; Gruhin, 1980; and, implicitly, Hazan in 1980 and Saul Cohen in 1981.) This position is based on juridical and political considerations (extensively discussed in Ch. 1). It is noteworthy that the majority of the post-1949 proposals affirm Israeli control of *west Jerusalem* or suggest that this situation should remain in the future as well. However, Hamas (Islamic Resistance Movement) claims Arab sovereignty over all of Jerusalem, and indeed over the entire territory of Israel. This position is dictated by radical religious arguments (see: "Position of Hamas").

Some authors who proposed a federation or confederation between Israel, Jordan, and the Palestinians, pointed to the possibility that Jerusalem would be the seat of the joint institutions, though without prejudice to its status as the capital of Israel (Gottlieb, 1989, Elazar, 1991, and see also the UNSCOP minority report, 1947).

Some proposals advocate dividing the city between Israel and an Arab state. One variation on this theme was the idea of restoring the situation that existed on the eve of the 1967 Six-Day War (the *status quo ante*), when Israel controlled the western sector and Jordan the eastern sector of the city (Sweden, 1950). Proposals advanced in the last decade have suggested that sovereignty in east Jerusalem should accrue to a Palestinian state (Caradon, 1981; Draper, 1981; King Fahd, 1981; Mallison, 1981; Cassese, 1986; Israeli-Palestinian peace activists, 1991; and, implicitly, Khalidi in 1981. Egypt, too, is in favor of leaving west Jerusalem under Israeli control, but insists that the autonomy regime contained in the Camp David agreements be applied also to east Jerusalem, which in this view should revert to Arab sovereignty). Some of those advocating the city's division called for its demilitarization (Sweden, 1950, Caradon, 1980, Khalidi, 1988), but it should be emphasized that demilitarization does not affect sovereignty (see Lexicon, Ch. 4).

A cardinal issue in the resolution of the Jerusalem question relates to its status as a capital city. Naturally, advocates of Israeli sovereignty also believe that Jerusalem should remain the capital of Israel, while those who propose that the city (or part of it) should be placed under Palestinian sovereignty believe it should become the capital of the Palestinian entity. Several authors proposed in the past decade that Jerusalem should serve as the capital of both Israel and the Palestinian entity (Ish-Shalom, 1987; Boyle, 1992); these plans generally also included a proposal to establish a "borough system" (Littke, 1988; Cidor, 1989; Whitbeck, 1989; Nusseibeh and Heller, 1991). The borough system is more thoroughly discussed in the section on Municipal Administration.

The aspiration to find a solution that would meet the demands of both Israel and the Arab world, while leaving Israel sovereign over most of Jerusalem, led some authors to suggest that the city's boundaries should be expanded and sovereignty shared between two states. These proposals would add areas not previously included in the city, and grant Israel sovereignty over the areas included in the enactments that unified the city in June 1967, while sovereignty in part of the remaining areas would accrue to an Arab state. The Benvenisti proposal (1968) refers to Jordan as the Arab state, while Benkler (1972) apparently refers to either Jordan, a Palestinian state, or a federation between them. An important element of these proposals is the granting of some degree of administrative autonomy to the boroughs (see the section on Municipal Administration, below).

The dispute over sovereignty in Jerusalem led many authors to propose an international regime (see Lexicon, Ch. 4) which would not be subject to any of the parties involved in the Arab-Israeli conflict. This approach seeks to bypass the sovereignty question and thus to preclude the negative feelings liable to be generated if sovereignty is granted to one of the parties in a city which is sacred to three faiths. Internationalization was advocated by major figures in the Christian world who wanted to prevent Jewish or Muslim control over Christian Holy Places (Archbishop of Canterbury, 1949; the Vatican position; and see also George, 1978). The desire to deny control of the city to the parties involved in the Arab-Israeli conflict was in some cases accompanied by proposals to strengthen its international character by its demilitarization or neutralization (on *neutrality* see Lexicon, Ch. 4). (UNSCOP, 1947; Partition Resolution, 1947; Statute prepared by Trusteeship Council, 1950; Boyle, 1992.)

The city's internationalization was proposed already in the 19th century and the idea gathered momentum with the adoption of the Partition Resolution by the U.N. General Assembly in November 1947. This proposal was extensively elaborated in the proposed Statute prepared by the Trusteeship Council in 1950 upon the request of the General Assembly. Internationalization has not been mentioned in U.N. resolutions since 1952, leading some experts to conclude that in practice the organization has abandoned the idea (see Ch. 1).

The proposals for internationalization include major variations which are of considerable significance. The cardinal difference relates to the geographic applicability of an international regime. In the past some argued that the regime should encompass large parts of Palestine (Sykes-Picot, 1916), or all of Jerusalem, possibly with adjoining areas (UNSCOP, 1947; Partition Resolution, 1947), while some would be content to internationalize the Old City only (Archbishop of Canterbury, 1949; Jones, 1968; Wilson, 1969; Draper, 1981; Boyle, 1992, regarding responsibility for security in the Old City; Abu Odeh, 1992). In some proposals the emphasis was on internationalizing only the Holy Places, in order to preserve religious interests in them (State of Israel, 1950; George, 1978; Littke, 1988). Among the advocates of internationalization were some who suggested combining the international regime with the city's division between Israel and an Arab state. Wilson (1969), for example, proposed Israeli rule for the western sector, Jordanian rule for the eastern sector, and an international regime for the Old City (Jones, 1968, also contains elements of a combined approach).

Another key difference among the internationalization proposals lies in the identity of the body that would be granted effective control in the city. Some plans would place control in the hands of the U.N. (UNSCOP, 1947; Partition Resolution, 1947; Statute of the Trusteeship Council, 1950; State of Israel, 1950; Wilson, 1969; Littke, 1988; Boyle, 1992, regarding resonsibility for security). Others advocated the creation of an interfaith committee comprising representatives of Judaism, Islam, and Christianity to administer the internationalized area (George, 1978; Cattan, 1981; Abu Odeh, 1992).

Advocates of internationalization are also divided over its duration. Some consider it a permanent solution (UNSCOP, 1947; Partition Resolution, 1947 – though a referendum and modifications after ten years are envisaged; Wilson, 1969; George, 1978; Littke, 1988). For others, though, it is merely an interim stage until the final resolution of the Arab-Israeli conflict (Cattan, 1981; Mallison, 1986).

The desire to vest Jerusalem with a special status, separate from the parties involved in the conflict, was given far-reaching expression in the proposal to make the city a separate state on the model of the Vatican: Nixon (1967) referred to the Old City only, and this was also probably what Fulbright (1974) had in mind, although he did not say so explicitly. Neither of these leading American statesmen elaborated on their idea, and our survey accordingly concentrated on an analysis of the status of the Vatican (see also Lexicon, Ch. 4).

C. Holy Places

A major cause for the intensity of the dispute over the future of Jerusalem stems from its sanctity for Judaism, Islam, and Christianity. The city's sacred character is also the reason for the widespread interest in its status. The existence of holy sites sometimes produced an uncompromising position regarding sovereignty over them (notably that of Hamas). The majority of the authors recognized certain basic principles that should serve as guidelines for whoever is in charge of the Holy Places: freedom of access and of worship, their administration by clerics, and, in some cases, preservation of the *status quo*. In this sphere the parties to the conflict have shown greater flexibility toward compromise than they have in others.

Various proposals display a striking similarity between the regime suggested for Jerusalem as a whole and that suggested for the Holy Places. In some cases, however, the religious character of these sites has given rise to proposals geared especially for them (often as compensation for granting sovereignty over the entire city to a perceived "alien" element). This section of the present chapter focuses mainly on proposals recommending the establishment of a special regime for the Holy Places.

Recognition of the religious interests of the various communities in the Holy Places, and the objection by each faith to its sacred sites being controlled by authorities of a different faith, led some authors to suggest that sovereignty at the Holy Places should be removed from the parties involved in the conflict and vested in an international body (see *Internationalization* in the Lexicon, Ch. 4). Such plans were generally accompanied by the hope that an impartial international body would best be able to maintain the interests of all the religious communities and to decide fairly between rival demands at certain sites (see, for example, the position of the Vatican).

Among the proposals, some recommend territorial internationalization while others favor functional internationalization. Territorial internationalization refers to the establishment of a political entity on an international basis; functional internationalization refers in this context to the idea of entrusting certain religious functions at the Holy Places to an international body (on both terms, see Lexicon, Ch. 4). The best-known proposal for the *territorial* internationalization of the Holy Places (as part of an international regime for the entire city) is the one included in the Partition Resolution (1947). Among later proposals the most notable is that of the Trusteeship Council (1950), which put forward a detailed statute relating to the Holy Places (and see also George, 1978; Littke, 1988; proposals for the internationalization of the Holy Places as part of an international regime for the entire Old City are found in: Jones, 1968; Wilson, 1969; Draper, 1981). The most detailed proposal for the *functional* internationalization of the Holy Places was contained in the Swedish plan submitted to the General Assembly (1950); it would have transferred supervision over religious functions to the U.N. Commissioner in the city, including the authority to resolve disputes relating to the Holy Places (functional internationalization is also one of the alternatives adduced by the Brookings Institution, 1975; and by Gruhin, 1980; see also State of Israel, 1950).

Not everyone who wished to remove control over the Holy Places from the parties to the Arab-Israeli conflict proposed internationalization. Some suggested various international mechanisms for supervising certain of the functions at the Holy Places (Archbishop of Canterbury, 1949; Akzin, 1967; Wilson, 1969; Reisman, 1970; Caradon, 1980; Rafael, 1983; Khalidi, 1988). Several authors suggested that a U.N. representative should supervise the access to, worship at, and protection of the Holy Places (Wilson, 1969; Berkovitz, 1978; Caradon, 1980). Others proposed that supervision of certain functions be entrusted to a committee composed of representatives from the three relevant faiths (Akzin, 1967; Hazan, 1980; Khalidi, 1988).

An additional method that was suggested for separating the arrangement for the Holy Places from the geopolitical conflict between the parties was to entrust the ongoing administration of each site to adherents of the religion for which it is sacred (a kind of autonomy of the Holy Places). The most notable proposal along these lines was made by Lauterpacht (1968), who suggested that representatives of the religious communities should administer the Holy Places and exercise jurisdiction over their personnel in certain spheres; representatives of the territorial sovereign would be prohibited from entering these sites without the consent of the head of the religious community in question (another detailed plan similar in certain aspects to Lauterpacht's was proposed by Berkovitz, 1978; see also Wilson, 1969; Reisman, 1970; Benkler, 1972; Brookings Institution, 1975; Gruhin, 1980; Cohen, 1981; Prittie, 1981; Cohn, 1981; Cidor, 1989; Albin, Amirav, and Siniora, 1992).

The idea of granting diplomatic immunities and privileges to the Holy Places and their personnel was meant to create another means for consolidating the independent status of the sites and their officials *vis-à-vis* the sovereign power in the city (the most notable proposal of this kind was that submitted by the State of Israel to the U.N. after the 1967 war; see also: Berkovitz, 1978; Gruhin, 1980; Cohn, 1981). It should be noted that conferring diplomatic immunities on the Holy Places or on the clerics serving at them does not amount to the transfer of sovereignty or internationalization at these sites, since the granting of diplomatic privileges does not confer sovereignty or control on their recipients nor does it entail ex-territoriality (internationalization could be accompanied by the granting of immunity).

A more extreme attempt to assure the independent status of the Holy Places was undertaken by several authors who proposed that these sites should be granted "extraterritorial" status. This proposal was generally accompanied by a suggestion to transfer sovereignty in the city to a state "alien" to the adherents of the religion for whom the sites are sacred. Thus Benkler (1972), Hazan (1980), and Cohen (1981) proposed that sovereignty in the city be vested in the State of Israel, but that the Islamic Holy Places should be granted extraterritorial status. Walid Khalidi (1988) would have sovereignty in east Jerusalem transferred to a Palestinian state, with the places sacred to Judaism given extraterritorial status. No details for these proposals were elaborated, and the intention seems to have been to grant extremely broad powers to the clerics administering the Holy Places, as well as establishing an independent status for the sites *vis-à-vis* the authorities of the state which would enjoy sovereignty over the city.

The majority of the plans that referred to the status of the Holy Places in Jerusalem included a proposal to ensure freedom of access to and worship at these sites, and even those authors who did not say so explicitly would probably assent to this. Some proposers believe that the future regime in the city must guarantee the preservation of the *status quo* (see Lexicon, Ch. 4) at the Holy Places (British Mandate, 1922; UNSCOP, 1947; Partition Resolution, 1947; draft Statute of the Trusteeship Council,

1950; proposals by Sweden, 1950; Levontin, 1967; Lauterpacht, 1968; Berkovitz, 1978; Littke, 1988; Israel/Palestine Center for Research and Information, 1994). The purpose of this proposal is evidently to assure the religious communities (especially the Christian communities) that have custody of the Holy Places in the city that the authorities will not assist any particular community to change the status at these sites at the expense of another community.

D. Municipal Administration

Most of the plans for the future of Jerusalem that were drafted in the more distant past paid little attention to municipal administration. However, this topic has gathered momentum in the past two decades. Many recent proposals consider the future structure of the city's municipal administration to be a crucial component in finding a solution which will satisfy the demands of most of the parties to the Arab-Israeli conflict. The major innovation in these plans is the suggestion to vest the institutions of municipal administration with considerable powers and to consolidate their relative independence *vis-à-vis* the state authorities. Some of the proposers advocate granting considerable tasks to bodies that represent subsidiary units in the city (generally boroughs) in order to balance the granting of sovereignty over the city to a particular state. In some cases it has been proposed that the subsidiary units be granted an "autonomous" status (see Lexicon, Ch. 4), thus reducing the effect – in daily life – of vesting sovereignty in a particular state. Some authors have tried to sidestep the thorny problem of granting sovereignty to a particular state by proposing the establishment of "administrative sovereignty" (Prittie, 1981); such proposals exceed the boundaries of "municipal administration" and spill over into the sphere of national aspirations. An additional objective which is apparent in some plans that focus on municipal administration is to preserve the city's municipal unity even if agreement is reached on a division of sovereignty between two states (see, for example, the position of Egypt). Special attention should be drawn to the detailed proposal by retired Supreme Court Justice Haim Cohn (1981) which could serve as a source of inspiration for additional municipal models in the future.

The majority of the proposals that referred to municipal administration advocate the city's internal-municipal division into subsidiary units which would operate in cooperation with a central roof-municipality. The units would enjoy a certain degree of autonomy in the day-to-day administration of the boroughs' affairs (e.g., in planning and building, environmental protection, education and sports), while the central municipality would supervise the functioning of the subsidiary units and be responsible for providing common services (see the detailed description in Cohen, 1981, and see also: Arlosoroff, 1932; Fitzgerald, 1945; Benvenisti, 1968; Benkler, 1972; Aspen Institute, 1975; Le Morzellec, 1979; Hazan, 1980; Prittie, 1981; Littke, 1988; Khalidi, 1988; Whitbeck, 1989; Cidor, 1989; Elazar, 1991; Palestinian and Israeli peace activists, 1991; Albin, Amirav and Siniora, 1992; Israel/Palestine Center for Research and Information, 1994). Special importance also attaches to the degree of independence (or subordination) of the subsidiary units from the central municipality. Some of the plans vest the units with broad powers, and limit the responsibility of the central municipality to the supervision of common services (Khalidi, 1988; Position of Egypt; and this would also seem to be in accordance with the spirit of the draft Statute of the Trusteeship Council, 1950). Others give the central municipality a dominant position, with extensive powers of supervision over the subsidiary units (Fitzgerald, 1945; Benvenisti, 1968; Cohen, 1981; and this is also in the spirit of the Albin, Amirav and Siniora proposal, 1992).

The proposals differ regarding the basis for the city's internal division and on the number of subsidiary units to be established. Some advocate division on an ethnic – Arab and Jewish – basis (Allon, 1976; Littke, 1988), others on a geographic foundation, i.e., the city's western and eastern sectors (Peel Commission, 1937; Fitzgerald, 1945; Khalidi, 1988; Position of Egypt), and still others espouse a combined geographic-ethnic division (Benvenisti, 1968; Benkler, 1972; Rafael, 1980). As for the number of subsidiary units, the range is from two to twenty (two are advocated by Fitzgerald, 1945; Rafael, 1980; Khalidi, 1988; Littke, 1988; Israeli and Palestinian peace activists, 1991; and Position of Egypt; five units are proposed by Benvenisti, 1968; Benkler, 1972; Aspen Institute, 1975; nine units are suggested by Justice Cohn, 1981; and twenty units are proposed by Albin, Amirav, and Siniora, 1992).

One of the alternatives mentioned in the study by Daniel Elazar (1991) proposes that present-day Jerusalem become a "county," with territorial units within it being given municipal status. The relationship between the county and the municipalities within it could be "hierarchical, federal, contractual, or some combination of all three."

Finally, we should mention the plan adduced by Terence Prittie (1981), which proposes the creation in Jerusalem of a special regime of "administrative sovereignty" under which the city authorities would have broad municipal powers, on the model of those which accrued to West Berlin before the unification of Germany. In this regime the State of Israel would function as a "trustee" for Jerusalem. As noted above, this proposal goes beyond the sphere of municipal administration – at least in the narrow sense of the term – and suggests vesting sovereignty over the city in a municipal (rather than a state) body. This, of course, in conjunction with an internal division of the city into boroughs with a common central authority over them.

Chapter Four
LEXICON OF TERMS

1. Annexation

This term is used in several similar although not identical meanings.

1. In the broad sense it refers to the acquisition of territory by a State by any means.

2. Addition of territory to a State as a result of an agreement transferring title, i.e., cession.

3. Acquisition of territory through unilateral appropriation by a conquering State.

In the past it was accepted that a State could annex, by unilateral action, territories which it had conquered in a war, provided the other side had ceased to exist or was incapable of continuing to fight (*debellatio*, subjugation). Annexation was effected by means of a unilateral declaration. In the absence of absolute victory, the conquering State was not permitted to annex the territory and acquire sovereignty (q.v.) by means of a unilateral action, its rights being limited to those of a military occupant. The fate of the captured territory was decided in the peace treaty.

History has known many instances of unilateral annexation, such as those undertaken in the aftermath of World War II.

Nowadays, with the prohibition on the threat or use of force foreseen by the United Nations Charter (Article 2 (4)), opinions differ as to whether the right of unilateral annexation still exists in the aftermath of an absolute victory. All experts agree that the aggressor State may not annex territories, since it should not be allowed to profit from its illegal acts. As for the question of whether unilateral annexation is permitted following a full victory in a war of self-defense, some commentators would permit annexation in those conditions in order to preclude a situation in which an aggressor State has nothing to lose. Most authors maintain that even victors in a war of self-defense do not have the right to annex territory that they have captured, but only to control it as a military occupant until a peace agreement is concluded. Some would permit unilateral annexation if a conqueror acting in self-defense has a valid claim to the territory.

Questions relating to annexation arose following the Knesset's enactment of legislation applying Israeli law, jurisdiction, and administration to east Jerusalem after the Six-Day War. The first question was whether this was indeed an act of annexation or only the application of Israeli law. At the time it was stated in the international arena in the name of the Government of Israel that it was only an administrative act, but under Israeli law the courts in Israel ruled that as a result of the Knesset's act east Jerusalem had become part of the State of Israel. This attitude encountered opposition from the U.N. and the international community. The act was again condemned by the Security Council in 1980, following the adoption by the Knesset of the Basic Law: Jerusalem the Capital of Israel. It should be noted that Israel's claim to east Jerusalem is not based only on a military victory (see Chapter 1). In 1981, following the adoption of the Golan Heights Law, 5742-1981, which applied Israeli law, jurisdiction, and administration to that territory, the same question arose: was this annexation, and if so was it legal? That law was also condemned by the U.N.

The question of the legality of the acquisition of territories by war also arises in connection with the interpretation of the preamble to Security Council Resolution 242, which mentions "the inadmissibility of the acquisition of territory by war".

2. *Autonomy*

Etymologically, "autonomy" derives from two Greek words: *auto* = self, and *nomos* = law, or legal rule.

Present-day usage of the word extends to three spheres. In philosophy the term denotes the individual's ability to define himself and his will. In the natural sciences it means organic nondependence, or actions which are not dependent on will or consciousness. In law and in political science the term is used in several senses: some use it as a synonym for independence; for others it means a general power to act in accordance with one's discretion; for some it is a synonym for decentralization; and for a fourth group it denotes a regime in which a certain region is granted exclusive powers in the fields of legislation, administration, and adjudication in specified spheres.

The purpose of *territorial* political autonomy is to grant a certain degree of self-determination to a group which is geographically concentrated and is different from the majority of the State's population, but constitutes a majority in that region. Autonomy thus helps ensure the rights of ethnic minorities, indigenous populations, and peoples who for various reasons are unable to enjoy full self-determination.

Autonomy arrangements in the past, as well as those currently in existence, differ greatly from one another. Therefore the survey that follows does not pretend to reflect accurately all the possible cases.

A cardinal question in every autonomy regime relates to the division of powers between the central government and the autonomous authorities. The powers of an autonomy regime are generally confined to matters of culture, economics, and social affairs. Still, there are varying degrees of autonomy, and the powers vested in the autonomous authorities can range from the minimal to the maximal in the relevant spheres. Foreign relations and external security are usually the exclusive purview of the central government, though it may consult with the autonomous body if an issue of foreign affairs particularly concerns the autonomous region. Some autonomous entities do have limited powers in the sphere of foreign relations.

It is desirable to define clearly the powers and responsibilities of the autonomous authorities from the outset. Generally, there are four spheres of powers: those retained by the center, those fully transferred to the autonomous entity, parallel powers, and powers that can only be exercised jointly.

Still, not even the most meticulous care taken in formulating the division of powers at the time the autonomy regime is established can prevent difficulties at a later stage. For example, there may be differences of opinion on the question to which category of powers a certain practical matter belongs; similarly, a new problem may arise concerning an area for which responsibility has not been established in advance; or how to handle questions that involve several areas of responsibility, some of them held by the central government and others by the autonomous region (e.g., if it was agreed that tariffs and customs are under the authority of the central government, while criminal justice is a matter for the autonomous regime, who is authorized to deal with customs offenses?).

In order to ensure the level of cooperation needed for the exercise of certain powers, and to solve problems such as those described above as well as others, in many cases a joint body is established in which both the central government and the autonomous authority are represented. Similarly, agreement may be reached in advance on procedures for the peaceful settlement of disputes between the center and the autonomous body.

As mentioned, the autonomous authorities usually receive powers of legislation, adjudication, and administration in the spheres for which they have been given responsibility. In some cases, however, adjudication may remain entirely in the hands of the central authorities. Legislation enacted in the autonomous region usually requires confirmation by the central government, although this is normally a mere formality unless there has been an excess of power or the act endangers the security of the State.

The assumption is that in the autonomous area the representatives of the local population themselves exercise the relevant powers. Nevertheless, there is often a need for coordination between the center and the autonomous authorities regarding the appointment of some of the high-ranking officials, or at least one of them, such as the representative of the central government in the autonomous region or the head of the local administration. That official is in many cases appointed either jointly or by the center with the consent of the elected representatives in the autonomous area, or vice versa.

Acts of the autonomous entity in the areas for which it has responsibility are normally not subject to any control by the central authorities other than in special cases such as an excess of power or a breach of State security.

In many cases the introduction of changes in the autonomy arrangements requires the assent of both the central authorities and the autonomous ones.

An autonomy regime can be established by an international convention, by a constitution, a statute, or a combination of some of these sources; perhaps it may even be established by custom.

A second form of autonomy – other than territorial – is *personal* autonomy (sometimes called cultural autonomy). This is a regime applicable to members of a particular group – generally an ethnic, linguistic, or cultural minority – irrespective of their place of residence in the State. A group possessing personal autonomy may preserve and promote its distinctive character through institutions which it establishes, vested with powers to take binding decisions and even to levy taxes from the members of the group. Personal autonomy usually applies to the realms of culture, language, education, religion, and charity.

Examples of territorial autonomy are: the Aaland Islands, situated between Sweden and Finland, since 1920; Memel (Klaipeda) in Lithuania between the two world wars; Greenland since 1979; Alto Adige-South Tyrol, since 1948; South Sudan from 1972 to 1983; and Eritrea from 1952 to 1962. It should be emphasized again that there are considerable differences between the various examples.

Examples of personal autonomy are the minority regime that existed for a time in the Baltics following World War I, and the *millet* system in the Ottoman Empire.

Autonomy resembles self-government, though some authors consider it to be a narrower form of self-rule, while others consider it to be a broader one.

The Jewish people has a close affinity with the notion of autonomy. Historically, some Jewish communities enjoyed personal autonomy for certain periods – in some cases lengthy ones – primarily in the diaspora but also in Palestine when it was under foreign rule. During the period of Ottoman rule the non-Muslim religious communities enjoyed personal autonomy (the *millet* system); the terms of the British Mandate for Palestine (1922) stipulated that the Mandatory power should develop "self-governing institutions" of the Jewish community (Article 2) and "encourage local autonomy" (Article 3); during the Mandate period and in the State of Israel certain powers relating to personal status have been vested in the recognized religious communities; in the "Framework for Peace in the Middle East Agreed at Camp David" (1978) Israel and Egypt pledged to work for the establishment of full autonomy for the Palestinian Arabs in the West Bank and the Gaza Strip as an interim solution to last five years; and the "Peace Initiative by the Government of Israel" (May 1989) proposed granting the Palestinians "self-rule," again for an interim period. In their Declaration of Principles signed in September 1993, Israel and the PLO agreed to create a temporary regime of self-government, initially in the Gaza Strip and the Jericho area, and afterward throughout the West Bank and the Gaza Strip. The Agreement on the Gaza Strip and the Jericho Area was signed in May 1994, and in August 1994 the Agreement on Preparatory Transfer of Powers and Responsibilities in the West Bank was concluded. As this manuscript goes to press, the parties are negotiating on the establishment of self-government in the West Bank.

3. Buffer Zone

"Buffer zone" is not a technical legal term. It describes an area situated between demarcation lines of various kinds, such as borders, ceasefire lines, and armistice lines; or an area placed under a special regime in order to separate two States. There are buffer zones of various types which possess different legal characteristics, such as demilitarized zones (q.v.), neutralized areas (q.v.), "undefended zones," an "area between the lines" (i.e., a no-man's-land between two warring sides), and others.

The Arab-Israeli armistice agreements of 1949 established demilitarized zones and "defensive areas" (i.e., areas on both sides of the Green Line – Israel's 1949 armistice lines – where limitations were placed on the size of the forces permitted). The agreements also referred to the area between the lines, in the sense of no-man's-land. Areas of the latter type also existed in Jerusalem, notably the Pagi neighborhood in the north, the area opposite Jaffa Gate, the Abu-Tor neighborhood, and a narrow strip in the demilitarized zone on Mount Scopus. The area of Government House was a demilitarized zone, and the entire city was part of a zone where only defensive forces were permitted.

Security Council Resolution 242 (of 1967) mentioned demilitarized zones as an example of measures to be adopted in order to guarantee the territorial inviolability and political independence of the various States in the area (see also entry *Demilitarization*).

The 1974 Egyptian-Israeli Agreement on Disengagement of Forces established an area between the lines in a different sense – a "zone of disengagement." In this area the U.N. force (UNEF) was stationed, while in areas on both sides limitations existed on armament and forces.

The 1974 Agreement on Disengagement Between Israeli and Syrian Forces on the Golan Heights referred to "an area of separation" in which the U.N. force (UNDOF) would be stationed, with "two equal areas of limitation in armament and forces" in the adjoining areas on both sides.

The Agreement between Egypt and Israel of 1975 created a "buffer zone" in the Sinai. In this zone the U.N. force (UNEF) operated. On either side of the zone limitations on armament and forces were foreseen. In addition, early-warning stations were set up in the buffer zone, one each operated by Israel, Egypt, and American civilians. Access to the stations was subject to supervision by the U.N. force. The agreement also stipulated the establishment of various special "areas" on the east bank of the Suez Canal.

The 1979 Treaty of Peace between Egypt and Israel established four zones of limitation of forces in the Sinai and in the southern Negev (see entry *Demilitarization*), but no similar provision has been included in the 1994 Treaty of Peace between Jordan and Israel.

4. Capitulations

This term is used in two completely different senses. In the area of the rules of war, capitulation means surrender. However, in the context of the status of foreigners, capitulations (from the Latin *capitula* = chapters) were agreements that removed foreign nationals from the jurisdiction of the local authorities and left them subject to the laws of their country of origin through a quasi-exterritorial arrangement. Powers of adjudication over these foreign nationals were entrusted to the consuls of their States or to special courts, in some cases of mixed composition.The consuls were also in charge of the protection of those nationals.

The great trading powers of the Middle Ages – Genoa, Venice, Pisa – received jurisdiction over their nationals in the Middle East from the Crusaders in the eleventh and twelfth centuries, and afterward from the Byzantine Empire. The Ottoman Empire, which sought to improve its commercial ties, granted privileges to Genoa (1453), Venice (1454), France (1535), and England (1583). The United States was granted capitulations in the nineteenth century. Far Eastern countries too granted capitulations to nationals of Western States.

If at first the capitulations were a means to encourage commerce and prevent discrimination against foreigners adhering to a different faith, in time they practically led to a kind of colonialism and generated contempt for the local sovereign power after it had become extremely weak.

At the end of the nineteenth century various territories began to be released from the burden of capitulations. Initially these were territories which had seceded from the Ottoman Empire. The process was not completed until the mid-twentieth century.

The British Mandate (q.v.) for Palestine provided that the capitulations regime would not apply in Palestine (Article 8). However, it added that States which had previously enjoyed capitulations and did not renounce them, would regain those privileges again upon the expiration of the Mandate.

The U.N. General Assembly Resolution of November 1947 on the Future Government of Palestine (Part IV) invited States which had formerly benefited from capitulations to renounce them in the Arab and Jewish States to be established and in the City of Jerusalem.

During the Ottoman period the consulates in Jerusalem dealt with foreign nationals on the basis of capitulations granted by the Ottoman Empire.

5. Church of the Holy Sepulcher

According to Christian tradition, the Church of the Holy Sepulcher stands on the hill of Golgotha and its surroundings, where Jesus was crucified, buried, and rose again to life. Consequently, this is one of the holiest sites for the Christian world. The four last stations of the "way of sorrows" (via dolorosa) of Jesus are located inside the church.

The first Christian building on the site was erected during the Byzantine period by Helena, the mother of the Emperor Constantine. During a pilgrimage to Jerusalem in the year 326 C.E. she found what she believed were the remains of the "true cross" on which Jesus had been crucified, and in 335 a church was dedicated at the site. The present-day structure combines remains from the Crusader period and renovations carried out in the nineteenth and twentieth centuries.

The Church of the Holy Sepulcher is sacred to most Christian rites, but some Protestant groups believe that Golgotha was actually at a different location – a place known today as the Garden Tomb, which is outside the Old City, not far from Damascus Gate.

The arrangements regarding possessory rights in the various sections of the church, the right to repair or clean certain areas or the items located there, and the arrangements for worship have given rise to disagreements among the different rites and have even generated international conflicts among the Great Powers.

The Sultan of Turkey, in a number of *firmans* (royal decrees), of which the most important was issued in 1852, ruled that the *status quo* (q.v.) – i.e., the arrangements which had previously existed – must be maintained in the church (and at certain other Christian Holy Places.)

It is interesting that for centuries the key to the Church of the Holy Sepulcher has been entrusted to a Muslim family.

6. *Condominium*

The term – from the Latin: *con* = together, *dominium* = ownership – refers to a regime in which two or more States control a particular area on a basis of equality and in accordance with a specific arrangement to which they have agreed. It would really be more accurate to speak of *co-imperium* – joint rule. In some cases each of the two controlling States maintains parallel governing institutions, while in others there are joint institutions. A number of proposals for solving the Jerusalem problem mentioned the possibility that certain parts of the city would be under a regime of condominium.

Some authors distinguish between two types of condominiums: that of a border region, and a colonial or quasi-colonial condominium. An example of the former is Moresnet, a condominium of Prussia and Holland that was established in 1816 due to ambiguity and disagreement regarding the border demarcation. The regime was abolished in 1919 and the area annexed to Belgium. Other examples are the French-Spanish condominium on Faisans Island in the Bidassoa River (since 1856) and in Andorra (since 1278; in 1993 the powers of the two co-princes were considerably reduced).

An attempt has been made to apply the concept of condominium to maritime boundaries as well. This occurred in 1917 when the Central American Court of Justice ruled that the waters of the Bay of Fonseca belonged jointly to the three littoral States: Salvador, Honduras, and Nicaragua. The arrangement was again confirmed by the International Court of Justice at The Hague in 1992 in a different case. It also bears recalling that Austria claimed in the past that part of Lake Constance situated between Austria, Germany, and Switzerland is a condominium.

Examples of colonial condominiums are the Russo-Japanese condominium over Sakhalin Island (1855-1875); the Franco-British condominium over the New Hebrides (1906-1980, today the independent State of Vanuatu); and the Egyptian-British condominium over Sudan (1899-1956.)

7. Corpus separatum

This term carries no special political or legal meaning. It indicates the existence of a separate body without indicating its juridical status. The term was used in the U.N. General Assembly Resolution of November 1947 on the Future Government of Palestine. The recommendation was that Jerusalem should be a *corpus separatum* but nevertheless a part of the economic union between the Jewish and Arab States which were to be established.

8. Demilitarization

Demilitarization exists when two or more States agree not to introduce armed forces and weapons into a particular territory and not to fortify it. The scope of demilitarization, or the limitation of forces, is determined by the agreement. Since demilitarization is established by agreement, it does not detract from the State's sovereignty. Demilitarization can apply to a territory which is part of a State (e.g., the Rhineland under the Treaty of Versailles, 1919; and demilitarized strips in Korea and Kashmir), or to territory which is not part of any State (e.g., Antarctica under a 1959 treaty, and outer space under a treaty of 1967).

Demilitarized zones and neutralized zones (q.v.) are similar and related, though not identical, concepts. Whereas it is forbidden to maintain armed forces, weapons, or fortifications in a demilitarized zone – either completely or above certain levels – in a neutralized zone there is a ban on hostilities. In many cases an area is both demilitarized and neutralized, such as the Aaland Islands and the Spitsbergen Islands.

Some authors use the comprehensive term "non-military zones" to denote areas that are both demilitarized and neutralized. Such zones may be established in order to serve as areas of shelter during hostilities, or as an area in which negotiations can be conducted and a ceasefire supervised.

A demilitarized zone can constitute a temporary solution when there are conflicting claims to sovereignty and it can reduce tension along a demarcation line through a separation of forces. Demilitarized zones may also be intended to prevent the outbreak of a war.

The 1977 Geneva Protocol I Additional to the Geneva Conventions of 1949, Relating to the Protection of Victims of International Armed Conflicts, deals with the establishment of non-defended localities (Article 59) and of demilitarized zones (Article 60).

The General Assembly Resolution of November 1947 on the Future Government of Palestine recommended the demilitarization and neutralization of Jerusalem, which was intended to be a separate body under international administration: "The City of Jerusalem shall be demilitarized; its neutrality shall be declared and preserved, and no para-military formations, exercises or activities shall be permitted within its borders" (Part III, C, 4).

At the end of Israel's War of Independence agreement was reached to demilitarize certain areas. The Israel-Syria armistice agreement (1949) demilitarized the territories which had been captured by Syria in the war and from which Syria was to withdraw under the terms of the agreement; the armistice agreement with Egypt left the Nitsana area demilitarized; and the armistice agreement with Jordan called for the demilitarization of the area around Government House in Jerusalem. Earlier (July 1948) Israel and Jordan had agreed on the demilitarization of Mount Scopus. The various disengagement of forces agreements of 1974 and 1975 also in fact created demilitarized areas, although that term was not employed (see also entry *Buffer Zone*).

The Israel-Egypt peace treaty of 1979 established a limitation of forces in the Sinai and in the southern Negev – supervised by the Multinational Force and Observers. The latter institution was established in 1981 by agreement of Israel and Egypt, with the assistance of the United States.

It should also be noted that Security Council Resolution 242 (November 1967) recommends "guaranteeing the territorial inviolability and political independence of every State in the area, through measures including the establishment of demilitarized zones" (par. 2(c)).

9. Diplomatic Privileges and Immunities

Some proposals seek to solve the problem of the Holy Places by granting them and the clergymen serving in them diplomatic status. It is, therefore, useful to examine what that status entails.

The inviolability of diplomatic envoys is a rule that goes back three thousand years, and the rule on the inviolability of the premises of a diplomatic mission crystallized in the seventeenth century. Nowadays the matter is dealt with primarily in the 1961 Vienna Convention on Diplomatic Relations.

The inviolability of the *premises of a mission* has two aspects: the agents of the "receiving State" (i.e., the country in which the mission is located) may not enter those premises to carry out searches or deliver legal documents without the consent of the head of the mission. Moreover, the receiving State has a special duty to take the necessary measures to protect the premises of diplomatic missions. This obligation is not absolute, but in the event of damages the receiving State usually compensates the "sending" State (i.e., the country that the mission represents.)

Only those parts of the mission that are "used for the purposes of the mission" enjoy diplomatic privileges. In the event of borderline cases, such as a cultural center or a tourist office being located in the building, the two States have to make arrangements by agreement. Premises used for commercial purposes do not enjoy the special rights of a diplomatic mission.

The sending State and the head of the mission are exempt from all dues and taxes in respect of the premises of the mission, other than dues representing payment for specific services rendered. The archives and documents of the mission are inviolable wherever they may be.

It seems that diplomatic asylum may be granted in the diplomatic mission to political offenders. This rule is especially prevalent in Latin American States, while other States tend to limit its applicability to extreme cases of an immediate threat to life.

The mission has the right to maintain free and secure communication for official purposes, though the use of a wireless transmitter requires the consent of the receiving State. In principle, diplomatic correspondence (the "diplomatic bag") may not be opened or detained. In practice, however, the transit or entry of diplomatic bags has sometimes been prevented when serious grounds existed for suspicion that they contained drugs, currency, or arms and explosives. Although the screening of the "bag" by means of X-rays may perhaps not be prohibited – since this does not constitute search, opening, or detention of the bag – many States do not permit their diplomatic bags to be screened.

Subject to exceptions based on national security considerations, the receiving State must allow the members of a diplomatic mission free movement in its territory – a rule that was not always honored during the Cold War.

As for the immunities of *diplomatic agents*, it should be emphasized that they are of a procedural nature, i.e., immunity from jurisdiction of the courts and from attachment of property. However, diplomats must obey the laws of the receiving State and may not engage there in professional or commercial activity for personal profit.

As will be detailed below, diplomats, their residence, and their property enjoy personal inviolability, immunity from criminal jurisdiction, immunity – subject to certain exceptions – from civil and administrative jurisdiction, and immunity from execution, as well as exemption from social security payments, from many taxes, from public service, and from customs duties.

The inviolability of diplomats has two aspects, similar to those surveyed above relating to the mission's premises. Diplomatic agents may not be arrested or subjected to a search, and samples of their blood may not be taken against their will, other than in a case of self-defense. At the same time, the receiving State has the duty to protect them. Their place of residence is immune from search and may not be entered without permission. Like the mission's documents, the diplomat's property, papers, and correspondence are also protected.

As already noted, the diplomat has full immunity from criminal jurisdiction of the receiving State, but he is of course liable to face trial in the sending State. Although the receiving State cannot try a foreign diplomat, it can ask the sending State to recall the suspect, or it can declare him *persona non grata* – an undesirable individual – in which case the sending State must terminate his functions with the mission and recall him.

There are three exceptions to the immunity from civil jurisdiction: a real action relating to private immovable property situated in the receiving State; to succession; or to professional or commercial activity exercised by the diplomat in the receiving State "outside his official functions." A diplomat "is not obliged to give evidence as a witness," but frequently the diplomatic staff assists in the doing of justice by giving evidence voluntarily, perhaps in writing.

The sending State may waive both immunity from jurisdiction and from execution. The initiation of proceedings by a diplomat precludes immunity from jurisdiction in respect of any counterclaim directly connected with the diplomat's original claim.

The diplomat enjoys immunity from the moment he enters the receiving State to take up his post until he leaves the country (or until expiry of a reasonable period after his functions have ended if he has not left). He retains immunity for acts which he has performed in the exercise of his official functions.

The exemption from taxation does not apply to the following taxes: "indirect taxes... which are normally incorporated in the price of goods or services"; taxes on private immovable property; inheritance duties; taxes on private income having its source in the receiving State; "charges levied for specific services rendered"; and registration and court fees, stamp duty, etc. relating to private immovable property.

The exemption from customs duties applies to articles for official use of the mission and to articles intended for the personal use of the diplomat and his family. Personal baggage (in contrast to the diplomatic bag) may be searched in the diplomat's presence if there are "serious grounds" to suspect that it contains items that are not exempt from customs duties or goods which are barred from import by the receiving State.

The members of the family of the diplomat who are part of his household and are not nationals of the receiving State also enjoy diplomatic privileges and immunities.

The privileges and immunities described above apply to the members of the diplomatic staff of the mission. The other staff members enjoy a lesser degree of privileges and immunities, and they are divided into three categories: the administrative and technical staff, the service staff, and private servants of members of the mission.

As for diplomats and members of the staff who are premanent residents or nationals of the receiving State, their immunities are extremely limited.

It should be noted that the diplomatic agents of the Pope (usually known as "nuncios") also enjoy the privileges and immunities described above.

The preceding survey dealt with diplomats. The staff of a *consular mission* also enjoys immunities and privileges, but on a far more limited scale. The status of consular missions and their personnel is dealt with primarily in the Vienna Convention on Consular Relations, 1963.

It should be emphasized that the privileges and immunities are granted in order to facilitate the performance of a diplomat's functions (the functional approach) and in order to respect the foreign State that he represents, but not for reasons of prestige or personal benefit.

Finally, a word on the *status of the diplomatic mission.* In the past the mission was thought to possess exterritorial status, i.e., it was not considered to be located in the State where it was, in fact, situated. This approach is nowadays completely rejected. The mission is considered to be situated in the territory of the receiving State and subject to the local sovereign, but it possesses certain privileges and immunities granted by international law and by the local sovereign.

10. Enclave

Some authors use this term to denote a State, or part of a State, or an entity of some other type, which is wholly surrounded by the territory of another State. It was in this sense of the term that Jerusalem was intended to become an enclave under the partition plan adopted by the U.N. General Assembly in 1947 in its Resolution on the Future Government of Palestine.

Others limit the use of the term to describe an area belonging to State A (though not constituting most of its territory) which is wholly surrounded by territory of State B, such that any movement between the area and the mother-country (State A) involves transit through the surrounding country (State B). If a geographical connection exists between the area and the mother-country, but direct transit is practically impossible due to topographical reasons (high hills, etc.), the term used is "quasi-enclave." Some authors do not use the term "enclave" if the area is surrounded by the territory of another country (State B) but has an outlet to the sea.

History knows many enclaves, though their number has greatly declined in our time. Examples are the Baarle-Hertog area – a Belgian enclave in the territory of Holland; Campione d'Italia – an Italian enclave inside Switzerland; and Llivia – a Spanish enclave surrounded by French territory.

The enclave is for all purposes part of the mother-country. The main problem concerns the right of passage through the State whose territory surrounds the enclave. The modalities of a right of passage are often established by a special agreement, otherwise the rules of customary international law apply, as crystallized in a 1960 judgment of the International Court of Justice at The Hague in the case of *Right of Passage Over Indian Territory*. The case concerned Portugal's right of passage through Indian territory to certain Portuguese enclaves. According to this judgment, private citizens, officials, and to some extent armed police have the right of passage to an enclave (though only insofar as this is necessary to maintain normal life there). There is no right of passage for military forces or passage via the airspace of the country which surrounds the enclave. Although this decision was based on the special circumstances of the case, the principles laid down by the Court have been considered to incorporate general customary rules.

There is no custom that permits passage via an enclave to the territory of the surrounding State.

From 1948 to 1967 the northern part of Mount Scopus in Jerusalem was an Israeli enclave inside territory which was under Jordanian control. Access to the area was arranged by the Israel-Jordan agreement on Mount Scopus (7 July 1948) and by several subsequent arrangements. In principle, a U.N.-escorted Israeli convoy was allowed passage to and from the enclave every two weeks.

11. The Holy Places

The question of the Holy Places in Israel is often discussed in connection with the Jerusalem question, since the entire city, or certain places in it, are considered sacred by Judaism, Christianity, and Islam. It should be noted, however, that there are holy sites elsewhere in Israel and the West Bank as well (e.g., the Church of the Anunciation in Nazareth).

The term "Holy Place" has no generally recognized definition. Moreover, for every event depicted in the New Testament there are at least two or three churches each of which claims sanctity for its location. The Supreme Court of Israel has ruled that the test in each case is factual-religious. In some enactments the term Holy Place can have a flexible meaning to be derived to a great extent from the attitude of the community for which it is holy. Hence it is also possible that due to historical and geographical changes the physical confines of a Holy Place may be reduced or enlarged in accordance with the conception of the relevant religious community and in view of the terms and object of the specific enactment. In fact, the term Holy Place may have different connotations in different texts. The U.N. has prepared various lists of Holy Places though none is binding.

For places that are sacred to only one religion, an arrangement can usually be found under which the adherents of the religion in question are allowed to administer the site autonomously in accordance with their traditions. The difficulties arise when a site is sacred to more than one faith. Well-known examples are the Temple Mount, which is holy for Jews and Muslims, and the Church of the Holy Sepulcher, which is holy to many Christian rites.

Already in the nineteenth century the Ottoman Empire tried to solve the problem by providing that the *status quo* (q.v.) had to be maintained in several locales that were hotpoints of dispute between various Christian communities. The *status quo* came to be applied to the following seven sites: in Jerusalem – the Church of the Holy Sepulcher and its dependencies, the Convent of Deir as-Sultan, the Sanctuary of the Ascension (on the Mount of Olives), and the Tomb of the Virgin (at Gethsemane); in Bethlehem – the Church of the Nativity, the Milk Grotto, and Shepherds' Field. The *status quo* sought to determine and preserve the powers and rights of the various rites in the above-mentioned places, an arrangement which had been laid down in several *firmans* (Ottoman royal decrees) of which the most important was that issued by Sultan Abdul Majid in 1852. Following the Crimean War the *status quo* received international recognition by the Conference of Paris (1856) and was reconfirmed by the European Powers at the Congress of Berlin (1878). The term "*status quo*" was first used in this context in Article 62 of the Treaty of Berlin: "... [I]t is well understood that no changes can be made in the *status quo* of the Holy Places." During the period of the British Mandate (q.v.) the *status quo* was extended to cover also Rachel's Tomb near Bethlehem and the Western Wall (also known as the Wailing Wall) in Jerusalem. Israel and the Holy See declared their adherence to the *status quo* in the Fundamental Agreement of 30 December 1993 (see entry *Vatican*).

Certain difficulties exist in implementing the *status quo*. The rights at the Holy Places have occasionally been modified due to pressure exerted by various Powers that have granted their protection to certain churches respectively. The question, then, is what is the relevant date on which a particular right at a Holy Place had to exist in order to deserve protection. An additional problem is the difficulty of preserving a certain situation when other circumstances change.

Under the Terms of the Palestine Mandate, Britain was responsible for the Holy Places and the religious buildings or sites in the country. This included the duty to preserve the existing rights at those places as well as freedom of access to and worship at them, subject to the requirements of public order and decorum. On these matters Britain was responsible solely to the League of Nations. Britain was not authorized to interfere in the management of purely Muslim sacred shrines (Article 13). At the same time, Britain was asked to appoint a special commission – subject to approval by the Council of the League – "to study, define and determine" the rights and claims of the different religious communities relating to the Holy Places in Palestine (Article 14). Moreover, Article 28 stipulated that should the Mandate be terminated, the Council of the League would make arrangements to ensure the safeguarding of the above-mentioned rights secured by Articles 13 and 14.

The commission, however, was not set up since the States concerned could not reach agreement as to its composition or powers. Britain administered the Holy Places in accordance with the *status quo*. In 1924 Britain promulgated the Palestine (Holy Places) Order in Council which removed questions related to the Holy Places from the jurisdiction of the courts and authorized the High Commissioner to deal with them.

Because of the sacred character of Jerusalem and its Holy Places, the U.N. General Assembly recommended in 1947 that the city be a separate entity under U.N. administration. The Administering Authority was to protect the unique spiritual and religious interests of the three monotheistic faiths and to ensure order and "religious peace." In addition to his duties in Jerusalem, the Governor of the City of Jerusalem, who was to be appointed by the U.N. Trusteeship Council, was also authorized to make decisions in cases of disputes relating to the Holy Places in the Jewish and Arab States slated to be established according to the General Assembly's recommendation.

During the period of Jordanian rule in east Jerusalem (1948-1967), the Holy Places of Islam were fostered, but Christian sites were neglected and most of the Jewish sites were destroyed (many synagogues and gravestones in the cemetery on the Mount of Olives). Contrary to what had been agreed upon in principle (subject to further negotiations) by Article VIII of the Jordan-Israel armistice agreement of 1949, Israelis were denied access to the Holy Places situated in the area under Jordanian control.

On 7 June 1967, immediately after Jerusalem was reunified in the Six-Day War, Prime Minister Levy Eshkol informed the heads of the different religious communities in the city that Israel would prevent any impairment to the Holy Places and would maintain regular contact with the heads of the faiths so that their spiritual activities could proceed unhindered. He also noted that at his request the Minister of Religious Affairs had issued directives according to which the Chief Rabbis would determine the arrangements at the Western Wall, a council of Muslim clergymen would determine the arrangements for the Islamic Holy Places, and similarly a council of Christian clergy would make the arrangements for the Christian Holy Places.

Within a few days the Knesset enacted the Protection of the Holy Places Law, 5727-1967, which safeguards all the Holy Places against desecration and ensures free access to them. These principles were reaffirmed in 1980 by the Basic Law: Jerusalem the Capital of Israel. A similar commitment was undertaken by Israel with regard to Catholic sacred places by the Fundamental Agreement between the Holy See and Israel, of December 1993 (see entry *Vatican*). In a letter by Israel's Minister of Foreign Affairs to his Norwegian counterpart (October 1993), the role of certain Palestinian institutions in east Jerusalem was recognized, as well as the importance of the Christian and Muslim Holy Places.

According to the 1994 Washington Declaration and the 1994 Peace Treaty between Israel and Jordan, "Israel respects the present special role of... Jordan in Muslim Holy shrines in Jerusalem. When negotiations on the permanent status [of the West Bank and Gaza] will take place, Israel will give high priority to the Jordanian historic role in these shrines."

In practice, Israel acts according to several principles:

1. Israel protects all the Holy Places against desecration and damage, and ensures free access and worship, subject to the safeguarding of public order. This principle is based on Israeli legislation, and with regard to Catholic sacred places it has also been foreseen in an international agreement.

2. The courts have no jurisdiction to deal with disputes relating to rights at the Holy Places (such as questions of ownership and possession); that power resides with the government.

3. Although Israel has not undertaken by any express legislation to uphold the *status quo*, in practice the latter is normally preserved. The authorities ensure that

160 *Lexicon of Terms*

there are no deviations from arrangements and accepted usages, subject, however, to changes that were introduced in order to enable Jews to reach and pray at their Holy Places. In the Fundamental Agreement concluded on 30 December 1993 by the Holy See and the State of Israel, the parties undertook to respect the *status quo* at the Christian Holy Places to which it applied.

4. Administration of each Holy Place is entrusted to the religious community for which it is sacred.

5. Israel provides financial aid for the maintenance and renovation of Holy Places.

6. The Holy Places enjoy certain fiscal privileges.

12. *Internationalization*

Internationalization occurs when a certain area, or a river, etc., is removed from the exclusive jurisdiction of the State in which it is located, and is placed under the jurisdiction or control of certain States or the community of States. Three elements characterize internationalization: abolition, suspension, or limitation of the powers of the territorial State; creation of a regime that serves the interests of several or all States; and establishment of an international institutional framework, i.e., an international administration.

There are wide variations among arrangements of internationalization, and the details are worked out in each case by the relevant agreement.

A distinction is generally drawn between territorial internationalization, which involves the abolition or suspension of the State's powers over the area; and functional internationalization, which entails only a limitation of those powers.

Some authors distinguish between three types of functional internationalization: first, the exercise of limited powers by the international community within a State, e.g., the historical European commission of the Danube; second – and this is the largest group – international control over the exercise by the State of certain powers, which have to conform with certain obligations that serve the interests of other States, e.g., arrangements regarding rivers, such as those for the Rhine and the Moselle; in these cases the national administration of the river is subject to international control exercised by a river commission; and third, a State may exercise certain powers for the benefit of the international community in connection with events that took place outside that State's territory, for example the power a State may exercise when a foreign ship suspected of polluting the open sea docks in one of its ports.

Examples of territorial internationalization are the Saar region from 1919 to 1935; the Free City of Danzig, 1919-1939; and the international zone of Tangier from 1924 to 1956. An attempt was also made to internationalize Trieste in accordance with the 1947 peace treaty with Italy, but the plan was not implemented. In November 1947 the U.N. General Assembly recommended the territorial internationalization of

Jerusalem, but this too was not put into practice. In the course of a later General Assembly debate on Jerusalem, Sweden proposed a certain functional internationalization for the city in order to ensure free access to the Holy Places (q.v.) under international supervision.

In the 1970s and 1980s agreement was reached on the internationalization of the ocean floor and its resources and of outer space, since these areas are considered to belong to all mankind. However, the term "internationalization" was not used in this context, perhaps because those areas never belonged to any particular nation.

13. Mandate

Following the end of World War I the question arose of how to deal with territories that had been wrested from defeated States, i.e., Germany's former colonies and extensive areas of the former Ottoman Empire. The victorious Powers were not inclined to annex these territories because of the rise of the idea of nationalism and the principle of self-determination; but those territories were not yet ready for independence. The solution that was adopted – and incorporated into Article 22 of the Covenant of the League of Nations – was to place the territories under a Mandate regime, to be administered by developed Powers. The basic principle was that "the well-being and development of such peoples form a sacred trust of civilization..." (Article 22 (1)).

The Covenant stipulated that the character of the Mandate would differ according to the stage of development of the people, the geographical situation of the territory, its economic conditions, and other similar circumstances. A distinction was thus drawn between three types of Mandate:

(a) "Certain communities" which had formerly been part of the Ottoman Empire and had reached a stage of development where their existence as independent nations could be provisionally recognized. They were to receive administrative advice and assistance from the Mandatory Power until they could function on their own. Type "A" Mandates, as these were known, included the British Mandate in Iraq and the French Mandate in Syria and Lebanon. Some commentators put the Palestine Mandate in this category, but, as we shall see, the status of Palestine was different.

(b) "Other peoples," especially in Central Africa, who were at a stage requiring more prolonged administration by the Mandatory Power. These type "B" Mandates included Tanganyika, Togo and Cameroon, and Ruanda-Urundi.

(c) Less developed "territories," such as South West Africa and certain islands in the Pacific Ocean (Carolines, Marianas, and Marshalls), were known as type "C" Mandates. They were administered by the Mandatory Power as an integral part of its territory.

The particular conditions of each Mandate were determined separately in agreements between members of the League of Nations or were defined by the Council of the League (Article 22 (8)).

The administration of the Mandate territories was supervised by the League Council's Permanent Mandates Commission.

The victorious Powers of World War I appointed Britain to administer the Palestine Mandate, for which the terms were approved in a resolution of the Council of the League of Nations on 24 July 1922 (the Mandate entered into force on 29 September 1923). *Inter alia*, Britain was made "responsible for placing the country under such political, administrative and economic conditions as will secure the establishment of the Jewish national home, ... and the development of self-governing institutions, and also for safeguarding the civil and religious rights of all the inhabitants of Palestine, irrespective of race and religion" (Article 2). Britain was also requested to facilitate Jewish settlement in Palestine.

Certain Arab jurists have argued that the terms of the Palestine Mandate went beyond the framework laid down in the Covenant of the League of Nations, since in their opinion Palestine was included in the type "A" Mandates, where independence of the local people could be provisionally recognized under Article 22 of the Covenant. However, other jurists contend that not all the "communities" that had been part of the Ottoman Empire were included in this category, but only "certain communities." Moreover, since – as already mentioned – the League of Nations Council was authorized to determine the distinctive terms for each Mandate separately, it did not exceed its authority by making Britain responsible for promoting the idea of a national home for the Jewish people. True, the League of Nations secretariat dealt with the Palestine Mandate as a type "A" Mandate, but this was a technical arrangement which did not prejudice the character of the Mandate.

The British Mandate for Palestine was terminated in 1948 in accordance with British enactments adopted in the wake of the U.N. General Assembly Resolution on the Future Government of Palestine (November 1947) which *inter alia* recommended the termination of the Mandate.

14. Neutrality and Neutralization

The term "neutrality" is used in at least five different contexts:

1. Regular neutrality – The status, rights, and obligations of a State which does not participate in a particular war. Whether a State will be neutral depends on its own political decision but also on the decision of the belligerents. If a State undertakes in advance to remain neutral in a particular conflict, naturally it loses its discretion on this question. The rules that apply to a neutral State have been laid down by international law. Generally speaking, a neutral State may not intervene or assist any of the sides involved, while the latter refrain from attacking the neutral State and from engaging in hostilities in its territory or its waters. Examples of this type of neutrality were The Netherlands in World War I, Sweden in World War II, and the United States in World War II until 1941.

2. Permanent neutrality – Sometimes a State assumes a general international commitment, which receives the assent of most other States, not to take part in any war that might break out. This State must not only refrain from participating in any war, but also from taking any action during peacetime liable to involve it in an armed conflict. However, a State in a regime of permanent neutrality does not have to be demilitarized (q.v.); it may establish an army and build fortifications for self-defense. Other States have the obligation not to attack a State under this regime, and in the past in certain cases some of the other States even were guarantors of this neutrality and went to war to protect it. Today two countries are in a regime of permanent neutrality: Switzerland (since 1815) and Austria (since 1955).

3. Neutralization – This term refers to the exclusion of a particular area from the theater of hostilities, with the consent of the parties involved. Examples are the Suez Canal under the 1888 Constantinople Convention, the Panama Canal under the 1977 treaty, and the Spitsbergen Islands under the 1920 Treaty Regulating the Status of Spitsbergen. During a war the belligerents may agree on the creation of "neutral zones" where no hostilities will be carried out and which are intended to serve as havens for the wounded, children, and the elderly (see also entries *Buffer Zone* and *Demilitarization*).

4. Neutralism – This term describes a political position, not a legal situation. During the Cold War the term "neutralism" was used to denote nonalignment with the major blocs.

5. Quasi-neutrality – This term is used by several authors to denote the status of a State which does not participate or intervene in hostilities short of war between other States (as differentiated from ordinary neutrality which exists during a war in the full sense of the word).

The U.N. General Assembly Resolution of 1947 on the Future Government of Palestine recommended that "The City of Jerusalem shall be demilitarized; its neutrality shall be declared and preserved, and no para-military formations, exercises or activities shall be permitted within its borders" (Part III, C, 4). During Israel's War of Independence there were a number of neutral places in the Jerusalem area.

15. Sovereignty

The question of sovereignty over certain areas in general, and over Jerusalem in particular, may become a fiercely contested issue in the negotiations between Israel and her neighbors. The concept of sovereignty developed in the late Middle Ages and served the territorial rulers in their efforts to free themselves from the influence of the Emperor on the one hand and the Pope on the other. It also helped them to consolidate internally their exclusive territorial jurisdiction in contrast to overlapping medieval personal jurisdiction.

The French author Jean Bodin (1530-1596) developed a comprehensive theory of sovereignty, writing: "Sovereignty is the absolute and perpetual power of a republic."

The term "absolute" connotes comprehensive legislative power, and the lack of a higher earthly authority. Bodin, though, conceded that the sovereign was subject to the laws of God and nature as well as to certain human laws common to all peoples. With Hobbes and his *Leviathan* (1651) sovereignty became an absolute concept. As a result of this absolutist perception, the term was sometimes used in support of totalitarianism and to justify wars of expansion at the expense of others.

This drift toward absolutism discredited the concept of sovereignty and led to its rejection by various twentieth-century scholars. Hans Kelsen and Georges Scelle, for example, proposed replacing the notion of sovereignty with the idea of the international legal order – the supremacy of a *Weltrechtsordnung* or a *civitas maxima* – while Charles Rousseau preferred to use the term independence instead of sovereignty.

Nowadays the absolutist perception of sovereignty no longer prevails and everyone agrees that sovereignty is subject to the rules of international law. Nevertheless, some commentators continue to regard sovereignty as an all-embracing and indivisible quality.

The conventional viewpoint today is that sovereignty is one of the traits that characterize the State. There are many opinions about the nature and attributes of sovereignty. Usually a distinction is drawn between the internal and the external aspect. The former refers to the highest and original power (i.e., which is not derived from another source) within the State. This power is not subject to the authority of another State or of any foreign law other than public international law. In contrast, the external aspect emphasizes the independence and equality of States and the fact that they are direct and immediate subjects of international law. It seems that there are three main elements in sovereignty. First, the sovereign is a full subject of international law; second, it is not under the control of any other State; and third, the sovereign is in fact able and free to exercise a fair amount of State powers.

In the past a number of phenomena were linked to sovereignty, of which we shall mention only a few: sovereign equality among States, the prohibition on intervening in the internal affairs of another State, the exclusiveness of territorial jurisdiction, the presumption in favor of a State's competence, the lack of an obligation to submit to binding third-party adjudication, the virtually unlimited right to wage war, and the positivist theory of international law under which the source of validity of that law lies solely in the will of the States. (On the changes that some of these phenomena have undergone, see below.)

The rise of democracy and federalism brought about a certain loosening of the concept of sovereignty, especially when determining who is the sovereign *within* the State. The American Declaration of Independence of 1776 favored popular sovereignty, the French constitution of 1791 declared that sovereignty resides in the nation, while according to John Austin, who was influenced by the British system, sovereignty was vested in a nation's parliament. The complex federal structure of the United States required recognition of the division of sovereignty in practice, if not in theory, between the union and the member-States (as explained in the famous *Federalist Papers*). These concepts led to the development of notions such as dual sovereignty, divided sovereignty, residual or *de jure* sovereignty, *de facto* sovereignty, pluralistic sovereignty, *souveraineté partagée*, *souveraineté-association*, and perforated sovereignty. New developments in the law of the sea led to the emergence of the concept of functional sovereignty – situations in which the State has sovereign powers to undertake only certain activities in a specific sea area.

These tendencies, which were based on the assumption that sovereignty is not monolithic and indivisible, have been reinforced in recent generations by both factual developments and normative changes. Interdependence in the economic sphere, the free movement of people across borders, the universality of worldwide systems of communications and the need for international cooperation in order to protect the environment reduce the relevance of sovereignty and of State boundaries. In the normative sphere as well, there have been far-reaching changes which narrow the scope of sovereignty: international law has drastically reduced the right of the State to resort to force in its international relations, and it has also imposed limitations on the State's right to treat its citizens at its discretion due to developments in the sphere of human rights. Moreover, it seems that with rare exceptions in which the borders of a State are identical with the borders of the nation, the principle of sovereignty clashes head-on with the right of peoples to self-determination. Perhaps these developments require a more flexible approach to the concept of sovereignty, such as will enable the existence of partial, shared, or functional sovereignty over certain territories.

16. Status quo *in Religious Matters*

Status quo literally means the situation as it is, and it denotes the preservation of the existing state of affairs.

In Israel the term refers to religious questions in two different contexts:

1. Preservation of the situation relating to the distribution of rights among the various communities at certain Holy Places (q.v.).

2. Compromise arrangements between religious and secular Jews on matters concerning the Jewish faith, such as: respect for the precepts of Judaism in public places and in the Israeli army; safeguarding the rights of the religious establishment; and application of religious law in marriage and divorce proceedings. The roots of the *status quo* lie in agreements reached within the framework of the World Zionist Organization and the Jewish community in Palestine before Israel's establishment. The religious-Zionist parties were especially active in this regard. A key official document in this matter is a letter sent on 19 June 1947 by David Ben-Gurion, Rabbi Judah Leib Maimon, and Yitzhak Gruenbaum to the Agudat Yisrael party. The letter, which sought to convince this Orthodox party not to oppose the establishment of a Jewish State, promised that the Sabbath would be designated the weekly day of rest, that all public kitchens would observe *kashrut* (dietary laws), that efforts would be made to meet the demands of religious circles regarding matrimonial laws, and that religious educational institutions would have an autonomous status.

166 *Lexicon of Terms*

Additional principles were added later: government support for religious services; availability of religious services in the army; exemption from military service for religious women and *yeshiva* students; extension of the jurisdiction of the religious courts to cover marriage and divorce proceedings of all Jews in Israel (including non-citizens); and the granting of exclusive powers to the religious establishment in matters of burial.

The *status quo* is often the subject of negotiations among political parties and leads to disputes. In fact, changes are sometimes introduced in it. Thus, for example, at a certain stage the religious parties requested that El Al, the national air carrier, stop flying on the Sabbath. On the other hand, as this book goes to press, the possibility of introducing changes in matters of burial is being discussed.

17. The Supreme Muslim Council and the Supreme Islamic Authority

During the period of Ottoman rule the affairs of the Muslim community were administered by the authorities of the Empire. However, the British Mandatory authorities who succeeded the Ottomans in Palestine, preferred to place the relevant powers in the hands of a communal-religious Muslim body. The result was the establishment, in 1922, of the Supreme Muslim Council, comprising five members elected indirectly. The Council performed functions of cardinal importance, including: the administration and supervision of Muslim religious endowments; proposing candidates for *Qadis* (judges) in the *Sharia* (Muslim religious) courts; appointment of Muftis; appointment – and dismissal, if needed – of all Waqf (q.v.) directors and officials; submitting claims to the government for the return of Waqf property; and introducing changes in the management of the religious endowments. The British authorities granted the Council broad autonomy.

From 1922 to 1937 the Council was headed by the Mufti Haj Amin al-Husseini, under whose impact the Council expanded its influence over Muslim life in Palestine. It also incited the populace against Jews and Zionism, frequently triggering violent clashes.

Because of the Mufti's inflammatory rhetoric and his involvement in the Arab Revolt which began in 1936, the Mandatory authorities in 1937 dismissed him from the post of President of the Supreme Muslim Council and disbanded the Council. From 1937 to 1948 British-appointed officials and personalities served on the Council. After the conquest of the West Bank and east Jerusalem by Jordan (1948), the Council was dissolved and its powers transferred to Jordan's Ministry of Waqf.

In July 1967, after Israel had conquered the West Bank and east Jerusalem, twenty-two Arab politicians and clergymen from Jerusalem met and drew up a memorandum to the Military Governor of the West Bank stating their opposition to the annexation by Israel of east Jerusalem, which they regarded as an integral part of Jordan. The twenty-two proclaimed themselves the "Supreme Islamic Authority" – sometimes also referred to as the Muslim Council. This is not an official body and is not recognized either by the Israeli authorities or under Jordanian law. In the 1980s the Authority was expanded to include all *Qadis* and many political personalities.

18. The Temple Mount

The Temple Mount, or *Har ha-Bayit* in Hebrew and *al-Haram ash-Sharif* (the noble sanctuary) as it is known in Arabic, is sacred to both Jews and Muslims. It is situated on a relatively high point in the Old City of Jerusalem, on Mount Moriah. According to Jewish and Islamic tradition, it was on the rock situated on this mount (the "Foundation Stone") that Abraham intended to sacrifice Isaac; according to some Muslim traditions, it was Ishmael and not Isaac who was to be sacrificed. The Dome of the Rock *(Qubbat al-Sakhara)* was built over this Foundation Stone by the Caliph Abd al-Malik in the years 692-697 C.E. Probably somewhat later the al-Aqsa Mosque was built. The Temple Mount is situated between two gulleys, Kidron Valley and Tyropoeon Valley. The southern section of the Temple Mount rests on an impressive system of pillars and halls built by King Herod to enlarge the area of the site, a system which from time to time has been renovated.

The Temple Mount is holy for Jews because both the First Temple (approx. 950-586 B.C.E.) and the Second Temple (515 B.C.E.-70 C.E.) stood there. According to Jewish tradition the *shekhina* – the Divine Presence – still abides on the Temple Mount. Religious Jews do not visit the site because the exact location of the Holy of Holies, where no one is permitted to enter, is unknown.

The site's sanctity for Muslims stems from their belief that the Prophet Muhammad visited it and ascended from there to heaven. It is the third holiest site in Islam, after Mecca and Medina. Of the many Muslim buildings situated there, the two most important ones are the al-Aqsa Mosque and the Dome of the Rock shrine.

The Temple Mount is administered by the Muslim authorities (headed by the director of the Department of Religious Endowments in the District of Jerusalem). Where security and public order are concerned, there are contacts and cooperation between the Israel Police, the Jerusalem Municipality, and the Waqf (Muslim religious endowment, q.v.).

At times during the period of Muslim rule in Palestine, Jews were not permitted to enter the Temple Mount precinct; under the Ottomans it was rare for Jews to be given access to the site. During the time of British rule – first military occupation (1917-1923) and then Mandate (1923-1948) – considerable tension was generated by a dispute over the Western Wall (q.v.), with certain Muslims claiming, *inter alia*, that the Jews were trying to gain control of the al-Aqsa Mosque.

Under Jordanian rule (1948-1967) Israelis were denied access to the Temple Mount despite the fact that Article VIII of the armistice agreement between the two countries (3 April 1949) had stipulated that there was agreement in principle (subject to further negotiations) about certain matters including free access to the Holy Places.

Following the Six-Day War and the ensuing Israeli control of the Temple Mount (1967), Israel left the administration of the site in the hands of the Muslim Waqf, but freedom of access was ensured to the adherents of all faiths at specified times. Nevertheless, to prevent tension, the Israel Police have not permitted Jews to pray in groups on the Temple Mount. The legality of this prohibition has been upheld by the Supreme Court.

The Protection of the Holy Places Law, 5727-1967, which guarantees freedom of access and protection, applies to the Temple Mount as it does to the other sacred sites.

As already mentioned, the Muslim Waqf is responsible for administering the site and maintaining law and order. Recently allegations were raised that the Waqf has been building new structures on the Temple Mount contrary to an agreement with the Israeli authorities, and that it has destroyed certain archaeological finds..

In September 1969 a deranged tourist from Australia tried to burn down the al-Aqsa Mosque. In 1984 the police prevented a Jewish underground organization based in the West Bank from blowing up the mosques and shrines on the Temple Mount. On 8 October 1990 a serious clash erupted on the Temple Mount after stones were thrown at Jewish worshippers at the Western Wall below. Eighteen Palestinians were killed during the efforts by the police to restore order and Israel was condemned by the U.N. Security Council. The Government of Israel appointed a committee to investigate the events (the Zamir Commission of Inquiry), while the Waqf conducted its own investigation.

Under the 1994 Treaty of Peace between Israel and Jordan, Israel recognized that Jordan has a special role in Muslim holy shrines in Jerusalem (see entry on *Holy Places*). This of course applies mainly to the Temple Mount. This provision has aroused criticism on the part of the Palestinians. However, according to some press reports, Jordan intends to transfer the custody of the Holy Places to the Palestinians once the latter acquire a certain control of the city in the framework of the permanent status of the West Bank and the Gaza Strip to be negotiated later.

19. *The U.N. Trusteeship Council*

Following the end of World War II the Allied Powers had to decide what to do with the territories they had wrested from the defeated States, and with territories held under Mandate (q.v.). The solution they adopted – and incorporated into the United Nations Charter – was to establish a trusteeship system. For each territory placed under this regime, a special agreement was drawn up, and it included the distinctive terms applying to the particular territory.

The objectives of the trusteeship system were: to further international peace and security; to advance the inhabitants of the trust territories toward self-government or independence; to encourage respect for human rights without discrimination; and to ensure equal treatment in social, economic, and commercial matters for all U.N. member-States and their nationals.

Among the trust territories were British Togo and Cameroon, French Togo and Cameroon, Ruanda-Urundi (under Belgian trusteeship), Tanganyika (British trusteeship), New Guinea (Australian trusteeship), and certain islands in the Pacific Ocean under United States strategic trusteeship. The administration of these territories was subject to supervision by the U.N. Trusteeship Council. The latter was one of the principal organs of the U.N. and was composed equally of States that administered trust territories and others that did not.

For all practical purposes the Trusteeship Council no longer functions, since all the former trust territories have gained independence or freely merged with another State.

In 1948, when it became obvious that the General Assembly Resolution of November 1947, which recommended the partitioning of Palestine, could not be implemented peacefully, there were calls to place Palestine under a trusteeship system. However, the proposal was abandoned when the establishment of the State of Israel was proclaimed.

Under the terms of the 1947 Resolution, the City of Jerusalem was to be a *corpus separatum* (q.v.) under a special international regime to be administered by the U.N. The Trusteeship Council was "designated to discharge the responsibilities of the Administering Authority on behalf of the United Nations" (Part III, A). The Council was also requested to draft a "Statute of the City" (III, C); it published such a draft on 21 April 1948 and a more detailed proposal on 4 April 1950.

20. The Vatican

Until 1870, the Pope was the sovereign of the Papal States and the Popes ruled their own territory. As a result of the conquest of Rome by Italy, the Pope lost his territorial basis. Nevertheless, he continued to have a partial international personality and his right to send and receive diplomatic representatives as well as to conclude international treaties was recognized. In 1929 a series of agreements (the Laterano treaties) were concluded by the Pope and Italy: a political treaty, a concordat on the status of the Catholic Church in Italy, and a financial agreement. The Laterano Treaty established the State of the City of the Vatican, headed by the Pope. The area of the "State" is extremely small and citizenship in it is merely functional – i.e., it is acquired as a result of one's fulfilling a function at the Vatican and forfeited upon the termination of that function. Responsibility for the preservation of order and security is in the hands of Swiss guards, while public services are provided by Italy.

In the 1929 agreement "Italy recognizes the sovereignty of the Holy See in the international domain as an attribute inherent in its nature, in accordance with its tradition and with the requirements of its mission in the world" (Article 2). The Pope, for his part, pledged to stay away from temporal rivalries between States and not to participate in international meetings convened for that purpose unless he is asked by the parties in conflict to intervene in order to fulfill his peace mission (Article 24).

For example, the Pope, at the request of the parties involved, mediated a dispute between Chile and Argentina over the Beagle Channel in 1979-1984. The Lateran treaties also stipulated that the Vatican City would always be a neutral and inviolable territory (Article 24). A later agreement, concluded in 1984, altered the provisions of the 1929 concordat but not the political arrangements.

It was not until the end of 1993 that the Holy See officially recognized the State of Israel. Prior to that time, the Pope was represented in Jerusalem by the Apostolic Delegate who in effect was a diplomat but was not accredited to the State of Israel owing to the absence of diplomatic relations. In this connection we should also mention the Custos, the head of the Franciscan Order, which for centuries has safeguarded the places holy to Catholicism. In contrast, the Latin Patriarch is the head of the Latin Church for religious purposes – i.e., matters pertaining to worship and observance – but is not in charge of the rights of Catholics at the Holy Places. At the end of 1993 the Holy See and the State of Israel concluded a "Fundamental Agreement" in which they affirmed their continuing commitment to support freedom of religion and conscience. In addition, they undertook to cooperate in combatting all forms of anti-Semitism, racism, and religious intolerance. Israel recognized "the right of the Catholic Church to carry out its religious, moral, educational and charitable functions, and to have its own institutions... to these ends," while the Church recognized "the right of the State to carry out its functions such as promoting and protecting the welfare and the safety of the people" (Article 3.2). The parties affirmed their continuing commitment to maintain and respect the *status quo* in the Christian Holy Places to which it applies (Article 4.1), and Israel agreed "with the Holy See on the obligation of continuing respect for and protection of the character proper to Catholic sacred places, such as churches, monasteries, convents, cemeteries and their like" (Article 4.3). Both sides expressed support for Christian pilgrimages to the Holy Land (Article 5.1). The right of the Catholic Church to establish, maintain, and direct educational institutions at all levels was recognized; this right has to be "exercised in harmony with the rights of the State in the field of education" (Article 6).

In the spirit of the 1929 treaty between the Pope and Italy, the Holy See "deems it opportune to recall that, owing to its character, it is solemnly committed to remaining a stranger to all merely temporal conflicts," and added that this "principle applies specifically to disputed territories and unsettled borders" (Article 11).

The parties decided to establish diplomatic relations: at the ambassadorial level on Israel's part, and by an Apostolic Nuncio on behalf of the Pope. Issues not yet resolved, involving property as well as economic and fiscal matters, would be negotiated and settled in an additional comprehensive agreement.

21. Waqf

Waqf (in the plural Awqaf) is a Muslim religious endowment. Property endowed as Waqf is granted in perpetuity and may not be the subject of a transaction involving a transfer of rights, such as transfer of ownership or possession, long-term leasing, mortgage, or lien. Still, Muslim law apparently permits the exchange of Waqf property for other assets of better or at least equal value. Income from the property is earmarked for a particular purpose which is indicated in a special deed. From this point of view a distinction is drawn between two types of Waqf: that from which the income is devoted to public purposes (Waqf *khayri*), and that from which the profits are earmarked for family purposes (Waqf *dhurri*). Each Waqf is directed by a trustee (*muthawalli*) who is appointed by the person who established the Waqf; the Sharia (Muslim religious) courts have exclusive jurisdiction over Waqf affairs. Endowed property does not become sacred unless it is designated to serve for worshipping.

During the twentieth century various Arab States have attempted to reduce the Awqaf because they were perceived to hamper economic development. In Mandatory Palestine the government preferred not to intervene in the affairs of the Muslim community and entrusted the administration and supervision of all Waqf matters to the Supreme Muslim Council (q.v.). Articles 52, 53, and 54 of the 1922 Palestine Order in Council of the King of Britain placed religious endowments under the exclusive jurisdiction of the religious courts (Muslim, Jewish, or various Christian, respectively.)

Following Israel's War of Independence the Awqaf in east Jerusalem came under Jordanian rule. The Jordanian Waqf Law of 1966 placed the administration of the Waqf under the Ministry of Religious Endowments and Muslim Affairs, headed by the Minister of Waqf.

As for Waqf assets that were in Israeli territory (inside the "Green Line" – the 1949 Armistice lines), most were designated as absentees' property under the Absentees' Property Law, 5710-1950, because the managers or the beneficiaries were absentees. In 1965 the Knesset enacted the Absentees' Property (Amendment No. 3) (Release and Use of Endowment Property) Law, 5725-1965. Under this law, ownership of Waqf property (i.e., not only the right to administer it and to enjoy the benefits) is vested unreservedly in the Custodian of Absentees' Property. It was also determined – in accordance with the evolving reforms in the Arab States – that if the Custodian releases immovable property of a family Waqf, he may transfer full ownership to the beneficiaries, while Waqf properties devoted to public purposes could be transferred to boards of trustees appointed by the government for various areas (Tel Aviv-Jaffa, Ramla, Lod, Haifa, Acre, Nazareth, Shefar'am). The government may designate additional localities where boards of trustees are to be established. The boards must use the income generated by the property for relief of the poor, scholarships, health, religious instruction, worship or custom, all for the requirements of the Muslim inhabitants within the board's area of operations. Waqf property not released by the Custodian and the income from that property must be used by the Custodian for the same purposes.

For Jerusalem no board of trustees has been foreseen. Property in the city's eastern sector was not transferred to the Israeli Custodian of Absentees' Property after 1967, but was left in the hands of the Muslim managers. Waqf property in the western sector belonging to religious endowments managed in the eastern sectors had been vested in the Custodian of Absentees' Property already in 1950, and was not transferred to Muslim authorities in east Jerusalem after 1967.

Following the Six-Day War an effort was made to integrate the Muslim institutions and clergymen in east Jerusalem into the Muslim-religious establishment in Israel, but this was fiercely opposed by Muslims. Consequently, Israel has maintained the full autonomy of Muslim institutions, and in effect the Waqf in east Jerusalem has been under the authority and supervision of the relevant authorities in Jordan. However, since the Fall of 1994, the Palestinian Authority established under the Agreement on the Gaza Strip and the Jericho Area (of May 1994) has tried to acquire control over the Muslim religious establishment in Jerusalem, and has appointed its own Mufti (see also entry on the *Temple Mount*.)

22. The Western Wall

The Western Wall (in Hebrew *ha-Kotel ha-Ma'aravi*) is part of the supporting structure of the platform on which the Second Temple stood – a section of the exterior western wall. Only some of its stones date from Herodian times; the higher layers were added in later periods. In languages other than Hebrew the wall is also known as the "Wailing Wall," the "Wall of Lamentations," or the "Wall of Mourning." In Arabic the area of the wall is known as *al-Buraq*, the name of Muhammad's horse which, according to Muslim tradition, was tied to the wall while the Prophet made his night journey to heaven.

The site is most sacred to the Jews, who for centuries have come to the wall to pray and to lament personal and national catastrophes. For Muslims the site was apparently less holy, but in the 1920s, as the Arab-Israel conflict in Palestine became more intense, its sanctity to Islam was stressed.

The area directly adjacent to the Western Wall was inhabited by families of Moroccan origin (Mughrabis) who benefited from the Waqf of Abu Midian, dating from the twelfth century. Attempts by Jewish philanthropists and Zionist institutions to purchase the area were unsuccessful.

Under Ottoman rule Jews were permitted to pray at the Western Wall, though subject to many restrictions. A 1912 order, for example, prohibited the placing of chairs and the erection of tents or a partition at the site.

The British Mandatory authorities applied the principle of the *status quo* (q.v.) – i.e., the continuation of the existing situation – to the Western Wall. In the Mandate period the dispute over the site also assumed a political-national character. The controversies in this period focused mainly on the following subjects: Muslim demands for a right to make repairs in the Western Wall; disturbances to prayer caused by Muslims, who passed by with mules during Jewish worship; noise made by Muslims during Jewish prayers; and stone throwing by Muslims at Jewish worshippers. The Jews, for their part, wanted to install benches, various appurtenances of worship, as well as a partition at the site, and to sound the *shofar* (ram's horn) at the end of Yom

Kippur (Day of Atonement). The highly charged dispute over the Western Wall sparked the disturbances of 1929. Following the findings of a commission of inquiry (1930), Britain adopted the Palestine (Western or Wailing Wall) Order in Council, 1931 which determined that the Muslim Waqf had exclusive ownership of the site, but recognized the right of Jews to worship there, subject to severe restrictions. Jews were permitted to bring certain appurtenances of worship, but were forbidden to install benches, carpets, or a curtain, nor were they permitted to sound the *shofar*. Political activity at or near the Western Wall was also prohibited by the Order in Council.

Between 1948 and 1967, when the Old City of Jerusalem was under Jordanian rule, Israelis were denied access to the Western Wall, contrary to the agreement in principle (which was conditional on further negotiations) contained in the Israel-Jordan armistice agreement of 1949 (see entry *Temple Mount*).

Following the reunification of Jerusalem in 1967 the area of the Western Wall was renovated and the plaza in front of it was broadened considerably. Those who were evacuated due to that expansion were offered full compensation or alternative housing.

Today free access to the Western Wall is guaranteed for everyone. Prayer is conducted according to the Jewish Orthodox tradition, and this has generated friction with Jews who adhere to other traditions.

Like the other Holy Places in Israel, the Western Wall is subject to the Protection of the Holy Places Law, 5727-1967, and to the Regulations for the Protection of Places Holy to Jews, 1981. In recent generations the Western Wall, in addition to its status as a sacred site for Jews, has also become a national symbol.

* * *

For the preparation of this lexicon, the author has used many sources. The most relevant ones are:

1. R. Bernhardt (ed.), *Encyclopedia of Public International Law*, 12 volumes, North Holland, Amsterdam, 1981-1990;
2. B. Lewis, V.L. Ménage, Ch. Pellat & J. Schacht (eds.), *The Encyclopedia of Islam*, Vol. III, Brill, Leiden and Luzac, London, 1971;
3. H.A.R. Gibb & J.H. Kramers (eds.), *Shorter Encyclopedia of Islam*, Brill, Leiden and Luzac, London, 1961;
4. S. Berkovitz, *The Legal Status of the Holy Places in Israel*, Thesis submitted for the degree of Ph.D. to the Hebrew University, Jerusalem, March 1978 (Hebrew);
5. Y. Reiter, *Islamic Awqaf in Jerusalem 1948-1990*, The Jerusalem Institute for Israel Studies, Jerusalem, 1991 (Hebrew);
6. L.G.A. Cust, *The Status Quo in the Holy Places*, 1929, reproduced in 1980 by Ariel Publishing House, Jerusalem.

SELECTED BIBLIOGRAPHY

Israeli Enactments

Law and Administration Ordinance (Amendment No. 11) Law, 5727-1967, Laws of the State of Israel (L.S.I.), Vol. 21, 5727-1966/67, p. 75.

Municipalities Ordinance (Amendment No. 6) Law, 5727-1967, L.S.I., Vol. 21, 5727-1966/67, pp. 75-76.

Protection of the Holy Places Law, 5727-1967, L.S.I., Vol. 21, 5727-1966/67, p. 76.

Law and Administration Regulation (No. 1), 5727-1967, Kovets Hatakanot (Collection of Regulations), 5727-1967, No. 2064, of 28 June 1967, p. 2690.

Basic Law: Jerusalem, Capital of Israel, L.S.I., Vol. 34, 5740-1979/80, p. 209.

Israeli Court Decisions

High Court of Justice 223/67, *Ben-Dov vs. Minister of Religious Affairs* (1968), Piskei-Din, Vol. 22(1), p. 440, 441-442. For an English summary, see R. Lapidoth & M. Hirsch (eds.), *The Jerusalem Question and Its Resolution: Selected Documents*, Nijhoff Publishers, Dordrecht, in cooperation with the Jerusalem Institute for Israel Studies, Jerusalem, 1994, pp. 487-488.

High Court of Justice 171/68, *Hanzalis vs. Court of the Greek Orthodox Patriarchal Church* (1969), Piskei-Din, Vol. 23(1), p. 260. For an English summary, see Lapidoth & Hirsch, *op. cit.*, pp. 489-490.

High Court of Justice 283/69, *Ruidi and Maches vs. Military Court of the Hebron District* (1970), Piskei-Din, Vol. 24(2), p. 419. For an English summary, see Lapidoth & Hirsch, *op. cit.*, pp. 502-506.

Miscellaneous Applications (Jerusalem) 186/87, *Attorney General vs. Yoel Davis* (1989)(3), Pesakim Mehoziyim, p. 336. For an English summary, see Lapidoth & Hirsch, *op. cit.* pp. 535-539.

International Treaties and Agreements

Sykes-Picot Agreement of 1916, in: J.N. Moore (ed.), *The Arab-Israeli Conflict, Readings and Documents*, Princeton University Press, N.J., 1977, p. 880.

Hashemite Jordan Kingdom-Israel: General Armistice Agreement, 3 April 1949, *United Nations Treaty Series*, Vol. 42 (1949), No. 656, pp. 304-320.

The 1961 Vienna Convention on Diplomatic Relations, *United Nations Treaty Series*, Vol. 500, p. 95.

Letters concerning Jerusalem exchanged by Egypt, Israel and the United States in connection with the conclusion of the 1978 Camp David Framework for Peace in the Middle East, reproduced in R. Lapidoth & M. Hirsch (eds.), *The Arab-Israel Conflict and Its Resolution: Selected Documents*, Nijhoff Publishers, Dordrecht, in cooperation with the Jerusalem Institute for Israel Studies, Jerusalem, 1992, pp. 204-205.

Treaty and Concordat concluded by the Holy See and Italy on 11 February 1929, in: Peaslee, *Constitutions of Nations*, Vol. III, 2nd edition, 1956, p. 668.

Agreement between the Holy See and Italy to Amend the 1929 Lateran Concordat, 18 February 1984, 24 *International Legal Materials*, 1985, p. 1589.

Fundamental Agreement between the Holy See and Israel, of 30 December 1993, 33 *International Legal Materials*, 1994, p. 153.

Books and Articles

S. Adler, "The Jerusalem Law - Legal Aspects", *New York Law Journal*, 22 and 23 September 1980.

A. Abu Odeh, "Two Capitals in an Undivided Jerusalem," 70 *Foreign Affairs* 183, 1990.

O. Ahimeir (ed.), *Jerusalem – Aspects of Law*, 2nd revised edition, The Jerusalem Institute for Israel Studies, Jerusalem, 1983 (Hebrew).

C. Albin, M. Amirav & H. Siniora, *Jerusalem: An Undivided City as Dual Capital*, Israel-Palestinian Peace Project Working Paper Series, No. 16, Harry S. Truman Research Institute for the Advancement of Peace and the Arab Studies Society, Jerusalem, Winter 1991/2.

M. Amirav, "Blueprint for Jerusalem," *The Jerusalem Report*, March 12, 1992, p. 41.

Y. Allon, "Israel: The Case for Defensible Borders," 55 *Foreign Affairs*, 1976, p. 38.

A. Antoninus, *The Arab Awakening*, Paragon, New York, 1979.

Aspen Institute for Humanistic Studies, *Jerusalem: A Proposal for the Future of the City* (unpublished), New York City, June, 1975.

S.M. Averick, *U.S. Policy Toward Jerusalem The Capital of Israel*, AIPAC Papers on U.S.-Israel Relations, The American-Israel Public Affairs Committee, Washington, D.C., 1984.

G. Baskin (ed.), *New Thinking on the Future of Jerusalem: A Model for the Future of Jerusalem: Scattered Sovereignty*, IPCRI, Jerusalem, June 1994.

G. Baskin, *Jerusalem of Peace: Sovereignty and Territory in Jerusalem's Future*, IPCRI, Jerusalem, 1994.

R. Benkler, "Proposals for the Solution of the Status of Jerusalem," 8 *International Problems*, 1970, p. 8.

R. Benkler, "*Pax Hierosolymitana*," 11 *International Problems*, 1972, p. 11.

M. Benvenisti, *Opposite the Closed Wall*, Weidenfeld & Nicolson, Jerusalem, 1973 (Hebrew).

U. Benziman, *Jerusalem – City Without a Wall*, Schocken, Jerusalem and Tel Aviv, 1973 (Hebrew).

S. Berkovitz, "The Legal Status of the Holy Places in Israel," Thesis submitted for the degree of Ph.D. to The Hebrew University of Jerusalem, 1978 (Hebrew).

H. Bin Talal, *A Study On Jerusalem*, Longman, London, 1979.

Y.Z. Blum, "Zion Has Been Redeemed in Accordance with International Law," 27 *Hapraklit*, 1971, p. 315 (Hebrew).

Y.Z. Blum, "East Jerusalem Is Not Occupied Territory," 28 *Hapraklit*, 1972, p. 183 (Hebrew).

Y.Z. Blum, *The Juridical Status of Jerusalem*, The Leonard Davis Institute for International Relations, Jerusalem, 1974.

E. Bovis, *The Jerusalem Question, 1917-1968*, Hoover Institution Press, Stanford University, Stanford CA, 1970.

F. Boyle, "The Future Peace of Jerusalem," 7 *The Arab-American News*, No. 335, Detroit, Michigan, 1-7 February, 1992, p. 4.

F. Boyle, "The International Legal Right of the Palestinian People to Self-determination and an Independent State of Their Own," 12 *The Scandinavian Journal of Development Alternatives*, Nos. 2&3, June-September 1993, p. 29, at 40-42.

M. Brecher, "Jerusalem: Israel's Political Decisions, 1947-1977," 27 *The Middle East Journal* 13.

The Brookings Institution, *Toward Peace in the Middle East*, December 1975, Report of a Study Group, The Brookings Institution, Washington, D.C., 1975.

Lord Caradon, *The Future of Jerusalem: A Review of Proposals for the Future of the City*, Research Directorate, National Defense University, Washington, D.C., 1980.

A. Cassese, "Legal Considerations on the International Status of Jerusalem," 3 *The Palestine Yearbook of International Law*, p. 13, 1986.

H. Cattan, *Palestine and International Law*, 2nd ed., Longman, London, 1976.

H. Cattan, *Jerusalem*, St. Martin's Press, New York, 1981.

H. Cattan, *The Palestine Question*, Croom Helm, London, 1988, pp. 324-326.

N. Chazan, *Negotiating the Non-Negotiable: Jerusalem in the Framework of an Israel-Palestinian Settlement*, International Security Studies Program, American Academy of Arts and Sciences, Cambridge, Massachusetts, Occasional Paper No. 7, March 1991.

S.B. Cohen, "Jerusalem Unity and West Bank Autonomy: Paired Principles," 8 *Middle East Review* 27, 1981.

B. Collin, *Les Lieux Saints*, Editions internationales, Paris, 1948.

B. Collin, *Le problème juridique des Lieux Saints*, Sirey, Paris, 1956.

B. Collin, *Les Lieux Saints*, 2e éd., Presses Universitaires de France, Paris, Collection "Que sais-je?", 1969.

B. Collin, *Pour une solution au problème de Jérusalem*, Maisonneuve et Larose, Paris, 1974.

B. Collin, *Rome, Jérusalem et les Lieux Saints*, Editions Franciscaines, Paris, 1981.

Y. Dinstein, "Zion in International Law Shall Be Redeemed," 27 *Hapraklit*, 1971, p. 5 (Hebrew).

Y. Dinstein, "A Reply to Mr. Dawiq," *Hapraklit* 27, 1971, pp. 292 (Hebrew).

Y. Dinstein, " 'And the Redeemer Was Not Redeemed,' or 'Not Demonstrations But Deeds,' " 27 *Hapraklit*, 1971, p. 519 (Hebrew).

Y. Dinstein, "Autonomy," in: Y. Dinstein (ed.), *Models of Autonomy*, Transaction Books, New Brunswick and London, 1981, p. 291.

Y. Dinstein, "Israel Cannot Annex the Territories According to International Law," *Ha'aretz*, 4 August 1988, p. 1 (Hebrew).

G.I.A.D. Draper, "The Status of Jerusalem as a Question of International Law," in: H. Kochler (ed.), *The Legal Aspects of the Palestine Problem with Special Regard to the Question of Jerusalem*, Wilhelm Braumuler, Wien, 1980, p. 154.

D.J. Elazar, *Two Peoples – One Land: Federal Solutions for Israel, The Palestinians, and Jordan*, University Press of America, Lanham, N. Y. and London, 1991.

P. Eliav, *The Political Struggle for Jerusalem*, Israel Information Center, Jerusalem, 1992 (Hebrew).

R. Falaize, "Le statut de Jérusalem," *Revue Générale de Droit International Public*, 1958, pp. 618-654.

Silvio Ferrari, "The Struggle for Jerusalem," 1 *European Journal of International Affairs* (Rome), 1991, p. 22.

Silvio Ferrari, "Le Saint-Siège, l'Etat d'Israël et les Lieux Saints de Jérusalem," in: J.B. d'Onorio (ed.), *Le Saint-Siège dans les Relations Internationales*, Cerf/Cujas, Paris.

Selected Bibliography

W. Fitzgerald, *Report by Sir William Fitzgerald on the Local Administration of Jerusalem*, 28th August 1945, Government Printer, Palestine, 1945.

Framework For a Public Peace Process, Toward a Peaceful Israeli-Palestinian Relationship, Stanford Center on Conflict and Negotiation and the Beyond War Foundation, Stanford CA., 1991.

J. George, "Jerusalem: The Holy City, A Religious Solution for a Political Problem," *International Perspectives*, April/March 1978, p. 18.

M. Gilbert, *Jerusalem – Illustrated History Atlas*, Macmillan, N.Y., 1977.

G.E. Gruen, *Some Suggested Approaches to a Jerusalem Problem* (1993 – unpublished yet).

A. Ginio, "Plans for the Solution of the Jerusalem Problem," in: J.L. Kraemer (ed.), *Jerusalem: Problems and Prospects*, Praeger, N.Y., 1980, p. 41.

M. Gmar, *The Negotiations on Establishing the Autonomy Regime (April 1979-October 1980) – Principal Documents*, Shiloah Institute for Middle Eastern and African Studies, Tel Aviv University, Tel Aviv, 1981 (Hebrew).

G. Gottlieb, "Israel and the Palestenians," 67 *Foreign Affairs* 109, Fall 1989.

M.I. Gruhin, "Jerusalem: Legal and Political Dimensions in a Search for Peace," 12 *Case Western Journal of International Law* 169, 1980.

J. Halpérin (préface), *Jérusalem – l'Unique et l'Universel, données et débats*, Presses Universitaires de France, Paris, 1979.

S. Hattis Rolef (ed.), *Political Dictionary of the State of Israel*, Macmillan, N.Y., 1987.

M. Hirsch & D. Housen-Couriel, *East Jerusalem and the Elections to Be Held in Judea, Samaria, and the Gaza Strip, in Accordance with the Israeli Peace Initiative of May 1989*, Jerusalem Institute for Israel Studies, Jerusalem,1992 (Hebrew).

G.E. Irani, *The Papacy and the Middle East 1962-1984*, University of Notre Dame Press, Notre Dame, Indiana, 1986.

Israel Information Center, *Speaking of Autonomy*, Jerusalem, 1981 (Hebrew).

Israeli-Palestinian Roundtable Forum on The Future of Jerusalem, *A Model for the Future of Jerusalem*, Israel/Palestine Center for Research and Information, Jerusalem, 1993.

S. Jones, "The Status of Jerusalem: Some National and International Aspects," 33 *Law and Contemporary Problems* 169, 1968.

A.S. Kaufman, "Memorandum on the Temple Area," 17.6.1979, unpublished.

M. Kaufman, *America's Jerusalem Policy: 1947-1948*, The Institute of Contemporary Jewry, The Hebrew University of Jerusalem, Jerusalem, 1985.

M. Khadduri (ed.), *Major Middle Eastern Problems in International Law*, American Enterprise Institute for Public Policy Research, Washington, D.C., 1978.

W. Khalidi, "Thinking the Unthinkable: A Sovereign Palestinian State," 56 *Foreign Affairs* 695, 1978.

W. Khalidi, "Toward Peace in the Holy Land," 66 *Foreign Affairs* 71, 1988.

M. Klein, *Arab Positions on the Jerusalem Question*, Jerusalem Institute for Israel Studies, Jerusalem, 1989 (Hebrew).

H. Kochler (ed.), *The Legal Aspects of the Palestine Problem with Special Regard to the Question of Jerusalem*, Wilhelm Braumuler, Wien, 1980.

T. Kollek, "Jerusalem: Present and Future," 59 *Foreign Affairs* 1041, 1981.

T. Kollek, "Sharing United Jerusalem," 67 *Foreign Affairs* 156, 1988.

T. Kollek, *Jerusalem*, The Washington Institute for Near East Policy, Washington, D.C., 1990.

T. Kollek & M. Perlman, *Jerusalem, Sacred City of Mankind: A History of Forty Centuries*, Weidenfeld and Nicolson, London, 1968.

M. Konopnicki & E. Ben Rafaël, *Jérusalem*, Presses Universitaires de France, Paris, Collection "Que sais-je?", 1987.

J. Kraemer (ed.), *Jerusalem: Problems and Prospects*, Praeger, New York, 1980.

R. Lapidoth, "Jerusalem and the Peace Process," 28 *Israel Law Review*, 1994, p. 402.

R. Lapidoth, "Jerusalem: The Legal and Political Background," 4 *Justice*, 1994, p. 7.

R. Lapidoth & M. Hirsch (eds.), *The Arab-Israel Conflict and Its Resolution – Selected Documents*, Martinus Nijhoff Publishers, Dordrecht, 1992.

R. Lapidoth & M. Hirsch, *Jerusalem – Political and Legal Aspects*, Jerusalem Institute for Israel Studies, Jerusalem, 1994 (Hebrew).

R. Lapidoth & M. Hirsch (eds.), *The Jerusalem Question and Its Resolution: Selected Documents*, Martinus Nijhoff Publishers, Dordrecht, in cooperation with the Jerusalem Institute for Israel Studies, Jerusalem, 1994.

E. Lauterpacht, *Jerusalem and the Holy Places*, The Anglo-Israel Association, London, 1968.

J. Le Morzellec, *La question de Jérusalem devant l'Organisation des Nations Unies*, Bruylant, Bruxelles, 1979.

G. Littke, "The Jerusalem Dispute: Settlement Proposals and Prospects," 11 *Middle East Focus*, Summer 1988.

J. Lucien-Brun, "Les Lieux Saints," 14 *Annuaire Français de Droit International*, 1968, pp. 189-197.

Y. Lukacs (ed.), *Documents on the Israeli-Palestinian Conflict, 1967-1983*, Cambridge University Press, Cambridge, 1984.

P. Malanczuk, "Israel: Status, Territory and Occupied Territories," in: R. Bernhardt (ed.), *Encyclopedia of Public International Law*, vol. 12, p. 149, Elsevier, North-Holland, Amsterdam, 1990.

P. Malanczuk, "Jerusalem," in: R. Bernhardt (ed.), *Encyclopedia of Public International Law*, Vol. 12, p. 184, Elsevier, North-Holland, Amsterdam, 1990.

W.T. Mallison & S.V. Mallison, *The Palestine Problem in International Law and World Order*, Longman, London, 1986.

R.R. Martino (Archbishop), "The Holy See and the Middle East," *Middle East Colloquium*, Fordham University, 10 April 1989.

M.H. Mendelson, "Diminutive States in the United Nations," 21 *International & Comparative Law Quarterly* 609, 1972.

T. Meron, "The Demilitarization of Mount Scopus: A Regime That Was," 1 *Israel Law Review* 501, 1968.

Y. Minerbi, *The Vatican, the Holy Land, and Zionism*, Ben-Zvi Institute, Jerusalem, 1985 (Hebrew).

Transcript of a Mock Arbitration on the Israeli-Palestinian Dispute, American Bar Association, 7 August 1990, 2 *Arbitration Materials* 5, December 1990.

E. Molinaro, "Gerusalemme e i Luoghi Santi," XLIX *La Comunità Internazionale*, 1994, p. 243.

J.N. Moore (ed.), *The Arab-Israeli Conflict – Readings and Documents*, Princeton University Press, N.J., 1977.

J.N. Moore (ed.), *The Arab-Israeli Conflict*, 5 volumes, Princeton University Press, N.J., 1974-1991.

U. Narkiss, *The Liberation of Jerusalem*, London, 1983.

Msgr. John M. Oesterreicher & Anne Sinai (eds.), *Jerusalem*, The John Day Company, N.Y., 1974.

Palestine Partition Commission Report, Cmd. 5854, H. M. Stationary Office, London, 1938, p. 73.

Peel Commission, Excerpts from the Report of the Palestine Royal Commission, June 22, 1937, in: J.N. Moore (ed.), *The Arab-Israeli Conflict, vol. III: Documents*, Princeton University Press, Princeton, N.J., 1974, p. 150.

R.H. Pfaff, "Jerusalem: Keystone of an Arab-Israeli Settlement," in: J.N. Moore (ed.), *The Arab-Israeli Conflict*, Princeton University Press, N.J., 1974, Vol. 1, p. 1010.

T. Prittie, *Whose Jerusalem?*, Frederick Muller Ltd., London, 1981.

J. Quigley, "Old Jerusalem: Whose to Govern?" 20 *Denver Journal of International Law and Policy* 145, 1991.

W.M. Reisman, *The Art of the Possible: Diplomatic Alternatives in the Middle East*, Princeton University Press, N.J., 1970.

A. Rubinstein, *The Constitutional Law of the State of Israel*, 3rd ed., Schocken, Jerusalem and Tel Aviv, 1991 (Hebrew).

D. Ruzié, "Jérusalem, capitale disputée," in: J. Halpérin and G. Levitte (eds.), *Jérusalem – l'Unique et l'Universel, données et débats*, Presses Universitaires de France, Paris, 1979, p. 89.

H. Sachar, *A History of Israel*, A. Knopf, New York, 1979.

H. Sachar, *A History of Israel*, Vol. II, Oxford University Press, New York and Oxford, 1987.

S. Schwebel, "What Weight To Conquest?" 64 *American Journal of International Law*, 1970, p. 344.

Seminar of Arab Jurists on Palestine, "The Palestine Question" (translated from French), Algiers, 22-27 July, 1967 (reprinted in J.N. Moore (ed.), *The Arab-Israeli Conflict*, Princeton University Press, N.J., 1974, Vol. 1, p. 311).

A. Shalev, *The Autonomy Regime – The Problems and Possible Solutions*, Jaffee Center for Strategic Studies, Tel Aviv University, Tel Aviv, 1979 (Hebrew).

N. Shur, *History of Jerusalem*, Vol. 3, Dvir, Smora-Bitan, Tel Aviv, 1987 (Hebrew).

S. Slonim, "The United States and the Status of Jerusalem, 1947-1984," 19 *Israel Law Review* 179, 1985.

R.P. Stevens, "The Vatican, the Catholic Church and Jerusalem," in: Hans Kochler (ed.), *The Legal Aspects of the Palestine Problem with Special Regard to the Question of Jerusalem*, Wilhelm Braumuler, 1980, p. 172.

E. Tal, *Whose Jerusalem?*, The International Forum for a United Jerusalem, Jerusalem and Tel Aviv, 1994.

S. Toledano, "Peace by Stages," Jerusalem, 1991 (Hebrew).

J.B. Tulman, "The International Legal Status of Jerusalem," 3 *International Law Students Association Journal* 39, 1979.

M. Van Dusen, "Jerusalem, the Occupied Territories and the Refugees," in: M. Khadduri (ed.), *Major Middle Eastern Problems in International Law*, American Enterprise Institute for Public Policy Research, Washington, D.C., 1978, p. 37.

J.H.W. Verzjil, *International Law in Historical Perspective*, Vol. 2, Nijhoff Publishers, Dordrecht, 1969.

B.J. Wersen, "Vatican City," *The New Encyclopedia Britannica, Macropedia*, 15th ed., Vol. 19, 1983, p. 36.

J.V. Whitbeck, "The Road to Peace Starts in Jerusalem," *Middle East International*, 14 April, 1989.

J.V. Whitbeck, "Confederation Now – A Framework for Middle East Peace," *Middle East International*, 27 May, 1994.

J.V. Whitbeck, "The Road to Peace Starts in Jerusalem: The Condominium Solution," *Middle East Insight*, September/October 1994.

J.V. Whitbeck, "The Road to Peace Starts in Jerusalem: The Condominium Solution," *Middle East Policy*, December 1994.

M.M. Whiteman, *Digest of International Law*, Vol. 2, Department of State Publications, Washington, D.C., 1963.

E.M. Wilson, "The Internationalization of Jerusalem," 23 *Middle East Journal* 1, 1969.